John Bryant's formal love affair with utes goes back to 1994 when he started Bluey's Ute World, the country's first ute-gear store. His passion for Aussie ute culture motivated him to sponsor the inaugural Deni Ute Muster, where the arrival of 2,839 utes amazed everyone. John's first book of ute yarns, *Real Aussies Drive Utes*, was published in 1999, with a second book, *Real Aussies Drive Utes II*, released in 2001. He has written about utes and their quirky owners in numerous publications, including *R.M. Williams OUTBACK* magazine. When he's not mucking about in his own ute, he indulges his other obsession: building medieval towers.

Great Australian
UTE
STORIES

edited by
John Bryant

ABC
Books

The ABC 'Wave' device is a trademark of the Australian Broadcasting Corporation and is used under licence by HarperCollins*Publishers* Australia.

Great Australian Ute Stories comprises new material and stories originally published in *Real Aussies Drive Utes* (1999) and *Real Aussies Drive Utes II* (2001).

First published in Australia in 2012
This edition published in 2014
by HarperCollins*Publishers* Australia Pty Limited
ABN 36 009 913 517
harpercollins.com.au

HarperCollins*Publishers*
Level 13, 201 Elizabeth Street, Sydney NSW 2000, Australia
Unit D1, 63 Apollo Drive, Rosedale, Auckland 0632, New Zealand
A 53, Sector 57, Noida, UP, India
1 London Bridge Street, London SE1 9GF, United Kingdom
2 Bloor Street East, 20th floor, Toronto, Ontario M4W 1A8, Canada
195 Broadway, New York NY 10007, USA

ISBN 978 0 7333 3330 9 (pbk)
ISBN 978 1 7430 9609 3 (ebook)

Cover design by Alicia Freile, Tango Media
Cover image © Newspix
Back cover images: photo on left by John Grylls, Corrigan WA; photo on right by
David Vyyro
Internal photographs © John Bryant, with the exception of photograph on page 40
by John Grylls, Corrigin WA; photograph on page 51 by Cherie Curtis, Yuleba
QLD; photograph on page 157 by Steve Turner, Oatley NSW
Author photograph by Heidi Wilson
Typeset in 9.5/14pt ITC Bookman by Kirby Jones
Printed and bound in Australia by Griffin Press
The papers used by HarperCollins in the manufacture of this book are a natural,
recyclable product made from wood grown in sustainable plantation forests.
The fibre source and manufacturing processes meet recognised international
environmental standards, and carry certification.

To my wife, Annette; my devoted companion, fervent supporter, friend and lover, who laughs at my humour when it's not really funny. Her quiet confidence in me has made me the man I am today. Love ya, honey!

Contents

Mud Crab

Jeremy Waltzord
Melbourne, VIC

Back in 2007 a rellie offered me his old Navara ute really cheap, so I bought it to use as a second vehicle. I thought it would come in handy for running rubbish to the tip and occasionally humping furniture around for family and friends. Although it happened to be a 4WD, I didn't need off-road capability. In fact, I didn't really understand what 4WD was all about and was perfectly happy trundling around town in 2WD mode, until ...

One day after Uncle Frank finished building an extension on his house, he asked me to cart the left-over rubbish to the tip. I loaded the ute with a pile of stuff and headed off. It had been raining so when I got to the tip the place was a bog hole with greasy mud everywhere. For the first time I engaged four-wheel drive and was amazed at the extra traction it gave me. I had such a ball sliding around the muddy tracks and slopes at the tip site that I forgot all about the time; so I was a little embarrassed when the tip supervisor chased me down and asked me to leave, telling me that this was not the place to practise four-wheel driving.

The next day I mentioned the fun I'd had to my workmate Nev. He reckoned that was nothing compared to the fun he and his mates had when they went four-wheel driving. He invited me to tag along on their next boys-only weekend, when a bunch of them would head out to the Cathedral Range State Park, north-east of Melbourne.

That night I trolled YouTube and came across heaps of 4WD videos. I couldn't believe some of the tricks that blokes pulled in the mud and dirt in their vehicles, so when I went to bed that night I was just itching to get out into the rough stuff and have a go myself.

The next weekend I went out and drove some fire trails, getting a feel for how my ute tackled rough terrain. After that I did a few short-term excursions into local wilderness areas to practise my skills. I bought 4x4 magazines that had articles on how to set up a ute for really rugged off-road driving. The more I read the more enthusiastic I became. With a bit of advice from Nev, I fitted my ute with a whole range of stuff: MT tyres, airbag suspension, gas shocks, bullbar and winch, CB radio, and other bits and pieces. And since most of the utes that were written up in the magazines seemed to have a name, I decided to christen my ute 'the Mud Crab'.

By the time Nev announced the next boys-only weekend I felt that I was ready to tackle almost anything. When the weekend finally came around, it had been raining heavily for a week. Normally I would have been disappointed but, as Nev's mates all pointed out, the conditions were perfect for a bit of frolicking on the slippery tracks.

We left Melbourne in heavy rain and it was still pouring when we arrived at our off-road destination. We pulled off the tar and onto a muddy track where we let some of the pressure out of our tyres to increase traction. I was feeling pretty confident because in the back of my ute I had my long-handled shovel, a snatch strap with shackles and cable dampers, a compressor, a tyre gauge, jacking plate, mechanical lift jack, airbag jack, and of course, out front, I had my Warn winch ready to pull myself out of the trouble that I was eagerly expecting. All in all, I was a mobile 4WD accessory emporium, ready for anything that nature could throw at me!

Since I was the least experienced four-wheel driver in the group I let them go ahead and took up the rear. The boys set off at a fairly brisk pace in the misty rain, heading down a winding dirt track that they knew well. I had some difficulty keeping up. Then I realised that I had another problem: the other four utes in the convoy were doing a great job of hacking up the muddy track, so I experienced a lot of difficulty just keeping my ute going in the right direction through all the slush. The pace seemed to get faster and faster. I could see the vehicles ahead of me fishtailing and sliding in the sloppy conditions but it was all I could do to keep my ute on the road. I looked at my hands; my knuckles were white from gripping the wheel. My armpits were wringing wet.

I started to panic, fearing I might lose sight of my mates, so I pushed along much faster than I should have in those treacherous conditions. I then lost sight of the vehicle in front, so I went even faster. I came tearing around a bend, wipers thrashing at full speed, when I completely lost traction in the mud. In a flash the ute spun 180 degrees, so I was now travelling at the same speed, only backwards. To make matters worse, I was racing down a muddy incline, frantically pumping the brake pedal, which had no effect whatsoever. I was totally out of control. The ute had a mind of its own as it speared off the track and suddenly hit something; probably a deep erosion channel. I was momentarily airborne! As the ute violently bucked up into the air, everything in the tray – including my swag, my Esky full of Bundy and Coke, and all my four-wheel-drive recovery equipment – ditched into the bush without my knowing. It all happened so fast I didn't realise that, even though I was travelling backwards, my wheels were stuck in deep ruts that acted like railway lines, preventing the vehicle from ploughing off into the bush. As I sat staring in horror, I could see in the rear-view mirror that I was heading towards a broad muddy pond at the bottom of the hill.

I don't know how fast I was going when the Mud Crab did a giant belly flop into that greasy bog, finally slithering to a standstill. My steaming ute had now morphed into a giant suction cup: it sat resting on its belly, its four wheels spinning uselessly, distributing mud in four huge arcs.

By then the boys had realised that I was in trouble and doubled back to check out my predicament. They sat next to the bog hole, killing themselves with laughter. After they'd had their bit of fun at my expense they broke out the snatch straps, hooked me up and started pulling. Unfortunately the massive suction of the mud turned my two-tonne ute into a ten-tonne deadweight. Nothing would budge it.

It was only when I went to get my shovel to start digging that I realised all my equipment had disappeared overboard. I got a shovel from one of the boys and started digging under my wheels like I had seen on the YouTube clips. Two hours later in the fading light, after laying small branches under each wheel, and with the help of multiple snatch straps, we finally managed to extract my ute from the mud.

I was absolutely exhausted, soaked to the skin, and completely covered in stinking mud. When I told everyone that I'd had enough and was going home, they were incredulous and said the fun had only just started. They reckoned all I needed was a hot fire and a beer. It was OK for them because they all had a warm swag to crawl into. But I'd lost all my camping gear. There was no way I was going to be able to find anything back there in the pitch black and pouring rain. The only thing that appealed to me at that stage was the thought of a hot shower and a night in my own bed.

I took it slowly as I drove back out along the bush track, leaving the boys to continue with their 4WD fun. I finally got onto the highway but as soon as I reached about 80kph the ute started shuddering. I went out to have a look underneath but remembered that my $69.90 rechargeable floating torch lay somewhere back in the bowels of the murky forest. So, crawling around by the glow of my cigarette lighter, I discovered that my mudguards and every other crevice beneath my ute were chock-a-block with greasy mud. Lying underneath the ute in the wet gravel, in the dark, I was able to gouge away enough mud so that the wheels were free to turn without vibrating. But I'd only gone another few ks when I suddenly noticed my temperature gauge had rocketed up off the dial. I was about to pull over to check the water when there was a loud noise and the engine died.

It took four hours for the NRMA bloke to arrive; it was after midnight. When he opened the bonnet and shone his torch around the engine bay, it was instantly obvious to both of us what had happened. The radiator fins were absolutely packed with mud, causing my engine to overheat to the extent that it seized. In short, what was left of my ute was completely stuffed.

Since there was nothing he could do to get me going again, the NRMA bloke drove off, leaving me sitting in the dark cabin with my forehead on the steering wheel. My head was full of negative thoughts; I was filthy, I was wet, I was cold, I was broke, and I suspected that I was a wimp. After spending a very uncomfortable night in the cramped cabin of the Navara, hardly sleeping, I hitchhiked home, grabbed a hot shower, ate the entire contents of the refrigerator, and slept for twelve hours straight.

I know there's an old saying that every bloke would like to think applies to him: 'When the going gets tough, the tough get going.' And to be honest, I'd love to say that it applied to me. But the next day I borrowed Dad's car and drove out to where my filthy Mud Crab stood like an overgrown white-ant nest by the side of the road. I resisted the urge to push it over the side of the embankment and roll it down into the bush, never to be seen again.

Instead, I unscrewed the numberplates and scrawled 'FOR SALE BEST OFFER' and my mobile phone number on the windscreen. The first bloke to ring later that day offered me just enough money, so I grabbed it.

After I save up I think my next vehicle will be a convertible sports car. Bugger utes!

Hot Pickup!

As told to John Bryant by Greg Medinas
Gosford, NSW

I think I caught ute fever when I was about eight years old. It was my dad's fault, because he used to let me drive his old Holden One Tonner when I was just an impressionable little kid. My dad was a lazy bloke and every time we returned home from anywhere, it was my job to get out of the ute and open the farm gate. After closing the gate again I'd jump onto Dad's lap and he'd let me steer the ute for a couple of ks down the winding dirt road to the house.

In school I used to draw pictures of utes and write stories about utes. Any time there was a ute muster in the district, I was there eyeing off the utes and envying the blokes and girls who owned them. For my fifteenth birthday my dad got me an old HiLux paddock-basher. It came from a farmer who owed Dad money and couldn't pay, so he offered the HiLux instead. I did a hacksaw conversion on it and turned it into a feral, complete with vertical exhaust stacks. One of my favourite tricks was to wait until the exhaust stacks were really hot and then pour old sump oil down them, turning the oil into dense clouds of black smoke. Dad told our neighbours that he was real proud of me, disposing of our waste oil in such an environmentally friendly way!

When I left school I got a mechanical apprenticeship with a car dealer in town. I loved it; even the tech course.

I was a natural at mechanics. I soon got a reputation for being able to fix almost anything. After I finished my apprenticeship I decided I wanted to work on utes, and only utes, so I wrote letters to specialist ute shops looking for opportunities. I got a reply from one that was located in Western Sydney, so in 1996 I packed up and moved to the big smoke. It was a bit of a shock after growing up in the bush, but I was compensated by the fact that my boss liked and encouraged me. After a while he told me that he thought I'd be more valuable in sales than on the tools. So, after only twelve months, I left the workshop for the showroom, swapping my greasy overalls and diesel fumes for smick gear and aftershave. For me, this was like being a kid in a lolly shop. All day long I did nothing but parley 'Ute' with people who were fitting out their vehicles with all sorts of stuff, like bullbars, lids, canopies, suspension kits, winches, lights and a zillion and one other interesting bits of gear.

I was very nervous at first, but to my surprise I was a really good salesman. Not because I was high pressure – the opposite. I found that because I loved utes so much, I was always enthusiastic when chatting with customers. They tended to trust me and accept my advice when choosing their ute gear. A lot of customers became good friends. My first year selling was so successful the boss gave me a $500 Christmas bonus and a gift voucher for the Lone Star Steakhouse. I was stoked!

One day, after I'd been working there about three years, the boss called me into his office. He shut the door and told me to sit down. I thought, 'Uh-oh, here comes trouble.' But I needn't have worried, because what he said completely blew my mind. He told me he was really pleased with my performance but that, as a company, we needed to broaden our horizons a bit. He said that Australia was about ten years behind America in terms of utes and accessories, and that he wanted to send me to a gigantic trade fair called SEMA, which was held annually in Las Vegas. The boss had attended the SEMA show in previous years, but thought that I would benefit from the experience. He wanted me to spend one week in Las Vegas at the trade fair, then a second week driving around the southern states of the US checking out retailers that sold the same sort of stuff as our store in Sydney.

The boss gave me one final piece of advice before I set off on my 'business trip'. He said: 'Over in the States they call a ute a pickup. Back here a pickup is a sport you young fellas play on Saturday nights. Don't get the two terms mixed up. While you're away keep ya mind on utes. Forget about picking up American girls. Over in Las Vegas there will be plenty of opportunities, but I'm not sending you over there to fool about. When you come home I want to hear that you've seen more utes than any other Australian that has ever left these shores.'

About six weeks later I took my first ever plane ride on my first ever trip outside Australia. I flew into Los Angeles then changed planes and headed to Las Vegas. I couldn't believe the place: there were even poker machines in the airport toilets! I checked into The Sands Hotel and Casino.

The SEMA show was way beyond anything I had ever experienced in my life. There were literally acres and acres of under-cover stands, manned by manufacturers and distributors of automotive gear from all over the world. There were thousands of people just like me, walking around, gawking, networking, making contacts, and doing deals. I almost thought I'd died and gone to heaven!

Even after a week at the trade fair I still hadn't seen everything, but it was time to collect the vehicle that my boss had rented for my road trip around the Southwestern states of the USA. And guess what? He had hired me an F-150 ute – or should I say F-150 pickup truck – the largest selling motor vehicle on planet earth at the time.

Early the next morning I climbed into the F-150's captain's chair and headed south out of Las Vegas on one of the interstates, country music pumping from the eight-speaker radio. I stopped off at numerous retail automotive stores where I was welcomed with open arms. I can't count the number of free meals and beers that came my way from a whole host of great people. One shop owner even invited me home one evening for a feed and to meet his family!

It was on about the third last night of my trip that I pulled into a motel in the town of Durango, Colorado, just after sunset. I was grabbing my bag out of the back of the F-150 when the owner of the motel walked up and said,'Hi.' As we chatted he asked me what I was doing in that part of the world. I told him I was from Australia and that I'd been at a big trade fair in Las Vegas. I mentioned that I was now scouring his local area looking for utes. He asked me how many utes I was looking for. I said that I was looking for as many utes as I could find. With that he got all excited and told me that there were more than 10,000 utes just over the next hill! Wow, 10,000 in one place – I could hardly believe my luck! The motel owner took me into the office and scribbled out a mud map of the location of the utes. The boss would be proud of me, I thought as I drifted off to sleep that night. I was really excited that I'd stumbled upon such a goldmine.

After a quick breakfast the next morning I gunned the F-150 and headed off in the direction indicated on my mud map. After a few twists and turns on back roads I finally came over the crest of the hill and was confronted by a huge sign that read:

The Southern Ute Indian Reservation

With the sun rising over the mountains and the burbling of the F-150's V8 ringing pleasantly in my ears, I looked out across the plains ... and there they were – thousands of Utes! Not motorised utes, but Native Americans belonging to the Ute tribe of Indians. There were hundreds and hundreds of tepees dotting the landscape.

A little over a week later, sitting in the boss's office back home, I recounted all I had seen and done during the most memorable trip of my life. My fellow workmates could only seethe with envy as I waffled on about the latest developments in the US pickup truck market. The boss seemed impressed, especially when I assured him that I had indeed seen well in excess of 10,000 Utes. 'Money well spent,' he muttered to no one in particular.

As I drove home that evening in my Commodore ute, my mind wandered back to the absolute highlight of my US experience; something that I had kept well and truly to myself. In fact I never breathed a word of it to the boss, or even to my workmates.

You see, during my time in Las Vegas I came across the most amazing pickup in America.

Her name was Millie; she was twenty-three. She was in Las Vegas on holidays with her parents. Her old folks had already gone to bed for the night when I stumbled across her in Bugsy's Bar at the Flamingo Casino. I've seen some hot utes on this planet, but Millie would have to have been the hottest pickup in the whole of the USA!

Unco

Brenda Leigh
Wagga Wagga, NSW

Unco's parents said that their son had always had the happy knack of turning any event into a disaster. That's why they nicknamed him Unco, short for 'uncoordinated'. Some of his disasters were harmless enough, like how he regularly dropped the dog's food in the dirt before getting it into the feed bowl. His dad reckoned that the dog ate more dirt than meat during Unco's childhood days; that's why they called the dog Skinny. Other disasters were a bit more serious, like when he put his right arm through a glass sliding door while playing ping-pong, requiring fifty-eight stitches.

Unco's family became even more aware of his clumsiness when he failed to make a single sporting team during the whole of his school career. He couldn't bat, bowl, catch, kick, throw, dribble, run or tackle if his life depended on it. By the time he was sixteen Unco had rolled a mate's Brumby into a gorge while doing circle work; it still sits there to this day, half submerged in the creek. He also managed to write off the family's Ranger ute by plunging it into a dam while he was still on his P plates.

When I was a twenty-year-old single female on the lookout for a man, I was blissfully unaware that people like Unco even existed. I later learnt that Unco's mates reckoned he would be the last one in their group to get married, apparently figuring that no woman could stand a loser who trashed everything he touched.

I first met Unco after I accepted an invitation from my best friend, Rachel, to be a bridesmaid at her wedding. As fate would have it, Unco had been invited by the groom to be a groomsman, mainly because he owned a ute, which they needed to cart tables, chairs and other stuff to the reception venue.

About a month before the wedding Rachel held a barbecue at her place so her four bridesmaids could meet the four groomsmen, some of whom had never met each other before. That was where I first met Unco, and I must say that he made quite an impression. I remember I was standing with a group around the barbecue when Unco arrived. Instead of parking out front he swung around the side of the house in his ute, accidentally clipping a very large concrete flowerpot just before he stopped. The flowerpot, knocked over onto its side, rolled down the driveway into the backyard, spewing potting mix and geraniums as it gathered pace.

I watched the carnage, horrified, thinking that the pot would stop when it hit the back fence. It didn't. It kept rolling, smashing through the fence into the neighbouring property and leaving a gaping hole where a dozen palings used to be. The boys cheered as Unco stepped out of his ute, grinning ear to ear. He seemed unfazed by what I thought was a major disaster.

After brief introductions Unco proceeded to unload his ute with bags of ice, a couple of slabs of beer, barbecue tongs and scrapers, and other bits and pieces. I then realised with horror that Unco appeared to be in charge of the barbecue. As we sipped our drinks and chatted, Unco cooked the steaks, snags, prawns and onions. Every now and again he would reach under the barbecue for a can and spray the barbecue plate. When we all sat down to eat, the meal looked fantastic, so somebody proposed a toast of thanks to Unco for his culinary effort. But to our combined horror, as we started to eat, the meat tasted like kerosene. It suddenly dawned on us that Unco had grabbed the wrong can and had sprayed the barbecue plate with Mortein instead of cooking oil. As we threw the meat in the garbage bin Unco's embarrassment was acute, and it showed. That moment was a turning point in my life. My heart instantly went out to this poor bloke; I felt worse for him than he probably felt for himself. Rachel whispered to me, telling me not to worry, as Unco had a reputation for clumsiness. She said that he always seemed to recover without undue stress.

The next time I saw Unco was at the wedding, when he rolled up with his filthy ute covered in white ribbons. Towards the end of the reception it came time for the speeches, which was when Unco had to make a toast. As he rose to his feet, tapping a glass for silence, he somehow managed to snag the tablecloth, dragging several plates and glasses crashing to the floor. My heart was in my mouth even before he started speaking. His speech went well enough, until he raised his glass in the air to toast the bride and groom. Instead of sipping his drink, his glass missed his mouth completely. His entire drink spilt right down the front of his tux jacket as a roar of laughter went up from the crowd. I watched as Unco cringed through a weak, embarrassed smile. The poor bloke – my heart bled for him! To help him escape that horrible moment I leapt to my feet, grabbed his arm and steered him onto the dance floor. As the band struck up I realised with horror that Unco was even clumsier as a dancer than he was a barbecue cook or proposer of toasts. My feet got mercilessly trampled. I was fortunate not to end up a cripple!

Towards the end of the evening Unco, with the bright eager eyes of a puppy, told me he'd like to see me again. I felt so bad for the bloke. I felt he needed nurturing. I wanted to mother him, bring a little joy into his life. So, I said ... Yes.

And speaking of puppies, I heard later that Unco had backed his ute over Rachel's dog when he was returning the tables after the reception. And not only that! To top off a disaster-ridden day he copped a speeding fine as he rushed the dog to the local vet.

After going out with Unco in his ute a few times, I realised that he had started to grow on me. He was just such a happy-go-lucky, pleasant bloke with a loving heart. Our dates were peppered with what I now call 'Unco moments'. He tripped over shopping trolleys, stubbed his toes on gutters, walked into tow bars and dropped hamburgers. Once he even forgot to apply his ute handbrake in a parking lot. He ended up chasing it fifty metres down an incline before falling over to watch it crash into a stormwater drain. But underneath that clumsy exterior beat a heart of pure gold.

After a while we sort of got to the point where we both accepted that we'd get married. So one clear winter's afternoon as we sat alone on the grass, alongside a creek, on the 'struggle rug' that Unco always kept folded neatly under the seat of his ute, he popped the question. I said yes. Unco got so excited that he knocked over my Sprite as he lunged for my hand. We both ended up lying in an intimate embrace in a puddle of sticky soft drink in the middle of his struggle rug ... How sweet it was!

When it came to planning our own wedding day, I went over all the details with meticulous care, eliminating all possible opportunities for Unco to perpetrate one of his disasters. He was pretty upset when I insisted that he leave his ute at home, on the grounds that he would be drinking alcohol at the wedding and I didn't want him driving. The truth was that Unco tended to run into a variety of objects almost every time he drove his ute, so I figured that it was one risk we just couldn't afford.

Looking back, I am delighted to say that Unco made it right through our wedding day without a single incident. Although we couldn't get into our hotel honeymoon suite after dinner because Unco had accidentally locked the key in the room.

Unco and I have now been married for almost seventeen years, and I think the secret of our success is the fact that from day one I insisted I have my own car. Unco still has his old ute, which is so covered in dings and scars it looks like it has been used as a terrorist gunship in Beirut. Whenever we go out together we go in my car, and I drive. I refuse to suffer the risk and embarrassment of riding in Unco's battered ute!

Hell Raisin' Ute

As told to John Bryant by Ronnie Grimaldo
Parramatta, NSW

When Rocky pulled up at a building site in his Rodeo ute, heads turned.

His monogrammed Hombre shirts clung to his muscular torso like a sheet of GLAD Wrap. His long black stovepipe Yakkas dribbled into the top of his Redback boots, which copped a ration of Dubbin at least once a month. His clothing, uncommonly tidy and well ironed for a tradie, was set off by his crowning glory – a magnificent head of thick, black, shiny, wavy hair. Rocky's luxurious mane was styled and oiled into an enormous Elvis sweep, culminating at the back of his head in the mother of all mullets. It was neatly complemented by his luxurious chinstrap and moustache, which he meticulously inspected and trimmed first thing every morning. Yes, Rocky was that type of lad who looked a million dollars even when he was broke.

In fact Rocky had been quite a lad ever since his apprenticeship days, when his mates had first taught him the art of wolf whistling at girls. Back then, way before he could afford his own ute, three or four of them would crowd into the boss's dual cab and go cruising the shopping-centre car parks at lunchtime, hooting and whistling at girls.

Rocky was a fast learner. He quickly discovered that, while a wolf whistle usually attracted attention, it was the way the whistler was packaged that would determine whether the whistle would turn into a date. He soon saw that clean, smiling, well-dressed, nice-smelling blokes were light years ahead of dirty, smelly lowlifes. He also observed that the one piece of hardware that testified to the status of any tradie was his ute. Yes, a good-looking ute was a crucial piece of girl-attracting hardware, as important to a tradie as a fishing rod to a fisherman.

As Rocky speared his Rodeo from one building site to another, all the while keeping his eyes open for girls, he firmly believed that the entire meaning of life came down to one simple activity – the challenge of 'getting dates'. And it wasn't easy. It was a competitive sport that required innovative strategies, total dedication, much practice and constant improvisation. There was no doubt about it, the wolf whistle was a good starting point; but the spoils of victory usually went to the tradie who could come up with the best follow-on technique. And when it came to follow-on techniques, Rocky's most important discovery came about quite by chance one day while he was on the job.

One of the tasks Rocky hated was getting rid of his rubbish at the end of each building job. Although he'd usually get a Bobcat operator to load the left-overs into the back of his ute, he'd then face the sweaty job of shovelling all the debris off the back at the local tip. Not only did it mess up his hair, but it also introduced BO into the cab of his ute, which sometimes lingered for days. So when his old Commodore ute lease expired, Rocky came up with the bright idea of changing over to a table-top ute, complete with a tipping rear tray. This meant that he could drive into the tip, push a button in the cabin and the hydraulic ram would raise the tray and automatically eject all the junk. He wouldn't have to lift a finger. It was fast, easy, no sweating involved, and he could sit in the cabin in air-conditioned comfort maintaining his hair in pristine condition.

One afternoon, not long after he got the table-top, Rocky was stopped waiting for the lights to change. Just then a pretty blonde in a Mercedes convertible pulled up in the next lane. She glanced at Rocky, who winked and smiled, but she ignored him, looked away and stared at the road ahead. Rocky let go a soft whistle. No response. Almost without thinking, Rocky reached for his tip-tray button, and slowly raised the tray. Startled, the blonde looked at the rising tray, looked at Rocky, then tried to stare straight ahead again. But she couldn't hold it in; she burst into laughter. With the tray standing almost vertical, they both held each other's gaze while laughing. It was the honking of car horns from behind that snapped them back to reality. They drove off, Rocky's tray slowly descending into its normal horizontal position.

After that definitive eureka moment, Rocky got into the habit of raising his tray whenever he wanted to capture the attention of a pretty girl on the streets. The technique almost always worked, breaking the ice with a number of strangers, some of whom turned into enjoyable dates. Rocky got so hooked on his tip-tray dating technique that he sometimes forgot when he had a load in the back. On one memorable occasion he was carting a pallet of hardware and had quite forgotten that there was a load on board. He stopped at a pedestrian crossing next to a bunch of high school girls in a Corolla and raised his tray. Unfortunately, his entire load ended up on Canterbury Road in peak hour, causing a traffic jam while he picked up his stuff.

But such minor hassles were nothing compared to Rocky's major disaster, which has since become a legend in the pubs around Western Sydney. It happened when Rocky and his team were working at a building site in Parramatta, where they were fitting out the kitchens in a large block of new home units. Parking space at the site was tight, with a host of tradies' vehicles all crammed haphazardly in the muddy forecourt.

Rocky had been out to collect several six-metre lengths of steel pipe, which he strapped securely to the top carry bars in the back of his ute. He was stopped in traffic, only a few metres from the entrance to the building site, waiting to enter. Just then a very attractive young lady in a miniskirt started to cross the road on foot. Threading her way between the stationary cars, she was headed straight for Rocky's ute. Remembering that he had securely strapped the steel pipes to his tray bars, Rocky knew it was safe to raise his tray without the risk of the pipes coming adrift. With an expectant smile on his lips, up, up, up went Rocky's tray.

Just as his tray reached its full vertical height, the traffic started to move, so Rocky had to forget about the girl and get going. He slowly turned into the building site, his tray still standing vertical, with the steel pipes pointing towards heaven. The top end of the pipes was nearly five metres off the ground as Rocky steered through the gate. Unfortunately he failed to notice a large bunch of overhead electrical wires, which were wrapped in yellow and black protective sheathing. The steel pipes snagged the wires as he continued to drive his vehicle forward. He felt his ute shudder as the snagged wires stretched to breaking point, followed by a noise that resembled a tremendous thunderclap. The ruptured wires shorted out, wildly whipping around and earthing on everything they touched in a shower of sparks. Dozens of power tools on the building site instantly fried. In the ensuing mayhem Rocky sat frozen in his ute, trying to figure out what had happened. Had lightning struck his ute? Maybe it was an earthquake? A gas explosion?

With his ute now draped in the severed live wires, panicked workers screamed at Rocky to remain frozen inside his cabin while they called the authorities to shut down the power. Ninety minutes later a shaken Rocky stumbled from his ute to learn that an entire section of the Parramatta district was without power, and that the building site would be shut down until a full investigation was undertaken.

Ever since that fateful day Rocky has become famous as the 'Parra Hell Raiser'. But he no longer raises his ute tray to the ladies, because he simply doesn't have the money to go out on dates – he's too busy paying off the damage and fines.

Garbage

Annabel LeHuene
Bathurst, NSW

Daryl dreaded Monday nights because that's when the council truck called to collect his rubbish. Living on a hobby farm, he had originally purchased his second-hand XG Falcon ute with a view to carting his rubbish bin up the 400-metre driveway to the street. However, ever since he had developed a bad back, he was no longer able to lift the bin into the tray of his ute. That meant he had to drag his wheelie bin up the steep driveway to the road by hand. Daryl sometimes thought he'd have a heart attack as he struggled up his rutted drive, sweating like a pig and pulling the loaded wheelie bin behind him. He often wondered what his wife, Doris, put in the bin; it felt like it was filled with concrete. But by the time he got up to the street he was simply too stuffed to open the lid and check.

Then one day, after struggling up his driveway yet again, he had a brainwave.

Why not make a metal bracket that would attach the wheelie bin to the tow ball on his ute? That way he wouldn't have to lift his bin. Instead, he could drive the ute up to the road, towing the bin behind him. After thirty minutes in the shed with his angle grinder and welder, the job was done.

The next Monday afternoon Daryl hooked his wheelie bin onto the ute's tow bar. He was just about to tow it up the driveway when Doris yelled out, telling him to go to the shops and grab some milk. With his wheelie bin in tow Daryl set off. He felt a surge of joy and achievement as he realised that his innovative little bracket was working perfectly. No heart attacks for this little black duck, he thought proudly to himself.

When Daryl got to the road he stopped to unhook the wheelie bin from his tow bar. But just as he got out of his ute, he noticed his attractive next-door neighbour putting her bin out too. He yelled hello, then wandered over to chat. After twenty minutes of flirting, Daryl jumped back in his ute, remembering that Doris had told him to bring back some milk, and headed off to the local shop. Of course after all his flirting he had completely forgotten that the wheelie bin was still hooked to his tow bar.

As Daryl gunned the XG, his Marty Robbins CD drowned out the sound of the small plastic bin wheels rattling up the road, and soon disintegrating. Without wheels, the bottom of the bin was left to grind away on the bitumen. When Daryl reached the 100 kph zone, the bottom had vanished, ground into little bits as it got dragged along the rough bitumen. If Daryl had bothered to look in his rear-vision mirror he would have seen a long trail of his own garbage stretching behind him, progressively pouring out of the half demolished bin – but he was too busy singing along with Marty. A couple of other vehicles tooted, but Daryl just waved, completely oblivious to the mayhem he was causing. By the time he reached the shop there wasn't much of his bin left, and the rubbish was all gone.

After picking up the milk Daryl set off on his return trip. It was only then that he noticed the rubbish strewn down the middle of the road. He was disgusted that anyone would trash his local district that way. 'Dirty buggers,' he muttered to himself.

When Daryl finally pulled into his carport outside the kitchen window, Doris looked out and saw a metal bracket and a wide green handle hooked to the back of his XG ute: it was all that was left of his wheelie bin. 'What's that love?' she asked. It suddenly hit Daryl like a sledgehammer, but he feigned ignorance.

It wasn't until a week later that someone at the local shops told Doris they had seen Daryl towing half a wheelie bin down the highway, spewing rubbish: 'Surely a bloke with a ute can cart his rubbish to the tip instead of trashing the environment.' Doris couldn't help but agree, but said nothing as the truth dawned on her.

She hurried home to give Daryl the severe tongue lashing she was sure he deserved.

In the Poo

Ed Caxton
Tumbi Umbi, NSW

Johnny and Jenny Johnson had a great business and a lousy marriage.

Johnson Constructions built architecturally designed homes and made a small fortune. Johnny spent his days in his ute, driving from job to job, supervising his fifty-eight apprentices and tradesmen. He was fair, firm, a straight shooter and totally honest. Every one of his blokes respected him and would have killed for him if necessary.

On the other hand Jenny ran the office with an iron fist and was generally considered a nasty piece of work. She rode her staff hard, twisted the arms off suppliers, cursed delivery drivers, abused her creditors and hated her accountant. She stocked the office café-bar with the cheapest tea and coffee she could find, knowing that this would dramatically reduce consumption and therefore cost. As testimony to her penny-pinching, no visitor ever accepted a second cup of tea or coffee; the foul aftertaste sometimes lingered for hours. It was no wonder that the staff had secretly nicknamed Johnny and Jenny 'Sweet and Sour' behind their backs.

When it came to their personal lives, the marriage had survived only because they lived in different worlds. Johnny had half a dozen motorcycles and went riding with his mates on weekends whenever the sun was shining. If it looked like rain, he'd jump in his 4WD Triton ute and head off-road down to the river to fish. None of this fazed Jenny, who had her hands full caring for their four children, as well as looking after a menagerie of animals that were scattered around their twenty-acre property. In fact it was Jenny's animals that caused much of the friction in their married life. Johnny often came home at night to find a new pen full of pigs, or a donkey, or an alpaca, or some other exotic new pet that had taken Jenny's fancy, installed in the backyard or blocking the driveway.

One Friday afternoon, after a tiring week when nothing had gone right at work, Johnny drove his battered work ute up his driveway on autopilot. Almost before he realised it, he had nearly run over two dozen fancy-looking chickens. As he parked his ute in the shed and chucked his battered Akubra in the back, he thought to himself, 'Dammit, here I am busting my gut to make a dollar, and all she does is spend it on bloody feathery pests that are designed to annoy the hell out of me.' However, after twenty-six years of marriage, Johnny had learnt the secret of a half-happy life was to keep his mouth shut – no matter what. So, biting his lip, he walked into the house and said nothing.

When Johnny and Jenny went to bed that night, Johnny had completely forgotten about the chickens. As he lay there listening to Jenny snoring, he gradually drifted off, still tossing up whether to trade his old work ute for a new Colorado.

Meanwhile, the twenty-four newly arrived chickens had been busy trying to find somewhere to sleep the night, and finally opted for the exposed rafters in the roof of the shed. As bad luck would have it, many of them perched directly above Johnny's ute. And as even worse luck would have it, a few of them were perched directly over Johnny's upturned Akubra that was lying in the back of the ute where he'd tossed it.

By the time the sun's first rays heralded the new day, Jenny's new chickens had all successfully emptied their bowels, many of them directly into Johnny's hat.

As the family awoke that morning Johnny could see that Jenny was not in a good mood. He figured his best strategy was to get out of the house for a few hours until she found somebody else to pick on. He had been putting off quoting a couple of new jobs, so he decided to kill two birds with one stone and skedaddle. In a futile effort to earn a couple of points, Johnny suggested to Jenny that he take their youngest son with him to give her a break.

Johnny sauntered out into the shed and, as was his regular custom, grabbed his Akubra and popped it on his head. As he sat in his ute about to turn the ignition he experienced an unusual sensation in his head. He sat there for a moment wondering whether he was about to have that stroke that he had long dreaded would take him out. But then he realised that the symptoms were not in his head – rather, *on* his head. He whipped off the Akubra and ran his fingers through his hair. Just as he smelt the aroma and identified the substance, little Timmy yelled, 'Hey, Dad, you've got a pile of birdshit on your head!'

Nobody could remember the last time Johnny had lost his temper, but as he climbed out of his ute he was blind with rage, ready to murder anybody or anything in sight – especially if it was wearing feathers. He reached into the back of the ute, grabbed his nail gun, yelled 'Bloody chooks!' at the top of his voice, and started loping towards the house, where the chickens were now pecking scraps near the back door.

With his left hand holding the safety mechanism at the front of the nail gun, and his right hand on the trigger, Johnny started spraying 100mm nails in the general direction of the chickens. The sounds of nails hitting the house, Timmy screaming, and the chooks chook-chook-arking brought Jenny bursting out the back door. Instinctively she vented her enormous lungs, exhaling the sound that Johnny feared almost more than death itself: '*JohhhhhhhhneeeeeeeEEEEEEEEEE!*'

Luckily for Johnny and the chickens, the nail gun emptied itself after only half a dozen sprays. All of the nails had missed the chickens, having ricocheted off the side of the house or lodged into the dog kennel. Johnny, emotionally exhausted, chucked his nail gun at the last of the disappearing chickens, turned around, and pretended to walk calmly to the shed.

He climbed into his ute, pulling little Timmy in with him. After wiping the remainder of the chicken crap off his head with a baseball cap that had been sitting on the dashboard, he slipped the ute into gear and drove off. He left the driveway with a screech of tyres and accelerated down the street, with wide-eyed little Timmy sitting next to him.

'Why did you do that, Dad?'

'Because I have shit for brains, son.'

'Where are we going now, Dad?'

'Anywhere the road will take us, son. And don't worry, mate, there's nowhere safer than inside a moving ute!'

The Joker

Jack Lewis, Secretary, Tipsy Rovers Ute Club
Sydney, NSW

His name was Artie but everybody called him the Joker. And if he hadn't been a founding member of the Tipsy Rovers Ute Club he probably wouldn't have any friends at all. However, all the blokes shared a passion for utes and uting, so the Joker's mechanical and customising skills had cemented him a place in the club despite his peculiarities. Most of the time the Joker was a pretty pleasant bloke; good for a laugh. It was only when he couldn't resist the urge to pull one of his stupid stunts that the victims found him less than scintillating company.

The Tipsy Rovers hung out at the local pub, where they carefully planned their official Ute Club functions. At least once each month they would set off in their utes to a different destination for an entire weekend. They usually spent their time fishing, hunting, camping and generally enjoying one another's company, all the while exhaustively discussing the latest goss about their beloved utes. Although a couple of the club members had serious 4x4 off-road type utes, the majority drove B & S show ponies, with a sick collection of fat wheels, humongous five-posters, lots of chrome, aerials, and enough lights to stage a rock concert. The common feature of every ute that turned up for a weekend of fun was a tray crammed with enough camping gear to turn a desert island into a five-star resort, complete with mandatory necessities like Eskies full of steaks, beer and ice. As the boys often admitted as they sat staring into the campfire in their tilt-back deckchairs sipping on Baileys, 'What's the use of putting up with hardship when we can enjoy the occasional luxury?'

Most of the Joker's practical jokes were harmless enough, entertaining everyone except the victim. One of his favourites was to insist that any new member of the club share his bowl of Coco Pops for breakfast on the first morning at a campsite. Even if they didn't like Coco Pops, all the blokes would assure the victim that this was part of the initiation into the club. It usually took the victim about four hours to realise that the Coco Pops had been doctored with a finely granulated laxative powder. While most of the blokes found this mildly funny, the Joker would collapse laughing with tears in his eyes every time the victim rushed into the bush with the mattock.

It was these types of incidents that got the blokes talking about how they needed to find a way to pay the Joker back. As they discussed the possibilities, they remembered that there was one thing the Joker feared more than anything else in the entire world: snakes. He refused to sit around a campfire at night, or even anywhere on the ground during the daytime, for fear a reptile may possibly be lurking nearby, waiting to attack him. Whenever the blokes pulled their deckchairs into a circle to eat or drink or chew the fat, the Joker would back his ute up to the edge of the circle, then assemble his deckchair in the back of his ute and sit up there, off the ground, safely out of reach of creepy-crawlies.

The other predictable thing about the Joker was that he would always indulge himself with a big barbecue lunch, during which he would usually consume at least a bottle of claret. He would then invariably fall asleep while sitting in his deckchair in the back of his ute. The blokes decided that this would be the ideal time to strike back at him; a time when he was both defenceless and least likely to expect anything.

Their opportunity came one weekend when they were camped out next to the Colo River in the bush north of Sydney. They had arrived Friday night, set up camp, and spent Saturday morning floating down the river on inner tubes. They returned to the campsite mid-afternoon, ravenously hungry, and ate a humongous barbecue. The Joker had consumed a couple of beers, as usual, and then washed the meal down with the traditional bottle of red. Come four o'clock on a beautiful summer's afternoon the Joker was in the back of his ute, propped up in his deckchair in the shade, fast asleep.

The Joker's deckchair was facing the tailgate, with the ute parked at the top of a small rise that led down a short dirt track to the water's edge. One of the blokes climbed into the Joker's ute, released the handbrake and very gently allowed the ute to roll backwards down the incline until the back wheels were in the water – all without waking the Joker. They carefully placed a large rubber snake in the Joker's lap as he lay there snoring, then drew their own deckchairs up on both sides of his ute to watch the fun.

The sense of anticipation was enormous as they sat there enjoying yet another beer while speculating on what the Joker would do when he awoke to see the snake. They chatted and laughed, intentionally getting louder and louder in an effort to wake him up. Finally he stirred, blinked, rubbed his eyes, and then looked around to see his buddies sitting on either side of his ute. He must have sat there for a minute or so, slowly waking up before deciding to get himself another drink. As he placed his hands on the arms of his chair, he happened to glance down, and that is when he spied the snake in his lap. With a piercing shriek he sprang to his feet, flicking the snake into the tray of the ute. Without waiting to assess the situation he took one giant leap over his tailgate, straight into the Colo River, fully clothed. Still unaware that the snake was fake, he pleaded with the blokes to remove it from the back of his ute so that he could safely return to dry land.

His mates staged a prolonged and convincing pretence of trying to catch the snake, racing around belting the Joker's ute with sticks, shouting, while the Joker stood up to his neck in water with his bottom lip quivering, his eyes rolling in fear. One of the blokes finally caught the snake and staggered around the campsite with it at arm's length, shrieking while all the other blokes jumped back, feigning horror. The snake catcher then twirled around and flung the snake in the direction of the Joker; it landed in the water just in front of him. The Joker didn't hang about. He did an excellent Thorpie impression, swimming to the opposite side of the river and scrambling up the muddy bank in a time that no one would have believed possible.

The Joker stood there yelling across the river, refusing to go back in the water for fear that the snake would get him. Finally he set out and walked three kilometres upriver to the Colo Bridge so he could cross over and walk back down to the campsite. As he arrived back at camp the sun was setting. To everyone's surprise the Joker announced that he would not be staying the night.

He said it was just too dangerous, especially as it was obvious that the campsite was riddled with snakes. As the Joker's tail-lights disappeared up the bush track, the boys cracked yet another beer and all agreed that they'd given the Joker a worthy dose of his own medicine.

Although the Joker continued to front up for the Tipsy Rover's weekend adventures, never again did he fall asleep in the back of his ute after a barbecue in the bush. 'Ya gotta keep your eyes peeled – it's just too friggin' dangerous!'

The boys never told him that it was a fake snake.

All-Purpose Ute

Wayne Connell
Gympie, QLD

I've spent a lot of years painting houses, all over the country, during which time I've come across some pretty darned interesting people, places and vehicles.

About twenty years ago I was contracted to paint a dairy farmer's house up near Gympie on the Mary River. The farmer reckoned that after milking twice a day, seven days a week for most of his life, he simply didn't have enough energy left to paint his own house. He personally couldn't care less that there was no paint left on the house, but he had been promising his missus a fresh coat of paint since he couldn't remember when. And because she'd been reminding him of his promise almost every day since, he figured the cost of getting me do the job was well worth the marital harmony that would hopefully follow.

Not long after I started his job I saw the old bloke driving around his dairy farm in a prehistoric Land Rover ute. I'm a bit of a ute enthusiast and I've seen a lot of vehicles in my time, but had never seen one quite like this. My curiosity got the better of me so I couldn't help checking it out and asking the old fella a little bit about it.

It turns out that he bought the vehicle brand new some time back in the 1940s; one of the first Land Rover utes to be sold in that part of the country, according to him. By the time I stumbled across it, it had done nearly half a century of hard labour. The odometer had packed it in at over 300,000 miles, but it appeared to still do its job as well as the day it was born.

One of the most intriguing aspects of this old ute was that it had a PTO (power take-off) facility incorporated into the differential, which facilitated the attachment of a range of accessories to do all sorts of useful jobs around the farm. When the old farmer ran into drought conditions he would drive the ute down to the river, hook up his pump to the ute's PTO and leave the vehicle sitting there, ticking over, delivering as much water as he needed. During flood times the ute was literally a life saver as it operated reliably in a metre of floodwater when most other vehicles simply couldn't make it through. The family reckoned it had saved their bacon back in the early '70s when they experienced major floods every January for six years in a row. The old fella also used the ute as a tractor, with a plough hooked up behind. Of course it did all the usual tasks too, such as transporting bulk fertiliser, chasing cattle, ferrying farm supplies and providing family transport.

I heard on the grapevine that the old dairy farmer retired about ten years ago, but at that time the prehistoric Land Rover ute was still going great. It got sold to a couple from Kilkivan, and to the best of my knowledge it is still in operation on a farm out there.

I have to smile when I look into the cabin of today's new utes and see acres of plastic, LEDs, buttons, knobs, GPS, mobile phones and Bluetooth/MP3 connectivity. All good stuff, but pretty blooming useless when the floods are a metre deep, the paddocks need ploughing, or the water needs pumping.

Hunk o' Junk!

Bec Day
Breeza, NSW

The funniest thing that ever happened to me in a ute was actually the result of two incidents that occurred within days of each other. But before I relate my story I need to tell you a little bit about the ute I was driving.

This ute was my father's, and I believe he'd had it since before I was born, fourteen years earlier. It was an old, whitish, '70s Holden Kingswood ute with an aluminium trayback. It rattled so much you could hear Dad coming from the back paddock. The front passenger footwell was so full of dirt that grass actually grew in it; and don't even think about turning on the fan, as you'd get covered with a shower of grass and stinking roger seeds. The gear stick had fallen out at some stage, so to change gears you had to use the screwdriver sitting on the middle of the dash, which was intentionally left there for that specific purpose. The driver's side inside door handle was broken, so the only way to open the door was to endure the squeaking serenade of the window winding down, then reach out and yank the outer door handle up while slamming your side into the door from the inside. This had to be timed precisely and coordinated properly or you had Buckley's of getting the bloody thing open.

OK, so now you have a picture of our family's ute: it was a typical old farm ute that mysteriously still had registration and was considered roadworthy. Now to the story.

I was about fourteen at the time. I had borrowed the ute to run down the back paddock to do a job. Being a silly teenager I thought I knew it all and wasn't watching where I was going. I reversed the ute into one of the drains and got it well and truly stuck. I trudged home to tell Dad what I'd done, expecting to be banned from driving till I was fifty. Dad simply smiled and handed me a shovel. 'Start digging.'

I had to dig the ute out of a drain that had been there since Dad was a young fella. It took forever! After a couple of days' digging I finally got the ute out and was bringing it home. As I tootled down the track to the shed I noticed a sinister hissing coming from the direction of the engine. The sinister hissing suddenly erupted into violent spitting and sizzling with torrents of what I thought was smoke beginning to spew out from under the bonnet. 'Holy shit!'

I slammed on the brakes, shoved the screwdriver in the gates to knock her into neutral and pulled on the handbrake. I tried to get the door open but, as previously mentioned, it required a certain degree of synchronisation. A panicking fourteen-year-old girl does not have that kind of coordination.

At the time all of this was taking place Dad had stopped in at the house for his morning smoko. He was standing at the kitchen sink making a cuppa when he looked up and saw me come to a sudden halt as clouds poured from under the bonnet. He continued to watch with curiosity as he saw me furiously winding down the window, reaching out and slamming my body against the door trying to get out.

I couldn't get the door open, no matter how hard I tried. After bruising my ribs from a couple of solid hits against the door I thought, 'Stuff this! It's gonna blow!' and proceeded to exit the ute via the window. I am well known among family and friends for my less than graceful manner. So rather than an athletic, balletic leap from the window, Dad saw me scramble out, get my shorts hooked on the door lock and end up sliding down the outside of the door, grabbing desperately at my pants as I fell to the ground. I then jumped up and proceeded to run as fast as I could, down the dirt road, away from the ute while hitching my shorts back up.

Dad had to sit down as he was laughing so hard. Not only did he witness my rather inelegant dismount from the ute window, followed by the comic vision of me running with my pants half on, but he knew exactly what had happened. The ute was in no danger of blowing up: it had simply split the radiator hose and was spewing steam.

I arrived back at the house rather panicked. I went straight to Dad and tried to explain what had happened in a way that wouldn't get me into any more trouble. Dad just shook his head, laughed, and explained what he knew had happened. It took years for me to live that one down! Unfortunately (or fortunately, depending on your perspective) we left the ute with the property when my parents sold up over twelve years ago. I dare say it found its way to someone's junkyard. It may have been the most ill-kept, difficult vehicle to drive but, as Mum always said, 'If you can drive that hunk o' junk, you can drive anything.' The legend of the old 'hunk o' junk' Kingswood ute is one that will be passed down to following generations.

The Duck's Nuts

John Grylls
Corrigin, WA

It all started when our town of Corrigin in WA, 235 kilometres south-east of Perth, decided to have a shot at breaking a ute record that had originally been established by a bunch of Victorians in 1997. In that year the ute owners of St Arnaud, Victoria, had established a record for assembling the largest number of utes with a dog in the back: 214 utes with 214 dogs, to be exact. The following year another Victorian mob, from Terang, north-east of Warrnambool, broke the St Arnaud record by lining up 325 dogs in utes. So far so good, but when Corrigin Apex president Bob Cooper heard about these efforts, he decided that his Corrigin Club should have a go at taking the record off the Victorians.

As planning for the event got under way, the attempt captured the imagination of people far and wide. Sydney-based Bluey's Ute World decided to get behind the Corrigin attempt by assembling a convoy of twelve very unusual utes and driving them right across Australia to the event. There was a Toyota Supra converted into a ute accompanied by all sorts of hacksaw conversions, including one ute with a two-metre tall fibreglass blue heeler mounted in the tray. The convoy drove from Sydney to Corrigin via Perth, arriving in time to join Corrigin's world-record attempt. On the way the convoy had rattled the can in pubs and clubs and raised over $40,000 for the Royal Flying Doctor Service.

Being a local ute-driving, dog-owning cocky I was more than eager to get involved in the world-record attempt, so on that day in October 1998 I joined hundreds of utes and dogs assembled in a paddock outside Corrigin. Once we got rolling, the procession of utes stretched several kilometres as it passed through the town, led by the local copper. I am proud to say that we did in fact achieve a world record by assembling a grand total of 699 utes in a queue, each with a dog in the back.

Smarting from the loss of their precious record, the Victorians regrouped and had another go, regaining the title in 2000 with 797 dogs in utes. Of course we Corrigians refused to accept defeat. So two years later, in April 2002, after scrupulous planning and months of hard work, we trashed the Victorians' efforts by stumping up 1,527 dogs in utes. I'm proud to say that I was there in my Tribute ute with my best mate at the time, a male Doberman named Chevy who has since passed on.

Although I've always been a ute enthusiast, I think it was the buzz surrounding the Corrigin events that caused me to think about making my own special statement about utes, dogs, farming, and the Aussie way of life. I started planning the creation of the most unusual ute that ever put wheels to earth.

I was aware that many blokes around Australia have had a shot at creating utes that were different from the mainstream, but for the most part they all started with at least an old factory-made ute, which they then modified to reflect their ingenuity and individuality. That wasn't good enough for me. I wanted my special ute to have as little trace of factory DNA as possible. It had to be a one-off original; so different from everybody else's effort that it could never be reproduced. The only way anyone else would ever get one like it would be if they stole mine!

The guts of my ute are made mostly from an old wheat elevator that had been rusting in one of my paddocks for years. Everyone had assumed the thing would never run again – but they hadn't taken into account that an old cocky with a pair of pliers and a roll of fencing wire can do just about anything. The engine is a Ronaldson Tippett single pot, which used to drive the elevator. While most blokes wouldn't give two bob for it, I reckon it's good for another half-million kilometres at least.

When I stopped to think about how I would fabricate the bodywork of my one-of-a-kind ute, I happened to be sitting on the dunny, which is where I usually come up with my best ideas. As I sat there, staring at the back of the door, I had a flash of sheer inspiration. My better half had been at me for years to demolish this old dunny. We had a new one inside the house, and this old one stood out like a sore thumb in the backyard. The only thing that had stopped me knocking it down was all the happy memories it held; all the times I'd spent in there alone with my thoughts. So, I thought to myself, why not use this old dunny as bodywork for my one-of-a-kind ute? I could please the wife and retain those happy memories all at the same time. So that's what I did. I got to work, demolished the dunny, and incorporated various bits and pieces to make the cabin and seats of my new ute.

When it came to the mechanics I plundered an old Falcon ute that had died behind my shed. I had trouble finding it at first: it was hidden under a mountain of kikuyu. I lifted the Ford Jailbar four-speed gearbox and lever clutch and stuffed it all behind the Ronaldson

Tippett engine. It fit perfectly with the help of a crowbar and sledgehammer.

I then cadged a Ford A front axle off a mate who wasn't using it, found a Centura steering column and linkages in someone else's shed, and used a Kenworth steering wheel that was lying around to provide the ute with that little bit of extra grunt.

I was able to extract the International angle gearbox from a header and match it to an XD Ford ute differential, which I installed upside down. This gave my ute one forward gear and four reverse gears – an incredibly handy feature when I want to reverse rapidly to escape a charging bull or a cranky mother-in-law. I am thinking of patenting this gearbox arrangement, as I feel most utes in the future will incorporate this type of advanced technology. For added safety I popped on an FB bumper. And of course, as every professional ute designer knows, aesthetics is an important design element. So I hunted around the shed and found an oil box and a host of other useless bits and pieces, which I installed to give the vehicle visual appeal.

After I had completed the ute there was one nagging fear that just wouldn't go away, and that was the question of vehicle security. I was concerned that if I left the ute parked in a shopping centre for example, any thief armed with a crank handle and an understanding of Ronaldson Tippett single pot engines, wheat elevators and Kenworth steering wheels, could easily jump in and reverse off into the distance before you could say, 'What the bloody hell was that?' To solve the security issue I installed a dingo trap immobiliser. It's a cranky and somewhat dangerous beast to set, but if the ute ever goes missing I know that I'll be looking for a person with at least one arm missing.

'I started planning the creation of the most unusual ute that ever put wheels to earth. It had to be a one-off original; so different from everybody else's that it could never be reproduced.'

So now to the final question of performance. I have to be honest and say that this vehicle probably outperforms ninety-five per cent of the utes out there. Whenever I go to start her up I usually draw a crowd that stands around in a wide arc, willing the engine to fire. Fortunately they are rarely disappointed as the Ronaldson usually kicks over after the first couple of turns of the crank handle. This is in severe contrast to modern utes that offer no starting challenges whatsoever; I mean, how often do you ever see a crowd standing around to watch a Commodore or Falcon ute start up? And the moment the Ronaldson Tippett fires up, the dogs howl, the kids come running, and the toothless old codgers sit around ogling with their mouths open.

Yes sir, my ute is just the duck's nuts for the smoko run, and not only a genuine tribute to the Aussie ute, but also a nostalgia trip for those who have ever enjoyed the peace and quiet offered by the old outback dunny.

Getting Even with Santa

As told to John Bryant by Anonymous
Name withheld to protect the guilty!

I was in trouble with the cops long before I was born.

Mum had gone to school with Colin (not the bastard's real name), who was just one of the many blokes in her circle of friends. Apparently he'd always had a bit of a crush on her but she didn't see anything special in him. In their late teens he would regularly ask her out on dates, but Mum was lukewarm and only went out with him every now and again when there wasn't much else to do in our small town in rural North Queensland.

As a young bloke my dad lived about thirty kilometres out of town on a large cattle station that had been in his family for well over a hundred years. When he was twelve he went to a Brisbane boarding school and didn't return until after he had finished a uni degree in Agriculture. When Dad arrived back in the district at age twenty-one, he and Mum fell in love and got married a year later. This really rankled Colin, who by that time had finished his training and been appointed a constable in our local two-man police station.

My family was highly regarded in the district and many people thought we were very wealthy, but anything we had was the result of four generations of blood, sweat and tears on the land. When I was in my teens I had a whole heap of chores that I had to do each day, but after they were done Dad would pay me ten bucks an hour for any time that I'd spent working with him on the property. By the time I turned eighteen and got my driver's licence, I'd saved up enough money to buy my first vehicle: a 1989 XF Falcon ute. I just loved that ute; every spare dollar I earned went on repairs or fuel.

I'd never taken much notice of Constable Colin until the first day I drove my new second-hand ute into town. I was just leaving the local servo after showing it off to the boys in the workshop when I heard a police siren and saw flashing lights in my rear-view mirror. I pulled over immediately. The police car swerved around me and pulled up slap-bang in front of my ute, as if I was an escaped convict who might try to flee at any moment. Constable Colin sauntered over to my window and asked for my licence. He then asked me who owned the vehicle. When I told him I had just bought it, he said, 'So, Daddy has bought his little boy a toy, huh?' I got really uptight but just sat there with my mouth shut, not realising that this bloke hated me simply because he was insanely jealous that my father had married my mother.

Well, that incident was the first of many where I got harassed by Constable Colin at every possible opportunity. Over the next twelve months he pulled me up for anything and everything, including a faded numberplate, a faulty tailgate latch, a stone chip in my windscreen, a crack in my headlight, a loose exhaust system, and a poorly aligned high beam. He also got me for an uncovered load when I was carting a pile of star pickets from town to home. They couldn't have fallen out of the tray even if I'd jumped over a bunch of double-decker buses. At one stage he arranged for his mate from the Roads Department to put my ute on the shaker to check the suspension and steering assembly.

Any time he saw my ute parked outside the pub he would come in and ask to see proof of my age. He did this countless numbers of times, always making a big deal of it, doing his best to belittle and embarrass me in front of my mates. And to top it off he seemed to be on regular highway patrol on the twenty-kilometre stretch of road between town and the turn-off to our property. Sometimes he'd be sitting concealed in the bushes beside the road, and sometimes he'd be travelling up and down. But whenever he spotted my ute he'd run his siren and flash his lights, and I'd have to submit to yet another licence or vehicle check.

I felt like arranging some sort of accident for Constable Colin, or if that failed, just shooting the man. I discussed this with my dad, who is a very wise man; I really respected him. He told me I should be pleased that I'd met my Nasty Bastard early in life; that I should be grateful for the excellent training I was getting in handling similar people I'd come across in later years. Dad's advice was to calm down, accept the fact that Colin was The Law and that, even though he was abusing his authority, there was nothing I could do that wouldn't get me into yet more trouble. I thought long and hard about his advice and concluded that even though I didn't like it, he was right.

However, Dad's advice didn't stop me dreaming of some sort of revenge. My mates sympathised with me too. We had countless discussions down at the pub as to how we should solve the problem. Jimmy, who had finished his apprenticeship as a butcher and loved cutting up meat, felt the best option was to capture Colin one night out on the highway, then simply shoot him and put his body somewhere nobody would ever find it. 'Cut him up, stuff him in a forty-four gallon drum, truck the Bobcat out there, dig a bloody great hole twenty kilometres off the main road in the middle of nowhere, pop a boulder on top. End of story.'

Jimmy's fantasy didn't attract any votes, but Gary had a better idea. We all knew that Constable Colin was single with a reputation as an emotional desperado, so Gary suggested that he could pose as a nineteen-year-old blonde bombshell on the dating website that Colin trolled for romance. 'I reckon I could get the bugger to fall in love with me online, and then I'd tell him that I live in South Africa. I'd entice him to sell everything and buy a plane ticket to come and live with me happily ever after.' We could all visualise that scenario with great relish, but at the end of the day, even though we all agreed Colin was a complete idiot, we didn't think that he was quite that stupid. However, as fate would have it, payback time came in a most coincidental manner. Maybe it was karma.

Every year at Christmas, Constable Colin tried to win a bit of public support by acting as the town's Santa Claus in the Christmas parade. He was the perfect Santa because over the years he had indulged himself with too many beers, resulting in an enormous gut. He had a ruddy face that was covered with tiny veins, resembling an aerial photograph of the tributaries to the Amazon River. And while his early years as Santa Claus had required quite a bit of padding inside the Santa suit, he now struggled like crazy just to get into it.

Each year Santa arrived in town in a different vehicle. One year he landed on Main Street in a mustering helicopter. Once he arrived in a horse-drawn carriage, and another Christmas he rode on top of a humongous John Deere harvester. This particular Christmas, because my Falcon ute was red, the guys asked if I would be prepared to drive Santa into town. They planned to sit him on a custom-made throne fixed to the back of the ute. They wanted me to drive slowly down Main Street while Santa threw lollies to the crowd, then stop at the town hall where he would make his traditional Christmas speech and pass out pressies to the kids while the old folks looked on.

My immediate thought was to say no, that I wanted nothing to do with the miserable Constable Colin. But as I discussed the issue with my mates they reckoned it could be the perfect opportunity to give our beloved constable a little taste of his own humiliation. The big attraction was that he would be out of uniform and off duty, therefore unable to retaliate in an official capacity. The more we discussed it the greater our excitement and the wilder the ideas became. By the time Christmas Eve rolled around we were well and truly ready. We could hardly contain our excitement.

The boys installed their new Santa throne in the back of my ute and then covered the whole vehicle with a heap of tinsel, 12V lights and other Christmas decorations. The ute looked a million dollars, especially since I'd even washed her for the occasion. At the appointed time on Christmas Eve I drove around to Constable Colin's flat, knocked on the door, and enjoyed his look of surprise when he realised I was his chauffeur for the evening. As he clambered up into the tray of my ute, he warned me to drive sensibly and slowly; that if I acted like a smart arse he'd see to it that I would regret it forever more. He didn't notice the liberal coating of quick-set adhesive on the throne when he sat down.

According to the instructions on the adhesive can, it would take fifteen minutes for the quick-set to reach full strength. Since the drive to the town hall was only half that, I had to delay my arrival by stuffing about on the way; I wanted him stuck good and proper. I drove incredibly slowly and took a couple of long cuts around town, ignoring Colin's knocking on the rear window as he shouted instructions. At a couple of intersections I stopped and gave way to vehicles that were half a kilometre away. When we reached the main street Colin must have thought I was the safest driver in the entire state. I stop-started all the way down the parade, almost frying my clutch while travelling at a snail's pace. Colin sat there oblivious, happily tossing lollies to the kids, who formed a jostling throng, running behind the ute as we approached the town hall. I glanced at my watch as I pulled up in front of the crowd, delighted that the drive had taken almost twenty minutes. That adhesive should be set rock solid by now, I thought to myself. The bastard won't be able to stand up to make his speech this year.

I jumped out of the ute and melted into the crowd to watch the fun. The entire town formed a large circle around my ute, with the mayor ready to make one of his boring speeches after Santa had handed out the pressies. The local newspaper reporter and photographer were busy scribbling notes and snapping photos.

Then the unexpected happened.

Santa went to stand up, but momentarily appeared stuck. He then put both hands on the arms of the throne and gave himself one almighty push upwards. To my dismay he stood, but to my surprise a huge roar of laughter went up from the crowd on the other side of the ute. He then started calling out the names of children to come forward for their presents while laughter continued to rumble around the crowd. Then I saw why. As he turned to face the other side of the ute, his back came into full view of where I was standing. A further peal of laughter went up from the people around me. I was stunned to see that a large piece of Colin's Santa Claus pants was missing: it was still stuck to the throne. Colin was oblivious to the mishap and obviously thought that everyone was laughing at his stupid jokes. The more they laughed the more he carried on with his antics, completely unaware that his fat buttocks were winking at everybody, barely contained by the pair of holey, yellowed Jockey underpants that must have been a hundred years old.

The crowd was enjoying the spectacle so much that nobody bothered to tell Colin his bum was on display. It wasn't until he had handed out all the presents and was about to clamber out of the ute that he spied the remnants of his Santa pants still stuck to the throne. With a gasp of horror his hand shot around to his bum. As he felt his barely underpanted buttocks he suddenly realised that he had been publicly unmasked. He struggled off the back of the ute then shot off down Main Street as fast as his wobbly legs could carry his fat gut, both hands behind his back trying to conceal the cause of his embarrassment.

My laughing mates piled into the back of my ute and we took off for a Christmas Eve party on the edge of town. I laughed so much that I ended up with a stitch in my gut; it couldn't have happened to a better bloke. We all agreed that I should probably leave town – if I thought my life was hell before, then that was nothing compared to what I could now expect from Colin. He would surely blame me for his public humiliation, and rightly so. We all went home that night thinking that that was the end of the fun. But more was to come.

When the local paper came out the following week, there was a page-three photo of my ute with a close-up of Colin's tattered bum in the foreground, surrounded by presents and kids. The headline read:

Christmas a bummer for Santa!

I kept a very low profile for the next few weeks and was surprised that I didn't run into Constable Colin once. Someone said he was on annual leave. Then the news broke that he had been transferred to another town. A few different rumours floated around: some said that he had applied for a transfer, others that his superiors had seen the newspaper photograph and decided he needed a change of scenery.

But I don't care either way. Not only am I a free man, but Colin's replacement treats me with respect. Maybe he'd heard what happens in our town when a cop picks on a young bloke in a red Falcon ute?

Reincarnated LandCruiser Ute

As told to Cherie Curtis by Jason Bell
Yuleba, QLD

It was love at first sight for me and my white 2003 LandCruiser turbo diesel ute.

Even after we'd spent many years together it still felt like we were on our honeymoon. She was always there, come hell or high water. Whether it was carrying motorbikes or work gear, rounding up cattle, getting through floodwaters or bushfires, or taking me to my chainsaw championships, she was simply there. There were even camping trips to the coast before the young ones arrived; come to think of it, maybe the LandCruiser helped the first one on its way!

Best of all was my ute's automatic GPS. Five ks before I reached home after work every night, the GPS would set off her right indicator and she'd veer off the highway until she came to rest and stall in front of the Yuleba pub. I couldn't even re-start her engine until I'd topped myself up with a couple of beers or rums.

Even my missus understood the special love I had for my ute. In fact she cultivated it, encouraging me to spend the night in it every time we had a barney. She was always very considerate like that. Just me and the girl under the stars; no wonder we kept the magic alive. Then one sad day in December 2011, my life changed forever ...

I was driving the sis-in-law back to Bundaberg (translation: finding an excuse to collect some rare drops of 100 Proof Bundy Rum). We were fourteen kilometres north of Murgon when a drongo, careening along in his Holden Rodeo pulling a trailer of sheep, failed to give way and merged onto the highway a split second in front of us. My life flashed before my eyes as I slammed on the brakes, my previous career as a speedway driver paying off at last. The screech reverberated through the cabin but we kept ploughing towards the Holden Rodeo – slower than before because of the brakes, but still out of control! I kept trying to veer away ...

Wham! We missed the Rodeo but slammed into the trailer. The tin flew through the air as my hands grappled with the steering wheel, trying to keep my fast-paced sliding girl on the highway. We sped towards a ditch and the countryside gyrated like the view from a thrown video camera. I had the little sister-in-law on board and I knew Granny, the mother-in-law, would be pissed if I let anything happen to her.

As we almost dived into the ditch on the other side of the highway, I jerked the gearbox into reverse and we skated backwards, away from the ditch, back onto the highway, across the white lines. I slowly brought her to a soft landing on the other side of the road as she finally ground to a gut-wrenching stop.

It took a bit of bull's balls to open my driver's door against the tangled steel panels that had ripped back against it. Metal ripped against metal and the door was finally open; I was out. The front of my beloved ute had taken a real beating – totally smashed up and barely recognisable. But sis and I were unscathed inside the cabin, and even sis's bloody luggage and kitchen table and chairs were still pristinely tied down in the back of the ute. My beloved LandCruiser had sacrificed herself to save her load.

Emergency crews arrived and the police gave the drongo a ticket for dangerous driving. His sheep had to be put down. I was relieved no one was hurt but devastated at what remained of my beloved ute. We found parts of her side rail 300 metres away; other bits we never found. Only the month before I'd spent thousands in extra modifications on her 'cos I thought we'd be together for the long-haul. All those dust bowls and floodwaters, long days of work and lonely nights away from home ... she'd seen me through life and death. Irreplaceable! And there were the many scrapes I never breathed a word to the missus about, since she's almost as scary as a Rodeo at top speed! It's not right for a grown man to cry so I just stood and stared, knowing that I'd never own anything as precious again. It was like my best mate had died.

Back home we searched the papers and websites for LandCruiser utes, but good condition LandCruisers with turbo diesel were as rare as rocking-horse droppings. Our insurance wouldn't come close and I wasn't prepared to waste cheap dollars on a later model without the turbo diesel. I've never been a man to settle for second best – just ask the missus! I was thinking of investing in an old battered ute; something that could just get me to work until I found a LandCruiser worth spoiling. But then we came across an advert that made our eyes pop. A blue 2003 LandCruiser turbo diesel ute, limited edition, only forty ever made, with a certificate of authenticity and hand-signed by Lee Kernaghan. This one was number eighteen and came with the name 'Bluey'. And only 80,000 on the clock! I was in love. I was stoked. I had to have this ute – no matter what!

So the missus and I sat with cuppas and calculators in the farm kitchen, wondering how much we could beg, borrow or steal. The mortgage would take a battering, but we'd made bigger sacrifices before for the things we loved.

We made it happen. I stepped out after the test drive and said to the wife, 'I'm in love,' and she knew I didn't mean her, not right then. 'It drives so well, even better than the old pigster.'

The deal was made. The missus, of course, worried about the dark blue colour: 'You're more likely to have an accident with the low visibility.'

I winked at her. 'The last one was white and didn't help much.'

Now she's wondering how many 'blueys' I might get in the mail. Not that I speed, of course, but when you've got a model this flash, it's easy to get distracted!

'A blue 2003 LandCruiser turbo diesel ute, limited edition, only forty ever made, with a certificate of authenticity and hand-signed by Lee Kernaghan.'

Anyway, it was only when I bought and collected Bluey and was driving her back to the farm that I knew she really was 'the one'. Five ks from the farm, her little right indicator flashed on and, out of my control, she veered off the highway, towards the Yuleba pub. She stopped and stalled, the smell of rum wafting through the air. Blimey. Just like my old ute. Not a GPS, but a GPPS: a Global Pub Positioning System. It's a love affair made in heaven and this time I have no intentions of losing her. Ever.

Boys' Night Out

Anonymous*, Sydney, NSW

I've never owned a ute, but I nearly died in one ...

I was in my late teens, living in suburban Sydney, when a Russian family moved in next door. They had just emigrated from Europe and were pretty hard-up financially, so they could only afford one family car. It was an old VW Beetle clunker, full of rust, which got shared between the four adults in the family – Mum, Dad, an older daughter, as well as a teenage son, Viktor, who had just got his driver's licence. Due to the fact that they all wanted the car all the time, Vik rarely got a turn at the wheel because he was lowest in the pecking order. This burned him up, so he devised a devious plan that would get him his fair share of time behind the wheel.

The highlight of Vik's life was Saturday night: party night. So Vik would wait until the family had gone to bed, then climb out his bedroom window. He'd sneak into the garage, get into the Beetle, then coast it down the drive and into the street before starting the engine. He'd then have a good six hours to get it home again before dawn. I often went with Vik on his weekend jaunts, roaming all over town to parties, mates' places, pubs and clubs; we had a ball.

Apart from Vik's dad occasionally complaining about how much petrol the Beetle used, his parents never suspected anything. Then one day his dad came home with a brand new HiLux dual cab ute, proudly announcing that he'd traded the old Vee Dub clunker and paid cash for the ute, which he could write off as a tax-deductible expense in his business. Everyone was excited, especially Vik, as he figured that a new HiLux ute was more of a chick magnet than the rusty old Beetle.

It wasn't long after the HiLux arrived that we got invited to a buck's night in a block of home units in North Sydney. We got to the party pretty late, picking up a portable barbecue on the way. The party was a blast, but as was typical at any buck's night, everybody had a bit too much to drink. Vik, however, had gone easy on the booze during the evening, as he had to get the ute home in one piece. We had left the party and were loading the barbecue into the back of the HiLux when a few of the blokes came up and asked for a ride home, rather than having to wait for taxis, which were pretty scarce at that time of the night. One thing led to another, and by the time we were on the road it was nearly 4 am: the barbecue was in the back and there were seven blokes crammed into the dual cab, all shouting, laughing and generally carrying on.

It was raining heavily as we started descending the hill that led down to the stone bridge in Northbridge. The road was slippery and dark. We're still not sure how it happened, but somehow Vik clipped the guardrail at the first of the S-bends. We ricocheted off the guardrail, and then the ute flipped onto its side and travelled maybe thirty or forty metres before hitting the guardrail again and flipping onto its roof. It continued slithering down the wet bitumen before rolling onto its other side, coming to a standstill when it hit the guardrail again.

Me and the other six blokes in the ute were stunned. There was total silence for a few seconds. Then somebody yelled out, 'She's on fire!' All of us, who at this stage were lying in a tangled heap on top of each other, started thrashing about in an effort to get out of the ute. Because it was on its side there was only one way out, and that was to climb up through the side windows. The doors were jammed due to the impact, so a couple of the blokes kicked out the side windows and everybody scrambled out to safety. Once we were on the footpath and able to survey the scene it was obvious that there was no fire, even though there was a fair bit of oil on the road. So the seven of us heaved the ute back up onto its wheels. None of the doors would open so Vik climbed back in through the driver's window and turned the key. It started! No one was injured, mainly because we had been packed in too tightly to roll around as the ute cartwheeled down the road. So the rest of us piled back in through the windows and Vik did the rounds, dropping the blokes off at their various homes.

It was almost 6 am, just as the sun was rising, when Vik and I pulled into our street. We were about to enter his driveway to quietly pop the ute back into the garage when the engine suddenly stopped. The petrol gauge told us we were out of fuel. Vik was freaking out of his brain because he worried that leaving the ute in the street would somehow give the game away. Undaunted, he kangarooed the ute up the driveway using the starter motor for propulsion. To our great relief he got it into the garage, closed the door, and we both went off to bed.

At about 8 am I was awakened by shrill screams coming from Vik's garage. I stumbled in there, and there was Vik and his whole family staring at the HiLux. Both sides were badly dented, two of the side windows were smashed, one side mirror was missing while the other dangled from a bolt. The roof was flattened to about ten centimetres lower than normal, with a horrendous gravel rash extending its full length. There were copious quantities of oil splattered around the front mudguards and bonnet. And, though I hadn't given it much thought before, it looked like it had been used to herd wild buffalo, taking quite a few hits in the process.

I'm proud to say that Vik and I got away with it, without even having to tell any lies. No one ever asked us whether we had damaged the ute. We weren't even suspects, so why would we be stupid enough to volunteer a confession? Nobody ever found out. Vik's dad reported the damage to the police who assumed that someone had stolen the vehicle, taken it for a joy ride, and then returned it again. As the cop said, 'Stranger things have been known to happen,' and we nodded in agreement.

The only real problem we experienced was that we lost the barbecue that was in the back of the ute when it rolled. When we went back to the scene of the accident it was nowhere to be seen. The seven of us all chipped in to buy the owner a new one. We told him that the original barbecue had fallen out of the back of the ute, which was 100 per cent true, but he didn't care how it had happened because he scored a brand new replacement.

The insurance company coughed up for the HiLux repairs, although Vik's dad was a bit dirty about having to fork out the $300 excess. We suffered a bit of stress because it was almost three weeks before the ute was repaired. We had an important twenty-first birthday party coming up and needed the ute to pick up the ice and a portable cool room.

Fortunately we got the HiLux ute back just in time, ready to sneak off to the twenty-first party the next Saturday night!

* He didn't have the guts to identify himself, fearing Vik's dad may recognise the circumstances!

Still Good Mates

A.G. Thomlinson
Toowoomba, QLD

I can't remember a time when me and Brad weren't good mates. We went through school together, starting in kindy and finishing at the end of high school. When it came to choosing jobs we both decided to do plumbing and got apprenticeships with two different plumbers. This was the first time we'd ever really spent much time apart. When we finished our apprenticeships we decided to go into business together, and opened the doors of Down Under Drainage. At first we drove worn-out old utes, but after two years our accountant suggested we lease new vehicles to help minimise our tax. After nearly a month of non-stop debate we finally decided to climb into two new 3-litre 4x4 Isuzu D-MAX single cab utes.

Although Brad and I had the same interests, we were very different. He was slow and serious and methodical, whereas I tended to rush into things a bit too quickly. The one thing we both enjoyed was taking the piss out of each other whenever possible, and our new utes provided an unexpected opportunity for a bit of fun.

One day Brad left his ute parked at my place overnight so I crawled underneath and fastened a large nylon cable tie around Brad's drive shaft. I didn't cut off the protruding end of the cable tie; I left it long. I then coiled the long loose end of the cable tie back around the drive shaft, and then wrapped a length of tape around it to secure it.

The next day we both took off in our utes to meet up at a job. As Brad got going the rotation of his drive shaft gradually frayed the tape, which eventually came off, leaving the loose end of the cable tie slapping against the underside of the ute. The noise of the slapping sounded like the transmission was about to blow up. Brad arrived at the job and then spent an anxious half-hour underneath his ute before he discovered the problem and removed the cable tie. He automatically assumed that the dealer had somehow forgotten to remove the cable tie before delivering the ute. That is, until a mutual friend whispered in his ear that I was the responsible party.

Unknown to me, Brad started plotting his revenge. He got hold of a small, round boiled-lolly tin, about 100mm in diameter. He gave the bottom a belt with a hammer, so that the middle of the base of the tin was slightly raised. He inserted four ball bearings in the tin, and then taped the lid on. When I wasn't looking he taped the tin underneath my passenger-side seat, out of sight.

The result was that most of the time the ball bearings slid soundlessly around the inside of the tin. But whenever I went around a sharp corner, or hit a decent pot hole, a metallic sound came from what sounded like underneath the ute. This noise drove me nuts. For months I searched the engine, transmission and suspension for a solution. I took the ute back to the dealer four times in two months. They couldn't even hear the noise, let alone fix it. After almost six months Brad decided he'd had enough fun, so he told me that he was going to fix the noise for me. I told him that I doubted he'd be able to fix it, as both the

'We both enjoyed taking the piss out of each other whenever possible, and our new utes provided an unexpected opportunity for a bit of fun.'

dealer and I had done absolutely everything possible to locate the source of the irritating noise, without luck. Brad bet me fifty bucks he could fix it overnight, so we swapped vehicles and each drove home. Of course he simply removed the tin from underneath the seat and returned my ute the next day. After a couple of weeks I was convinced that the noise was gone, so I handed over my money and was forced to admit that Brad was a mechanical genius.

It was only after we'd drunk the fifty dollars at the pub one Friday night that Brad confessed to the scam. I felt like killing him!

We're still good mates, but we have promised to leave each other's utes alone.

Gerty

As told to John Bryant by Rob Sherring
North Richmond, NSW

Brian and Dwayne were married to two sisters, which meant that they shared the same mother-in-law: old Gerty. While it was a reasonably harmonious family everyone was aware that old Gerty was absolutely loaded and that she didn't have long left on this earth. Consequently Brian and Dwayne were as nice as pie to the old duck, always going out of their way to help her, to curry favour, usually with clenched teeth.

Brian was pretty sure that he was ahead in the inheritance stakes. Being a switched on finance broker, he had helped Gerty with her many and varied investments, so it was only natural that she turned to him for advice when anything came up. On the other hand, Dwayne worked as a parks and gardens supervisor with the local council. He was smart enough in his own way, but the only time he seemed to be able to gain any real brownie points was when Gerty needed something shifted in his ute.

Just after Gerty's eighty-fifth birthday party, the family convinced her that she should sell up and move into a retirement villa. This presented Brian with a whole range of opportunities to display his wonderfully caring nature as he liaised with real estate agents, talked to the bank, corresponded with solicitors, negotiated with the retirement village, and generally made a huge fuss about the enormous workload that he was undertaking on Gerty's behalf.

Dwayne, on the other hand, watched all this with a feeling of helplessness. He had a sinking sensation deep in his gut that Brian had successfully wormed his way into Gerty's affections, pushing him aside. He feared that ultimately he and his wife would miss out when it came to Gerty's will. In fact Gerty's will was often the subject of discussion among her relatives, because the cunning old duck hadn't given anybody a clue where she was going to park her millions when she finally kicked the bucket. But by keeping them all guessing she was enjoying her old age to the max. Everybody was forced into being sickly sweet to her all the time, no matter how outrageous her demands or how cranky she got.

After Brian completed all the financial and legal arrangements it came time for Gerty to move from her old family home into her new villa. Brian was about to book a removalist when Dwayne suddenly realised that this was his big chance to jump in and demonstrate his undying love for the old girl. Although Gerty could have afforded to fly her household goods around the world in a jumbo jet if she'd wanted, she did love the thought of saving a dollar. So when Dwayne said that he and his trusty old ute would step up to the mark and move all her gear, she was genuinely delighted. Brian of course poo-pooed the idea, saying that there was too much stuff for Dwayne and his ute; and besides, he would probably damage the furniture and rupture his hernia in the process. Gerty listened to both sides of the argument but was finally swayed by the cash-saving, together with Dwayne's ironclad guarantee that nothing would get damaged, not even a scratch. And although Gerty would never admit it, she always liked to watch Dwayne sweat profusely on her behalf, especially when his hernia was playing up.

The day of the big move saw Dwayne arrive in his 1992 Mazda Bravo ute, pulling a large trailer that he had hired for the occasion. He was accompanied by a young bloke from work that he'd promised $150 cash for the day. Because Gerty's retirement villa was over an hour's drive from her old home, Dwayne decided he needed to maximise each load to cut down on the number of trips he would have to make. The first few loads went pretty well. They mostly consisted of the lighter items such as the bedroom and lounge furniture, together with lots of cartons and kitchen utensils.

Towards mid-afternoon Dwayne had shifted most of the stuff and was now facing his last load, which contained the larger, heavier items. As he walked through the house surveying the remaining items he felt a pang of concern as he noted the large old-fashioned refrigerator, separate freezer and a large slate-topped dining table. But perhaps the greatest challenge that confronted him was Gerty's old pump organ that had been in the family for nearly a century; it was big and it was heavy. Gerty had reminded Dwayne that very morning – at least half a dozen times – of all the good times they'd enjoyed standing around that old pump organ, singing their hearts out. 'Whatever you do, Dwayne, make sure you wrap that organ in blankets. If I see even one scratch on it there'll be hell to pay, m' boy.' With Gerty's threat lingering in his ears, accompanied by the thought of her many millions making it into his bank account, Dwayne realised this last load could make or break him.

Because the deck of the trailer was a lot lower than the deck of the ute, Dwayne decided to load the heavy items into the trailer; it would mean less lifting. In went the fridge, the freezer and the slate top of the dining table. Then Dwayne and his offsider grunted and groaned under the weight of Gerty's beloved pump organ, finally positioning it in the centre of the trailer and smothering it in a sea of blankets. Dwayne was pretty pleased. The trailer was now packed so tightly that he was tempted to not tie the load down, but decided to fasten a couple of ropes across it just in case.

After doing a quick scout around the house and picking up the last few odds and ends, Dwayne popped them into the back of the ute, slammed the front door of the house for the last time, and headed off on his last trip for the day. As he gunned the Bravo he felt the drag of the trailer, which he figured was probably loaded to its maximum capacity – or maybe a little beyond.

The route to Gerty's new villa took Dwayne down a secondary road that the locals referred to as the Big Dipper. A single lane in each direction followed a very steep gorge down to a creek, then up the other side at an equally steep angle. Since Dwayne had already driven the Big Dipper a few times that day, he didn't pay any particular attention to his speed, forgetting that his ute was towing a grossly overloaded trailer.

As the Bravo started to descend into the Big Dipper it quickly gathered speed. Dwayne gently applied the brakes, causing the heavily laden trailer to start pushing against the ute. Dwayne had to apply even greater pressure on the brakes to try to keep his speed in check. Then the unthinkable happened. Governed strictly by the laws of physics, the trailer decided that the ute was going too slowly and that it needed to overtake. All Dwayne knew was that the trailer was starting to fishtail, pulling the back of his ute one way, then the other. At that crucial moment Dwayne remembered a similar situation in a mate's vehicle some years ago: they had avoided jackknifing and survived only because his mate had accelerated to keep the trailer tracking evenly behind his vehicle.

Even though Dwayne was only a third of the way down the Big Dipper, he really had no option other than to hit the accelerator to prevent the violent fishtailing of the trailer. As the ute picked up speed the sickening sway of the trailer temporarily eased, but by this time Dwayne was doing over 100 kph and still had several hundred metres to go before reaching the bottom of the Big Dipper.

With the ute and trailer now rocketing down the steep hill at a highly dangerous speed, Dwayne experienced mental overload as the flow of data greatly exceeded his brain's capacity to process it. Instead of holding his nerve and trying to keep his ute gently accelerating until he hit the bottom of the descent, his common sense and rational thinking went on holiday. Without considering the implications of his action, he panicked and started stamping on the brake pedal, somehow hoping that the laws that undergirded the entire universe would be suspended for a brief moment in time. Dwayne's sudden panic-braking caused the trailer to resume its wild fishtailing, which in the last couple of hundred metres became so severe that at the very bottom of the Big Dipper the trailer jackknifed.

At an enormous speed that shall forever remain the subject of speculation, the ute didn't so much hit the guardrail – it simply flattened it. Like a derailed freight train, Dwayne, ute and trailer speared off into the bush.

Incredibly, by sheer good luck, the whole convoy missed the scattered gum trees and ploughed an enormous furrow into the slush for nearly a hundred metres before finally coming to rest. The Bravo's sump was shattered, taken out by an old tree stump during its wild ride.

Shaken, and whiter than the surrounding ghost gums, Dwayne and his offsider scrambled from the ute, hardly believing that they were in one piece after their terrifying ordeal. However, the worst was yet to come, for when Dwayne turned to survey the trailer, it was empty.

As his gaze rose he surveyed a trail of carnage where the fridge, freezer, dining table and other miscellaneous items had been scattered along the furrows left by the rampaging ute and trailer. Freaking out, Dwayne looked around for Gerty's precious pump organ, but it was nowhere to be seen. It wasn't until Dwayne walked back towards the road that he realised the organ had disintegrated into a thousand little bits; only an iron frame and a bird's nest of wires remained. There, lying in lots of little pieces in the dirt, were his chances of scoring anything at all from Gerty's will.

The police turned up, and after filling out their accident report they booked Dwayne for negligent driving. Then, as a 4WD recovery crane lifted his mangled Bravo onto a tilt tray, Dwayne said a silent farewell. She was uninsured, and he sure as hell didn't have the cash to replace her. He'd be lucky if he could scrape up enough cash to buy a second-hand 50-cc moped – and that's if Gerty didn't kill him first.

Gerty!

He'd almost forgotten the trouble he was in. How would he break the bad news to her? As he sat in a taxi, riding to her new villa, he dreaded confronting old Gerty and having to confess that he'd smashed up her pride and joy, her million-year-old family pump organ. When he arrived at Gerty's place they were just finishing a sumptuous barbecue.

'Where ya been?' everyone screamed at him. 'We thought you'd had an accident or sumfink.'

Dwayne's heart sank. There was Gerty, staring at him with barbecue sauce on her chin. 'Nuffin's happened to my old pump organ, has it, Dwayne? Dwayne? DWAYNE?'

Emotionally drained and still in shock from his horrendous ordeal, Dwayne felt like crying, so he did. Then, in the biggest voice he could summon, which was barely audible, he confessed. It was a long, garbled, sobbing, rambling confession. He held nothing back: he confessed all his sins, including the most significant, which was that the pump organ was in tiny pieces scattered over a few acres of swampland, never to be seen again. With his eyes closed, tears flowing down his cheeks, he finished his confession and waited for the torrent of abuse. But nothing – silence! He opened his eyes and there was Gerty, on her knees, her eyes rolled back in her head with only the whites showing, a daughter on either side holding her up. Everyone stood spellbound. Then, as Gerty slowly slid to the floor, Brian shouted,'Bugger me, she's fainted!'

Pandemonium broke loose as everyone screamed instructions at once. The ambulance arrived thirty-five minutes later to confirm that old Gerty hadn't fainted: she was stone cold, irretrievably dead. Heart attack!

Dwayne headed for the kitchen and grabbed a beer from the fridge, his mind numb as he tried to figure out whether he would perhaps be charged with murder.

Brian walked in and went to the fridge. Opening his beer, he winked at Dwayne and whispered, 'So you killed her, you clumsy bastard. I told you we should have used a removalist. But let's look on the bright side, mate: we're now going to get our hands on the old duck's cash.'

Two weeks later they were all assembled in Gerty's solicitor's office. The girls were weepy, but Brian was bright as a button, dressed in an expensive new business suit he'd bought for this special day; the day he anticipated he would at last become a millionaire. Dwayne was wearing sneakers and shorts because he had ridden there on his second-hand 125-cc Vespa scooter. All eyes were on the obese solicitor as he wiped his brow with a tissue and started reading out the last will and testament of Gertrude Heather Simpson.

First she bequeathed a house each to her two daughters, then $5,000 to her gardener, followed by a number of trinkets to the grandchildren. The solicitor droned on and on. A trust fund for Tweedy Bird, a new rotary clothes hoist for her ex-neighbour, a $500 hardware-store gift voucher for her butcher, a new pulpit for the church ... Brian was getting impatient and Dwayne was dreading having to witness Brian's joy when he copped a bucket load of Gerty's wealth. Then Dwayne heard his name.

'... *and to my dear son-in-law Dwayne Ronald Bennett, who, although not always blessed with the ability or capacity to render the services that others provide, has always been there for me when I needed him, especially with his trusty ute. I hereby bequeath the remainder of my estate.*'

* * *

Barely a month later Dwayne burbled slowly past Brian's house in his brand new $72,000 Maloo R8 SV Black Edition 6.2 litre ute. He smiled at Brian who was weeding his garden, waved, and then planted his right foot so savagely it almost went through the floor. Just before the fishtailing Maloo disappeared in a thick cloud of blue smoke, Brian caught a momentary glimpse of the personalised numberplate: GERTY.

He wept.

Stilettos and Fur Coats

John Bryant
Bilpin, NSW

Some owners treat their utes as lifeless objects – a useful tool for earning a living, a set of wheels to be trashed, or a beast of burden to be thrashed. They see them as mechanical devices made of steel, plastic and paint, to be used and abused as they see fit. The truth is very different.

Utes have feelings. Utes have names. Utes yearn to be loved and cherished. They need affection, respect, and must be faithfully maintained.

While the majority of utes live healthy, productive lives in harmony with their caring owners, a minority sadly find themselves in circumstances that can only be described as a never-ending nightmare. This case history has been released to expose the brutality often suffered by utes forced to live in abusive relationships, and to provide a warning to utes everywhere of the dangers of falling into the wrong hands.

And now to the sordid details of the lurid circumstances in which one innocent old ute found herself ...

The good Austrian doctor lived in a six-bedroom mansion on a five-acre manicured garden property in one of the better suburbs of Sydney. His six-car garage housed his $255,000 Lexus, his wife's $138,000 Audi, his $42,000 Honda Gold Wing motorcycle, a $15,000

Kawasaki jet ski, an $8,000 Bose surround-sound system, a massive 3D flat-screen TV, a leather lounge suite and a huge coolroom crammed with an impressive variety of very expensive imported wines. Better than most people's lounge rooms, the good doctor's garage was a stunning pleasure palace. He would often sit listening to his favourite music, or watching his favourite movies, sipping chilled white wine while gloating over the symbols of his success: his boy's toys.

Behind the good doctor's garage, out of sight, sat a crude, tumbledown, open-sided corrugated-iron shed. It housed left-over building materials and other junk. It also accommodated a 1978 Datsun 1200 ute. The old Datto, which had been purchased from its original owner for a mere $550, had enjoyed a wonderful life before falling into the hands of the good doctor. She had loved her previous owner but understood that he was too old to keep driving, so she looked forward to spending her remaining days in her new home. When she first rolled through the magnificent double gates of the doctor's impressive mansion she felt a shiver of excitement run through her drive shaft. She had never lived the high life before, so she assumed that this was going to be a fantastic place to slowly run out of rego during her declining years.

She was a little disgruntled when she was driven past the six-car garage and around the back, to be unceremoniously parked in the old shed in a position that left her open to the vagaries of the weather. Her anxiety escalated as she sat there, all alone, gathering cobwebs and dust, with her battery slowly ebbing away. For a ute that had been regularly washed, serviced and taken for a run, she felt dirty, neglected, old, sick, tired and unloved.

And that wasn't the worst of it. To her absolute horror she found that the good Austrian doctor and his petite blonde Austrian wife started throwing all manner of unwanted rubbish into her tray, including the occasional dead rabbit or rat carcass. While she hated to admit it to herself, she had been relegated to the role of a glorified garbage bin. During the long cold windy nights, she suffered nightmares, dreaming that she couldn't start, that her tyres had gone flat, that she had ended up as an old quadriplegic unable to power her own headlights. Her stress brought on a severe case of incontinence, resulting in a puddle of oil under her private parts. And while the Lexus and other expensive vehicles were washed weekly and serviced quarterly, she remained coated in filth, longing for a whiff of detergent. Her oil got so old and thick that it wouldn't leave the dipstick, even if someone had bothered to try coaxing it off with a rag.

The good doctor was ashamed to be seen in the old ute; he detested her. He would only take the Datto for a run under extreme circumstances, such as when the rear tub was so full, or so stinky, that his petite blonde wife nagged him to take a trip to the local tip. Before driving the ute, the good doctor would don sunglasses and a straw hat in an attempt to disguise himself. In the event he did ever happen to run into anybody he knew, he had already rehearsed an explanation as to how he was not, and never had been, related to or in any way associated with, this pathetic vehicle that common people refer to as a 'ute'. The good doctor's petite blonde wife had never ridden in the ute; it was simply beneath her dignity. It would mess up her ubiquitous all-white outfits: white underwear, white blouse, tight white leather slacks, white shoes, white dingle-dangle earrings, white nail polish on all fingers and toes. Yes, it would destroy her virginal social image if she was ever caught out in public in 'that pathetic old wreck'!

The only respite in the old girl's miserable existence were the occasional trips to the tip, which usually occurred only two or three times a year. She feared these excursions because they always commenced with the disguised good doctor, looking like a mad scientist in holiday garb, entering the shed wheeling his dreaded jump-starter. Like a Packer whacker zotting a human being, that jump-starter almost fried the old girl's wiring. Her guts sometimes started smoking before her clagged old engine coughed into life, gulping down draughts of stale unleaded petrol that were peppered with fine particles of rust.

The poor old ute had almost given up hope when the bushfires of 1996 rolled around. She was awakened one morning by the crowing of the rooster that always sat pooping on her cab roof, and noticed a mist of blue smoke hanging in the air. At first she attributed it to her failing eyesight, but then remembered back to a time when she had carried her first owner and his family to safety through a roaring bushfire. She heard the wailing of sirens, and then the sounds of helicopters overhead. She suddenly realised in horror that the surrounding bushland was on fire; and there she was, sitting with her tray stacked high with extremely combustible garden rubbish. To top it off, she was sitting right next to a 205-litre drum full of the high octane racing fuel that the good doctor used in his 1200-cc V4 go-kart. This, she thought to herself, was it. If she stayed parked where she was she would be gutted by the flames and probably blown to bits in a humongous explosion when the fuel went up. What an unpleasant end; she felt sick to the depths of her gearbox! But, she had to face it: there was no chance that anyone would even think about moving her out of harm's way. Not when the six-car garage was full of far more valuable vehicles that would be the focus of any rescue attempts.

As the fire front progressed rapidly towards the good doctor's boundary fence, the police bashed on the front door and ordered an immediate evacuation. Time was short. The good doctor and his petite blonde wife panicked. They raced around their mansion grabbing armfuls of cash and jewellery. He grabbed a one-week supply of his prostate pecker pills; she struggled under four of her favourite fur coats. They tumbled out the front door and headed for the six-car garage, her obscenely high stiletto heels clip-clopping along the verandah like a racehorse.

Unfortunately for the good doctor's petite blonde wife, she couldn't see where she was going with a pile of fur coats in her face. She tripped, disappearing over the verandah rail, spearing head-first into a forest of flowering hydrangeas in a flurry of fur coats. Meanwhile, the good doctor frantically pressed his remote control to open the garage doors but, to his horror, the doors stayed shut. Dropping his pecker pills, he tried to manually wrench the doors open, only to find that the electricity had been cut off by the fires. His growing panic turned into sheer terror when he realised that the Lexus and Audi were inaccessible. There was no escape; they were about to fry and die!

By this time his petite blonde wife had clawed her way out of the bushes, her fur coats bedraggled, her virginal white outfit and dignity shredded. As she realised their predicament she started screaming in terror. Slapping her savagely across the face to settle her down, the good doctor grabbed her by the arm and clip-clopped her around the side of the garage to the shed. 'Kvickly,' he screamed, 'get in ze bloody oot.'

Taken completely by surprise, the startled old Datsun nearly spat her dipstick as her two dishevelled owners crammed their sweating butts into her front seats. As luck would have it, the old girl had done a run to the tip two weeks before, so there was just enough juice left in the battery to fire up the engine. As the good doctor sat there cranking the starter motor, the old ute realised that she had come to a watershed moment.

Here she sat, having been abused, mistreated, neglected, and taken for granted for years. Now her torturers sat squirming inside her guts, trusting that she'd ferry them to safety. Suddenly the tables had turned. No longer was she dependent on them; their lives now depended on her!

Deep down at the bottom of her sump she knew that this was an opportunity to take a stand for abused utes everywhere. It was time to draw a line in the sand, to rise up, to nail her colours to the mast, to fearlessly declare what she believed in. She saw it all so clearly now. Her windscreen was crystal clear. She made her decision: it was time to act.

As the good doctor continued to frantically crank the starter and pump the accelerator pedal, the old Datsun sucked in her last breath. It was a looooong, slooooow, very deep breath. And once she had drawn that breath in, she held it. And she held it. She held it in for so long that air was prevented from passing through her carburettor and into her engine. In fact she held that last breath for so desperately long that she became dizzy, barely hearing the good doctor's frenzy as he screamed, 'Start zis bustard. BLOODY START ZIS BUSTARD!'

The old Datto slipped slowly into unconsciousness as the last few amps trickled out of her battery and died forever. As the roaring flames engulfed the old shed, the drum of racing fuel went off like a bomb. An orange plume billowed eighty metres into the air, accompanied by an explosion that started dogs barking five kilometres away. No one had a hope; the old Datto was gone. Her soul was already in the hands of the ute angel; ferried triumphantly up, up, up into glory in ute heaven.

Way back down on planet earth the Datto's twisted and lifeless carcass lay in the shed, white hot and engulfed in flames, providing a fitting funeral pyre for the pathetic doctor and his petite blonde wife.

The following day's newspaper told the story of the tragedy. The article bemoaned the fact that the charred remains of the couple could not be recovered due to the enormous eruption caused by the detonation of the racing fuel. The explosion and heat had converted them into billions of tiny molecules, which had been blown into the ether. The good doctor and his petite blonde Austrian wife now hung, invisible, in a thin mist in the atmosphere over the surrounding districts.

But travelling around Australia's car yards, moving even faster than a drum of exploding racing fuel, was the saga of the legendary Datto ute. She wasn't pretty to look at, she never won any races, she struggled to carry a one-tonne load, she could barely manage a burnout, she was just an old tip ute. But when push came to shove, she had the guts to stand up and be counted. To decide that enough was enough; that it was payback time!

Aussie Icon

'Hillbilly'
Mountain Lagoon, NSW

When thirty-two-year-old Alby bought his Holden One Tonner in the early seventies he paid the princely sum of $2,995. The ute's cast-alloy tray was one of the last manufactured in Australia in that era – it was constructed like a World War II tank. He often boasted, 'I could melt that sucker down and make four or five modern trays, there's that much meat in 'er.'

Business had been good to him back then. He was usually flush with cash because he used to siphon tax-free money out of his family-owned sawmill in the North Coast hinterland. As the years progressed, Alby resisted the urge to update the old Holden, even when the family sold the sawmill and he scored enough to retire. He didn't have to work, but he went out and got a job with the local council anyway; he became the 'Stop and Go' man in the local road maintenance crew. Driving from the council depot to the pub each afternoon, he often marvelled that his ute needed so little in the way of care and upkeep. He felt it was obscene to even think of ditching her in favour of some expensive bit of thin tin with mag wheels and a radio. Yes, he would wring every last ounce of value out of this old girl, and he would never part with her. Never!

As Alby progressed from middle age to old age, so did his ute. While Alby was slowly going bald, craters appeared in the ute's vinyl floor coverings, followed by a rusty hole where Alby's heel rested next to the accelerator pedal. His grime-covered Yakka overalls quickly wore away the factory seat coverings, eventually taking out the padding and leaving several springs exposed. This didn't worry Alby too much. It never occurred to him to pay for repairs or slip down to the wreckers for a second-hand seat. He'd occasionally throw another hessian bag on top of the springs to avoid getting spiked, because deep down he was a skinflint who hated spending money. Besides, he told himself, it added to his ute's 'character'.

His four hubcaps disappeared before the turn of the century, but Alby couldn't remember when or where. Somehow he always managed to get the ute registered with the cracked windscreen, chipped headlights and rust. When he originally noticed the rust, it was slowly munching its way around the windscreen, doors and sills – but Alby figured it was par for the course. If it didn't rust then it wasn't a genuine Holden! But in spite of all the neglect and lack of maintenance, the old Tonner started most mornings, even in the dead of winter. And if the battery, which was always thirsty for a drink, happened to be flat, the old ute would do her best to kick over as Alby kangarooed her down the hill for a clutch start. Yes sir, she was one hell of a ute, worth her weight in pure gold, and he loved her to bits.

By 2010 Alby was totally bald, his hearing and eyesight were shot, and he had shrunk two inches in height. His enlarged prostate forced him to have a pee once an hour, day and night. He was fully retired after being sacked from his council job for belting an impatient motorist's car with his Stop/Go sign. At the time he had been quite happy to cop the sack, because he was smoking three packs of cigarettes a day through sheer boredom. He reckoned his lungs were so full of crap that he could have won a gold medal at the World Coughing Championships!

Every now and again some young buck would approach him at the pub, usually during one of his hourly trips to the toilet, with an offer to buy his old Holden. In earlier days the young fellas only offered a couple of hundred bucks, which wasn't nearly enough to put a gleam in Alby's piggy red eyes. 'Bugger off,' Alby would tell them. 'I've been thrashing the old girl for the best part of forty years 'n' no amount of money would make me part with her. She's part of the family!'

But as the years passed by, the old Tonner slowly morphed from 'unwanted wreck' into a true-blue 'Aussie icon'. Body damage and rust didn't matter much any more; similar utes began bringing increasingly bigger bucks from young blokes who wanted to do them up. So as the supply of old Holdens grew thinner on the ground, the price of survivors continued to creep upwards.

Then one day it happened. Alby was leaning on the bar, half a schooner of VB in his hand, fag hanging from his lips, when a young bloke of about twenty, with a shaved head, tattoos and facial piercings, slouched down on the stool next to him.

'Your Tonner out there, old mate?'

'Might be. But she's not for sale!'

'Give ya three grand. Cash. Now.'

Alby might have been half stung, but jeepers – THREE GRAND! That was five bucks more than he paid for the old girl almost forty years ago! He slid the key across the bar as the young fella took a rubber band off the wad of hundred-dollar bills that he'd pulled from his pocket.

Alby had no idea what he'd do with the three grand, or how he'd get home that night, or what he'd do for transport tomorrow. But what he did know was that very few people make money out of an old ute.

Hounds from Hell

John Bryant
Bilpin, NSW

They were chasing after her and gaining fast as she crashed her way through the bush in the pitch black. Sheer terror pumped adrenaline through her veins, enabling her to leap obstacles that would otherwise have been impossible. The yelping and frenzied barking told her there were dozens of the beasts, unseen in the dark, about to reach her at any moment; to maul her to death in a bloody feeding frenzy.

Suddenly Cathy was awake, bolt upright in bed, eyes staring wildly into the dark. Her sheets were soaked with sweat. Could she still hear barking? Or was it just echoes from the nightmare she had escaped only seconds before? She reached out for reassurance, grabbing to feel for Owen, who was sleeping silently next to her. He was still there; she was safe. It was just that same recurring nightmare. As she tried to get back to sleep she told herself over and over that she was OK, that she had nothing to fear.

Cathy's nightmares had started about three weeks earlier, after she had suggested to Owen that they go down and pick up a load of mulch in his Triton table-top. It was coming to the end of spring and they had just finished planting about seventy new trees and shrubs on their ten-acre property. The old ute had been a great workhorse, carrying all their garden supplies without having to get their family car dirty. And now with a hot summer forecast, they needed to get mulch around all the new plantings to give their garden the best possible chance of survival when the hot weather hit.

But in all truth, it wasn't really her concern for the garden that motivated Cathy to suggest a trip to the local council tip for mulch. What Cathy really wanted was to catch a glimpse of her ex-husband, Tony, who worked there. She and Tony had divorced about three years earlier and gone their separate ways. She had only seen him twice in the last twelve months, both times at the tip when he was operating the machine that loaded the mulch into her ute. They hadn't spoken, but Cathy thought she caught a glimpse of longing when their eyes met. Cathy had remarried, thinking that she'd met her true love in Owen. But in recent months she had started to suspect that perhaps she'd made the wrong choice; that perhaps, deep down, Tony was the man she really wanted.

Tony had been horribly hurt when Cathy, without warning, had walked out on him to shack up with Owen. He'd always secretly thought that Cathy was a bit selfish and self-centred, but had been more than happy to overlook her shortcomings because he loved everything else about her. After she left, he went through his own private hell for over twelve months as he tried to cope with the loss of the only woman he had ever loved. His sanity wasn't helped by her lawyer's ferocious attacks, which were squarely aimed at cleaning him out financially. In the end they wore him down. He simply tossed in the towel and let her have the lot, including the Triton ute; he just didn't have the stomach to continue the fight. Even now, three years later, he lived in a rented unit with rented second-hand furniture. The only things he actually owned were a $500 WB ute and a couple of sets of clothes. That was it.

The first time Owen and Cathy had driven into the tip to collect a load of mulch, Tony could hardly believe his eyes. He'd been doing his best to put them out of his mind, even though he couldn't get Cathy completely out of his heart. He felt incensed that she would intentionally add insult to injury by flaunting her new man in his face at his workplace. But he said and did nothing; just loaded their mulch, turned around and drove off.

The second time they came he was equally unprepared. It was all he could do to restrain himself from smashing the huge front-end loader bucket onto the ute cabin, crushing them both like a pair of cockroaches. And of course it wasn't only Cathy he missed; he also missed the old yellow Triton ute that Owen was now driving. He had loved that five-speed manual gearbox coupled with that awesome diesel engine. Even though it was a bit of a top-speed slug, it had plenty of low-down grunt. He almost felt like a Formula One driver as he used to snick it up and down through the gears on his way to and from work; so much more satisfying than driving an automatic.

The third time Owen rolled into the tip with Tony's ex-wife to collect another load of mulch for Tony's ex-garden in Tony's ex-ute, Tony was preoccupied. He was just about to undertake one of the most unpleasant tasks that were part of his job at the tip.

Earlier in the day, just as Tony was about to take his lunch break, the van from the local animal shelter had pulled in with its cargo of euthanised animals. The van contained three dead dogs that had been put down earlier that day, unclaimed and unwanted. These and similar animals were regularly buried at the tip. Because

Tony had already washed up for his lunch break he asked the van driver to deposit the dead animals in the bucket of his front-end loader. He said that he would bury them after he had finished his lunch.

It was just after Tony's lunch break when Cathy and Owen drove in to pick up their mulch, and the three dead dogs were still lying in the bucket of Tony's front-end loader. Tony was just about to dump the dogs and go and load the mulch, when he noticed Cathy and Owen parked next to the mulch pile in the idling ute, waiting to be loaded. When he saw the lovebirds sitting there in his old Triton, something in his head snapped – although he later claimed that the devil made him do it. Ignoring the fact that he had three dead dogs in the bucket of his front-end loader, Tony took one run into the mulch stockpile, filled his bucket, and then dumped the lot into the back of Owen's ute. 'Hope they enjoy their new pups,' Tony thought to himself as he avoided eye contact and headed off to park the loader. Owen and Cathy, completely unaware that their load contained anything more than mulch, drove out the gates and headed for home.

When Owen and Cathy arrived home that Friday evening Cathy grabbed them both a cold beer. They sat out in the twilight in their garden discussing the next day's projects. Cathy had planned to trim the azaleas, but they decided that first thing next morning they would both get stuck into mulching around the new shrubs and trees.

They were out early the next day, eager to get started before the heat. Owen backed the ute up to one of the garden beds and dropped the tailgate, standing back so that he didn't get hit by the hungry board that toppled out as soon as it was released. Cathy, who had always been an animal lover, stood watching with her mulch fork in hand. As the hungry board and a small avalanche of mulch fell to the ground, the cascade was followed by the three dead dogs, which landed at Cathy's feet with a thump. She stood there frozen to the spot in absolute horror. She then emitted a long scream as she turned tail and raced into the house sobbing.

Owen, who had a stronger stomach than Cathy, was equally horrified and stood there with his mind racing, trying to figure out where the dogs had come from. His first thought was that it might have been a sick practical joke; but none of his mates had been anywhere near his ute since yesterday. Then he fleetingly suspected one of his neighbours had done it overnight as payback for a fencing dispute they'd had about a year before. But hang on, he thought, what ogre would murder some innocent dogs simply to vent his spleen? Owen couldn't figure it out so he walked inside to comfort Cathy, who by this time was bordering on hysteria.

After a while Cathy calmed down and together they went over Owen's movements since he had picked up the mulch. They finally concluded that Tony was the culprit. Owen was seething with anger as he got on the phone and called the tip supervisor to tell him what had happened. The supervisor was mortified. He undertook to conduct an immediate inquiry and sack the person responsible. With profuse apologies the supervisor immediately dispatched a vehicle to go and collect the dead dogs from Owen and Cathy's home.

After a couple of days had passed Owen wasn't overly upset by the whole affair, particularly as the tip supervisor insisted on supplying Owen with free mulch any time he wanted to call in and collect a load. On top of that, it was a great story to tell the blokes over a beer around the barbecue.

And Tony?

Cathy had already cost him his marriage, his home, his garden, his Triton ute, his superannuation and just about everything else her greedy lawyer could lay his grubby little hands on. It could be said that she had now also cost him his job. But when he analysed the situation he had to admit that he had given up his job willingly. Dropping those three dead dogs into Cathy's ute was the working man's equivalent of writing a resignation letter. So after dumping the dogs, he climbed in his battered old Holden WB ute, cranked up the stereo volume to a level where Willie Nelson filled his entire brain, and headed south into the Victorian high country. What was the point of hanging around town for the weekend, then turning up to work on Monday morning to give the boss the satisfaction of sacking him?

Unfortunately, it didn't pan out that easily for Cathy, who simply couldn't get the images of those stiff dead dogs out of her mind. She kept reliving the scene as they tumbled lifelessly out of Owen's ute and onto the garden with a thump, covered in mulch. She started having nightmares. It was always the same bad dream. The ghosts of the dogs were angry. They had sensed Cathy's terror and interpreted it as an admission of guilt. So most nights their ghosts gathered in Cathy's bedroom, leapt into her dreams and chased her ... panting, snarling, salivating, teeth flashing through their bared red lips, eager for revenge. In her dreams Cathy would run to take refuge with Tony in the safety of his old yellow Triton ute, but it always drove off before she could reach it, leaving her to the mercy of the hounds from hell!

The Ute that Fell Over

Lee Robertson
Darwin, NT

The ute sparkled in the bright Top End light as the early morning rays of sunlight danced on the drops of water clinging to the white duco. But the old Holden ute had seen better days. It had several dings where the front left mudguard had been dented in a collision with a gate; the right back mudguard near the bumper was bent and moulded to the body – a reversing mishap. The tailgate was imprinted with the trailer ball from endless drops. Scrapes, scratches and tears in the upholstery all testified to an eventful and productive life. But these were only small problems. The motor was sound and the air conditioner – its best feature – still blasted cold air in the hot, steamy north.

The ute was a work machine in a remote bush community and if it could've talked it would have told a great story: about the children it had carried in its tray, the dogs that had yapped and nipped at its wheels, and the weird and wonderful animals it had transported, including turtles, fish and even a dugong. And on one occasion, when it was young and sparkling, it had participated in a funeral; part of a solemn and tragic procession of painted Koori who wailed and cried, trailing behind the coffin in the ute's tray, covered with flowers and bark paintings.

Joe, the tall, thin Aboriginal man who washed the ute, was part of a local building team. His weekly washing ritual saw the red dust dissolve and the chrome shine for a brief moment. A couple of his dogs would lie nearby in the shade of the casuarinas, waiting for the job to be finished. The ute for them represented excitement and adventure; riding majestically in the back, nostrils flared and ears shredded in the wind, it was the highlight of their day. The only time they weren't allowed to travel was when the tray was loaded with timber or gravel or other materials. But even then, if they were quick enough, securing a position on top of the load was tolerated if done efficiently and quietly.

Joe had finished hosing the wheel rims and went to turn the tap off. The sunshine was starting to bite as the school siren confirmed that it was time for the white man's workday to commence. The dogs, recognising the signal, leapt over the tailgate and positioned themselves, one on each side behind the cabin. They were ready. Joe, noting their antics, yelled, 'Git outta there! Barge day and big mob things coming. Go on, git.'

The dogs glanced Joe's way but immediately sat down where they were, quietly communicating their intentional disobedience. Joe had already given up on moving them. He knew before he had opened his mouth that the order was destined to be ignored. He lowered his skinny frame into the driver's seat and wiggled the key till the old ute fired into life.

He pulled out of the driveway and onto the red gravel road, headed to the shop for breakfast. That was the best thing about going to work: the egg and bacon sandwich he had first thing every day, freshly cooked and washed down with coffee laced with plenty of sugar. No humbug lighting of fires and worrying about whether there were any groceries left in the house after his large extended family had been fed. He bought food at least once every week, including steak, onions and eggs for himself, and the rest to share. His nephew's son couldn't wait to get a job with the lure of breakfast at the shop each day. That daily breakfast and the occasional steak provided all the motivation he needed to get up off his bum and seek employment. Better than a thousand interventions, thought Joe to himself as he pulled up outside the shop.

Sam – his brother and workmate – was already eating a hamburger, seated on the low post-and-rail fence out the front. Joe was pleased to see the shop was open and the take-away in full swing. It was always touch-and-go as to whether the food supplies would last until the arrival of the next barge, and whether the staff would turn up instead of being off at some community event. The day was looking good.

Joe stepped up to the window of the take-away, nodding to his aunty-mother who worked there. He only had to appear at the serving window and she would automatically throw together a bacon and egg toasted sandwich and a coffee, into which she stirred four generous sugars. She usually expected him to leave some extra money so his niece could eat later in the day. As he was feeling generous that morning, he didn't wait for her to ask; he just handed her twenty dollars knowing he wouldn't see any change. She chattered on to the other women serving. 'Them pies be ready now, in that big oven.' Then to him, 'See you, son.'

When he returned to the ute his brother was already in the cabin.

'Mmm, hungry this morning. Barge day, yeah?' Sam said.

Joe nodded while still chewing. The sandwich tasted particularly delicious that morning and the coffee hot and sweet. Yes, he thought, the perfect way to start a day. There had been many days in his life that hadn't started this way – with food – so he expressed his gratitude by consciously appreciating each mouthful, chewing slowly and with concentration. He ate methodically then tossed the remnants to the dogs in the back of the ute. After a bit of a squabble they both secured some bits of crust and lay down, content.

The barge landing was a few kilometres out of town so they headed off in that direction. They could see plumes of dust both in front of them as well as behind, indicating that they were not the only vehicle heading for the barge ramp that morning.

Barge day created a sense of anticipation in the small isolated community. Shop shelves were replenished, the tuck shop served salad and some of the more fortunate occasionally took delivery of a new vehicle. There was no end to the excitement: new machinery, car parts, petrol, building materials of all kinds and crate after crate of goods packaged in plastic. Everything had to be manoeuvred on forklifts to waiting vehicles; it was fast and dynamic. It might have looked chaotic, but it was a carefully orchestrated operation that was governed by the rise and fall of the tide. All those participating in this community event were engrossed in following a precise order, otherwise the job would not get done in the time available.

The utes and troopies always vied for positions at the top of the boat ramp, getting ready for their turn to load. The sun sparkled on the water as it shone aqua blue on the beautiful Arafura. The approaching barge loomed large as a dirty swill of brown water spread underneath its turning propeller. The churning mud helped maintain what everybody called 'the barge hole', a permanent underwater dent in the local seascape.

On the ramp leading to the barge there was an imaginary down-lane and up-lane. Space was at a premium, and as time was of the essence the forklift needed to travel the shortest possible distance when offloading the barge and dumping the packages into the backs of the trucks and utes.

Joe's boss appeared. 'Glad to see you're here. We're fourth up, better get on the ramp. There's 'bout six we gotta get. They're late in and tide's already getting low. Gonna have to move it! I'll see you at the workshop.'

Joe nodded then headed to the top of the landing. All progress down the ramp was in reverse, so Joe positioned himself accordingly. Like everyone else, after his vehicle had been loaded, he would head back up the ramp, down the dusty track to town, then reappear for another load.

Joe had never liked reversing the ute down the narrow ramp, and the space seemed particularly cramped that morning. He needed to keep his right wheels close to the edge of the ramp, wary of the drop of about a metre and a half at the top. He inched down slowly, keeping a close watch on the edge of the ramp on one side, and the heavily laden trucks coming back up the ramp on the other.

The battered council truck had been loaded with long lengths of piping. In haste they had been loaded horizontally, so they hung over both sides of the dilapidated vehicle by about a metre. The wide truck and overhanging pipes were posing a real challenge to the other vehicles that were struggling to get down the ramp. Those backing down the ramp were instructed to move precariously closer to the edge to make room. Joe obliged, and then it happened in a split second.

The ute poised unsteadily on the edge of the ramp for a second, seeming to defy gravity. Then as the right wheels lost the surface, the ute lurched sideways off the ramp, sliding quite gracefully until it came to rest on its side in the damp sand. Joe's addiction to air conditioning meant the windows were up, so no damage was done to protruding limbs. Sam ended up on top of Joe, with both of them sandwiched against the bottom door. The motor was still running.

Joe managed to reach up to the key and kill the motor. Sam disentangled himself from Joe, clambered to the window above them, wound it down, and hoisted himself out. Joe followed, noting that both dogs were already heading for the shade of the casuarinas that lined the water. For them it was just another day out on the ute, their dingo speed and agility saving their bacon. Joe and Sam had silly grins on their faces as they stood there surveying the ute's novel position: lying on its side like a resting wallaby that wasn't quite comfortable. With its wheels off the ground, helpless, the ute pleaded for urgent assistance.

Recovering from their initial shock they both chuckled quietly.

'Shit.' Joe scratched his head as they both stared at the disabled ute. 'Tide coming. Better tell the boss, eh? Need to be quick-fast.'

Joe borrowed a mobile phone from his cousin who was in the crowd of people that now stood in an excited semi-circle around the disabled ute. It was dicey as to whether the phone would get reception this far from town. He dialled the workshop and to his relief his boss answered.

'Joe here. Got little bit problem. That ute … he fell over.'

Ute Balancing Act

Chris Anastasiou
Annandale, QLD

Quite a few years ago, when I was young and stupid, my brother and I bought a Holden V8 ute in Townsville. As we were driving it back home to Mount Isa, where we were living at the time, the motor blew up. We had no option but to leave it in Richmond for about a month until we could organise transport.

We prevailed on one of our friends who owned a six-cylinder 202 Holden ute to come to the rescue. He hooked up a car trailer to the back of his ute, and seven of us piled in to drive to Richmond. We left about midnight and drove all night, arriving after dawn. We chained the stuffed V8 ute onto the trailer and set off back to Mount Isa, picking up a hitchhiker on the way.

There were three of us crammed into the cabin of the 202 ute. The hitchhiker and another bloke were sitting in the open air out back, and another of the blokes was asleep next to them in the tray. The other two blokes were sitting in the cab of the V8 ute, which was chained to the trailer, listening to the radio as we made our way along the highway. We were in the middle of nowhere when the trailer started swaying violently, causing the driver to lose control. The trailer jackknifed into a causeway measuring pole, with the impact breaking the chains that held the V8 ute onto the trailer.

The 202 ute ended up blocking the highway, with the V8 perched on top of it facing the opposite direction. My sleeping mate woke up to see the undercarriage of the V8 just above his head. Nobody was hurt, but we ended up with two stuffed utes, a badly damaged trailer, and a freaked out hitchhiker who will probably never hitch again.

Hot Wired

Peter Sinclair
Goulburn, NSW

A day after the rain. The paddocks are running with water and the yard is a bog. What are we going to do to fill in the time till the sun shines again?

I know. Let's go over to Gary's and we can rip around his bottom paddock in that old HK ute he's got that's not registered! We can do all sorts of things, like slides and doughnuts and spinouts and that sort of caper.

Chris and I head on over to Gary's and it doesn't take much convincing to get him to take the old ute out of the back shed. The battery is a bit flat, but the three of us push start her and when she roars into life Chris and myself jump into the back and we're sitting on this bale of hay and Gary is fairly up it, full bore down to the bottom paddock.

Neat slide, Gary. Wow. Give her more, mate. See if you can fishtail her. Beauty, cobber. What a ripper three-sixty. Oh mate, this is tops! Flatten her, Gaz, and see how far we can slide. Go, go, go. Anchors out slide, slide sliding, still sliding, sliding, straight into ... the electric fence. You know the type. Four strands of wire, the top one is the hot one and every six metres or so is one of them wooden spacers.

The ute hits the fence and it moves upwards, the bumper goes under the bottom wire and the whole bloody lot goes up onto the bonnet, up past the windscreen. The wipers went missing some years ago. Over the cabin, and I copped it in the gob and Chris got belted in the chest.

Well, it flattened both of us. Set us on our bums across this bale and jammed us there. That flaming wire was as tight as any bloody guitar string and we were stuck there, and every four seconds ...

WHACK. 1, 2, 3, 4 ... ZAP ... 1, 2, 3, 4 ... WHACK.

Come on, you mongrel ... ARGH, Gary, for ^*$^%@# sake, move the ... ARGH ... c'mon you *%&^@# ...GARY, ARGH.

We're getting fried in the back and he doesn't care, does he? If the truth be known he knows exactly what's happening but he can't stop laughing, can he? He's literally rolling round the floor of the ute!!

We finally got mobile again and went back up to the house and put the ute away. Then we grabbed Mr Flamin' Hilarious and tied the mongrel up facing the strainer at the gate inside the PODDY calves' yard, slopped molasses all over him and ... see how long you laugh now, MATE!

'Anchors out slide, slide sliding, still sliding, sliding, straight into . . . the electric fence.'

The Sloth

As told to John Bryant by Damien Winder
Mudgee, NSW

The Sloth is about the weirdest ute driver I've ever met.

Me and the Sloth drive escort utes for heavy haulage trucks, almost always at night when there's no traffic. We work under contract for a large machinery supplier, and any time they want to move their bulldozers or tractors, me and the Sloth drive the escort vehicles. You may have seen us. Yellow flashing lights on top of our Falcon utes, with 'Wide Load' signs and all that sort of stuff. Usually I go out the front, with the Sloth coming up behind the low loader. We talk all the time on the CBs, warning each other and the low loader driver about approaching traffic. The Sloth doesn't actually talk, he has a sort of a grunt language that only me and some of the truckies can understand. The noise he makes on the CB is probably an echo caused by the Coke bottle that is usually in his mouth.

I'm a pretty average bloke, in that while I usually drive at night, I try not to sleep all day. The Sloth is different. Ever since I've known him, he sleeps all day and only comes out at night, sort of like a wombat or something. I doubt the Sloth has seen daylight for years, because if ever we're on the road towards dawn, he's desperate to either head for home or pull off the road and sleep. I once had a dream that he turned into an overstuffed turkey when the sunlight hit him ... maybe he would.

The Sloth has chucked the passenger seat from his XH Falcon ute so he can sort of twist himself into a sleeping position whenever he's not actually driving. I can't figure this out. I have a canopy on the back of my ute and it's set up for sleeping, with a mini fridge and stereo. The Sloth said that set-up wouldn't suit him because he'd get sick of walking from his ute door to the back of the ute, and back again. Yeah, I suppose it's a long walk!

We often spend a lot of time stopped at night, like while the Scalies (Roads and Traffic Authority) are weighing the low loader, or when the coppers are booking it. The Sloth can slip into a deep sleep in under five seconds, regardless of what's happening. One night the low loader got stuck under a bridge and pulled down some power lines, and while everyone else was watching the sparks and the frantic actions of the State Emergency Service and fire-brigade crews, the Sloth slept on.

We reckon that the Sloth must weigh over 150 kilos. He lives on a diet of Coke and chips. He's so overweight that he hardly ever gets out of his ute. He buys all his Coke and fries at drive-throughs, and I'm sure if ever they shut down the Sloth would die of malnutrition, except that it would take a long time because he has a lot of fat stored up in his tremendous gut.

The Sloth has some disgusting habits, too. Like he'll hardly ever leave his ute to visit the men's. He just does it in empty Coke bottles while sitting in his ute, and then lobs the 'fulls' into roadside bins. At least he's improved from when he used to do it onto the road. He used to simply stop his ute, swivel one leg out of the door, and pee from a sitting position. You could always see where the Sloth had been: wet patches of bitumen every 100 miles or so in the middle of the road.

Although he only grunts while driving escorts, I know the Sloth is really proud to drive a ute. The boss once suggested that he'd trade in our utes for a couple of those small Jap vans to save on fuel, and the Sloth nearly went off his head. He reckoned that real Aussies didn't drive Jap vans, and that he for one would go on strike if he ever lost his XH. It had the most comfortable seat in the world, he said. I've only ever seen the Sloth's ute seat once and it was a mess, completely collapsed from excessive driver weight. It happened when the Sloth had to leave the ute while it was being repaired. He'd dropped a french fry when leaving the drive-through one day. He slammed on his brakes and backed up to pick up the fry, and he ran into another vehicle. The Sloth believes even one fry is worth backing up for!

Because of all the time we spend together I reckon the Sloth would be one of my closest mates. Not that I really know him. He's a real loner. Come to think of it, I don't even know if he has a real name.

Probably the main thing we have in common is that we both drive XH utes ...

Beached Ute

Nick Smith,
Lane Cove, NSW

Mate, I've got a cracker. It involves myself, a few of my mates and my 1995 VRII ute.

It was about four months ago when four of my mates went across to Port Macquarie from Wee Waa to escape the floods and get on it for a couple of days. I decided to meet them up there, as I was living in Sydney, having previously lived in Wauchope for fifteen years on a dairy farm.

Anyway, after going out the first night we decided that a 'bender' was due and it was our duty to go out and make absolute idiots of ourselves, which we did. Our night finished at about 3.30 am and we all made our way back to the house.

This is where it gets very interesting. The house we were staying at was right on the beach. Very nice, really. As we all arrived back, one of my mates who is a diabetic decided that he needed to go for a run to get the grog out of him, because diabetics and piss don't go well together. We all said, 'Yeah, that's fine,' but when he hadn't returned an hour later we got worried. A mate and myself thought that he could have passed out on the beach.

Being the smart buggers that we are we got in my ute and drove it up onto a little cement ramp that goes down to the beach so we could shine the spotties on the sand to find our mate. Well, Tom wasn't there at all ...

Now, here was our problem. Being a little under the weather I didn't realise it but, as I tried to do a three-point turn, I had driven the ute just a little bit too far and my rear wheels were actually off the cement and in the sand. Needless to say, we were stuffed ...

I got out and started pushing while my mate was driving ... First mistake, he put the ute in reverse, not first. We rolled backwards and now all four wheels were in the sand. Now we were really stuffed. After trying for about twenty minutes with just the two of us, we realised that we needed the other two blokes. My mate ran up and got them while I sat in the ute shitting myself, worried that the cops would come and find my ute parked on Lighthouse Beach ... Not good, eh!

Anyway, the fellas turned up and we all started pushing. Inch by inch we got the ute further towards the cement ramp. To make matters worse, my ute has a stereo system in it and at four in the morning it is bloody loud. After trying for about an hour and a half and moving the car about four metres it was decided that we needed something to put under the wheels. I straightaway got the rubber tray mat out of the back and jammed it underneath. After pushing and pulling for another two hours, we finally got the bloody thing out.

You can imagine the sight ... six pissed blokes trying to push a Commodore ute off a beach at four in the morning is a bloody funny thing. Later in the morning I went down to check out the damage and only then realised how dumb we'd been. The windows had been down in the ute and being rear-wheel drive and in reverse I think there was half the sand on Lighthouse Beach in the cabin. Unbelievable – there was sand everywhere. But hey, at least we got out of it safely.

To add to this, we did actually find the mate we were looking for in the first place. He had passed out in a bus shelter about ten metres from the house.

The Stiff

As told to John Bryant by Gail Attwood
Schofields, NSW

Up Northern Territory way there are a few whistle stops that masquerade as 'townships' as you drive north up the main bitumen from Alice Springs to Darwin. They usually feature a general store with a post office agency and maybe a house or two, and a couple of shipping containers doubling as sheds.

I was heading up to Jabiru via Darwin one time, and stopped at one of those small-town general stores for a cold drink. As I walked around the shop savouring the air-conditioned comfort I spied these long, weird, meaty-looking things in the freezer display case.

'What are those?' I asked the shopkeeper.

'Skinned and frozen roo tails,' he said. 'The local indigenous population buy them. At $2.50 a piece it's easier than hunting roos.'

The shopkeeper explained that these frozen roo tails were famous round those parts; in fact they had entered into local legend. He then told me the story that had generated the legend.

A year back the local butcher had had a load of these frozen goodies in the back of his ute on his way to deliver them to the general store, and had stopped at the pub for just one very quick drink. While he was in the pub a fight had broken out. After landing a few good right hands, the publican had managed to get the combatants out of the pub and onto the footpath.

By that time the local cop had arrived, and was standing on the edge of the crowd trying to figure out which of the fighters was buggered enough to be arrested without being able to do him any damage. Just as he'd picked out his man, his man copped a head in the stomach and lurched back against the side of the butcher's ute. Spying the solid roo tails, he grabbed one, deciding he could wield it like a baseball bat and turn the odds back in his favour.

With a wild yell, his man swung the frozen roo tail in a great arc, intending to send the head-butting scumbag to the Promised Land. At that very instant the scumbag was decked by another bloke from behind, leaving the frozen roo tail with a lot of momentum and no legitimate target.

Well, it's a shame that the copper was standing so close to the action. The frozen roo tail completed its arc, and decelerated rapidly as it came to rest on the bridge of his not inconsiderable red nose. The cop didn't know anything about it for an hour, as he was knocked cold and taken to the hospital for treatment.

Funny part of the whole deal was that the cop scrambled out of hospital and arrested his man, charging him with 'assaulting a police officer'. To complete the arrest and make the charge stick he had to impound the frozen roo tail, which, after being thawed then refrozen, sat curled up in the police station freezer for two months, awaiting presentation to the travelling magistrate as 'evidence'.

'If that bloody butcher carried his meat in a van like everyone else this would never have happened, and my nose wouldn't have a double bridge. Health Department ought to create a law against carrying frozen roo tails in the backs of utes!' said the copper. He said this every time anyone mentioned roos, pubs, fights or utes.

Beating the Breathalyser

As told to John Bryant by Peter Munro
Arcadia, NSW

I've got this bunch of mates who always go to B & S balls as a group. If one can't go, then no one goes. And when we all go anywhere, we have all these routines that keep us laughing from the time we take off till the time we get home.

One of the best stories about our B & S group happened back just after drink-driving became a big issue with the country police.

We were all at this B & S ball in a New South Wales country town, and a police patrol had parked just down the road from the hall to catch anyone silly enough to drink and drive. The copper seemed to hate to see young people having a good time and was overzealous in nailing anyone who stepped out of line.

Late in the evening the police officer noticed a man leaving the hall so intoxicated that he could barely walk. The man stumbled around the car park for a few minutes, with the officer quietly observing. After what seemed an eternity of trying his keys on four or five vehicles, the man managed to find his ute. He got the door open, then stumbled around trying to figure out which leg to put into the ute first. He fell over twice before he finally climbed into the cabin. He was there for a few minutes as a number of other blokes and girls left the hall and drove off.

Finally this bloke started the ute, switched the wipers on and off (it was a fine, dry night), flicked the indicators on, then off, tooted the horn and then switched on the lights. He flicked up to high beam then back to low beam, and turned the lights off and then on again. He moved the vehicle forward a few inches, reversed a little and then remained stationary for a few more minutes as some more vehicles left. At last he pulled out of the car park and started to drive slowly down the road.

The police officer, having patiently waited all this time, now started up the patrol car, put on the flashing lights, promptly pulled the man over and carried out a breathalyser test.

To his amazement, the breathalyser indicated no evidence of the man having consumed any alcohol at all!

Dumbfounded, the copper said, 'I'll have to ask you to accompany me to the police station. This breathalyser equipment must be faulty.'

'I doubt it,' said the man. 'Tonight I'm the designated decoy.'

You Wouldn't Read About it!

Noel Glover
Moruya Heads, NSW

You wouldn't read about it! Some time ago a mate and I decided to go pig shooting out around the Pilliga scrub. We decided to leave after work on the Friday and share the driving through the night. Well, I should have seen the writing on the wall, but this is what happened.

I was driving trucks for a living at the time, and I went to work that Friday morning and found I had a stack of drops all around the city and suburbs. I was carrying steel mesh for concreting and the like, and my first drop was over at Palm Beach in Sydney's northern suburbs. I found the address and as I backed the truck up this bloke's driveway I felt the truck drop into a hole and get bogged down. I had broken through his new concrete path and had the back wheels firmly stuck in a cavity beneath, so I had to find a tow wagon big enough to move me and one that was available straightaway.

Three hours later one rolls up and pulls me free. I gave the owner of the demolished driveway my particulars and quickly took off, trying to make up the lost time. The day went from bad to worse. Anyway, I finally got back to the yard about six that evening and was feeling pretty knackered, but at least my mate could take over driving when I picked him up.

Unfortunately, when I got to his place he was out of it on the couch – thinking I wasn't coming, he had consumed most of the slab we had bought for the trip. Anyway, I loaded him into my trusty VC Valiant ute and headed for the mountains, having to stop on the way to pick up some bullets for my new Ruger. So I lobbed into Penrith, where there was a Mick Simmons store in those days that stayed open late on Fridays, pulled over and ran into the shop. After waiting for some old bloke who couldn't make up his mind I finally got my shells. Coming back to the vehicle I found a parking ticket under the wipers, for parking in a bus stop.

Anyway, after driving all bloody night we finally reached the Pilliga. As we stopped to walk around I noticed that the wide tyres I had on the beast had effectively sandblasted all the paint off the sills of the VC. Still, we soldiered on, and finally started to do some shooting. I was real proud of my new Ruger automatic, the first one I had ever owned.

The dogs had been after the pigs near the creek and one of the buggers was heading my way. As he broke through the long grass he had an ear hanging off from the dogs and he was none too happy. He sighted me and came at me. I aimed, pulled the trigger, and then the dreaded CLICK ... nothing! I had to act quick, because this mad pig was just about on top of me. I grabbed the rifle by the barrel and coshed the porker over the head. I stopped the bugger, but broke the butt of me new rifle as well. Smart move, eh?

Later on I tried to use my long-barrelled revolver, but after nearly shooting one of the other fellas decided to leave it in the back of the ute. But THERE'S MORE ...

After a bloody waste of time and money of a weekend we finally decided to head home. However, the bloke in the local service station wouldn't sell us any fuel because we had bought a couple of Koori fellas a few beers, and afterwards one of them rode this little pony through the local grocery store as he did his shopping. But these fellas were good blokes, and came to the rescue with a 44-gallon drum of fuel from somewhere. We filled up the VC and the jerry and took off down this short cut they told us about. The road was pretty rutted, so I was doing over 100 kilometres an hour when I came around this corner slightly sideways and saw that the road was cut by a wash-out. It was too late to brake, so I planted it in the hope of jumping the gap ...

Well, almost made it: the front wheels hit the edge, which splayed them like a skier going downhill. But the worst damage was to the fuel tank, which was lying on the road a few yards back. We used a bit of bush ingenuity and tied the fuel tank to a roof rack and used an old siphon (a bit of rubber garden hose) from the fuel line to the carby. The stench of petrol was overwhelming and after a few miles, with a ute that didn't want to steer any more, we both got these enormous headaches.

We finally made it into some town and were able to buy more fuel, and sure enough it started to rain. Couldn't shut the windows because of the stink, so we battled on. I forgot to mention that our little flying stunt had knocked the headlights out of whack, so every truck and most cars down the highway gave me a display of their high-beam power.

By the time I got home I was soaking wet, my head was pounding like a drum and my eyes were about the size of 20-cent pieces. My missus wouldn't speak to me, so I slept the rest of the night on the couch. I also got a serious dose of the flu and wasn't able to go to work for a couple of days.

My boss rang and said I had to come in, so I dragged myself off to work. I went into his office and he showed me the bill he copped for the bloke's driveway and promptly gave me the sack!

I said you wouldn't read about it but now you have and all the above is true. It actually did happen ... pretty funny, eh?

Love Hurts!

As told to John Bryant by Jason Blair
Lalor Park, NSW

Belle fell in love with Rory at first sight. She fell hard and fast, instantly infatuated the first time she laid eyes on him. Her girlfriends were really envious because she was so sure of her feelings so quickly. They asked her what was the big attraction. Deep down she knew, but to be honest she was too embarrassed to tell them. She couldn't bring herself to put it into words. Fact was, it all started long before she even met Rory.

Rory drove a slightly used HiLux ute. It was an '87 dual cab with five on the floor and 329,000 on the clock. He did all his own work on the ute, which was the only reason it still ran. That's not to say it was an unreliable ute; it wasn't. But you just needed to know which panel to bang, which wire to tug or which screw to tighten to make it start or stop or whatever.

It seemed whenever Rory worked on his ute, or anything else for that matter, he managed to inflict an injury on himself. Like one time when he replaced the HiLux's wiper rubbers, and he almost slashed his finger to the bone with his Stanley knife. When rotating his bald tyres the jack slipped and the tyre lever broke off the top of one of his two front teeth. Another time he was lying underneath the ute inspecting the holes in his exhaust system, and he managed to get dirt in his left eye, resulting in a trip to hospital to get it cleaned. He once got concussed when he caught his foot on the top of the tailgate while leaping out of the tray; he hit his head so hard on the grass that he passed out for a few seconds. 'Not the first time anyone was knocked cold by grass,' said his old man with a twinkle in his eye, hoping desperately that someone would catch his pathetic double meaning.

But perhaps the most significant and most painful injury ever suffered related to Rory's altercation with the HiLux's radiator.

Rory used to cart the most outrageous loads of stuff in his ute, and it was prone to overheating, especially on hot summer days. Being an ex-Boy Scout, Rory used to carry a 20-litre plastic drum of water in the back for whenever the radiator boiled. He knew the radiator leaked and that it probably needed flushing, but he doubted whether he could stand the injuries that such a repair job would inflict. Instead, he just waited until she boiled, then after a while he'd ease off the radiator cap and fill her up with cold water. He'd always keep the motor running so as not to allow the cold water to crack the overheated block.

Well, one hot summer's day Rory had a huge load on board. Paul, a mate, had talked him into using the ute to carry a load of ice for the local B & S ball, which was on that very night. They had loaded a small (but quite heavy) refrigeration unit onto the ute. They loaded it *onto* and not *into* the ute, because the refrigeration unit was too large to sit down on the floor, so they tied it down on the top rails, where it caused precarious swaying of the ute due to the high centre of gravity. The unit was filled with ice, and the load was way beyond safe loading limits.

As they approached the B & S venue, the poor old HiLux was labouring in third and started to boil. Paul didn't want to stop, because they were running late and the ice was melting. Rory knew that if he just kept going the ute might go off like a bomb.

'We'll pull over for a few seconds and ram some water into the radiator,' said Rory.

'Well, bloody hurry up, mate, we don't want this load of ice to turn to water before we can plug the fridge into the mains.'

Rory pulled off the road next to an old fence. He lifted the bonnet and steam was spurting out from a couple of cracks in the radiator, as well as from underneath the cap. 'Never seen her this hot before,' Rory moaned.

Rory was in favour of letting her cool off a bit to allow the steam pressure to subside, but Paul was impatient. After a short argument, Rory decided he'd better get the cap off pronto and throw some cool water down the HiLux's parched throat. Looking around the ute, he didn't have a rag to use as an insulator to protect himself from the steam, but he had a bright idea instead.

Climbing up onto the top of the adjacent post-and-rail fence, Rory balanced himself and placed his left foot down onto the radiator cap. 'Should be OK if I just ease her off,' he thought to himself. 'I can hold the cap down with me foot until some of the pressure escapes.' He was wearing a pair of pretty heavy-duty Redback boots with steel toecaps, so how could he get hurt?

As he stood down and twisted the cap, it let go under the enormous pressure of 100 cc of water boiling at a million degrees! The cap slewed sideways, and Rory's foot slipped off the radiator. A geyser of steam and boiling water shot skyward, straight up the left leg of Rory's shorts, knocking Rory off the fence and into the grass.

As he lay there clutching his groin, Rory's life flashed before him, and he entered into the true, awful and indescribable experience of Pure Pain. He'd had his balls knocked, kicked, ground and punched before in earlier accidents, but never before had he had them braised, boiled, cooked, roasted and fried, all at the same time.

It was nearly two months after this accident, after he'd just been released from hospital, that Belle had fallen in love with Rory.

Belle will never forget it. She was sipping a lemon, lime and bitters at the local beer garden when this young man caught her eye. First of all she just saw him from the waist up as he walked along behind the hedge, heading for the beer garden gate. He appeared tall, slender and tanned, and was wearing a red and white chequered shirt. He had a strange sort of swagger. Under his Akubra he also had a sort of cute grin, accentuated by his chipped front tooth.

As he swung through the beer garden gate, Belle saw Rory head-on for the first time. Below his shirt he sported a pair of tight blue Wrangler jeans, which fell away into his RM Williams boots.

However, the most stunning aspect of his appearance was that he walked with the most incredible bow-legged gait that she'd ever seen. She was swamped with thoughts of John Wayne, The Lawman, Reno, Nevada, Longhorns, Johnny Yuma, Lonesome Dove and Little Joe Cartwright, all rolled into one. She suddenly realised for the first time in her life that ever since she was a little girl she had subconsciously fantasised about being swept off her feet by her very own outback cowboy. NOW it had happened.

As they slowly got to know each other better, her outback cowboy impressed her more and more. They discussed everything as they rode around in his HiLux ute, making plans for the future. They even talked about sex once but, with tears in his eyes, Rory assured her that he was not interested, and was saving himself for marriage. He proved to her that he wasn't like all the other louts that she'd met in town. He was in no hurry to rush her into his swag in the back of his HiLux. He was a pure gentleman ... he respected her as a woman and as a person ... he treated her like a real lady! THIS, thought Belle, is TRUE LOVE.

Lucky Jack

Mick Quigley
Victoria Park, WA

Jack was one lucky bastard.

He always had been. Jack was the guy who, back when you all wagged school, would *never* get caught. He was the bloke who, when he paid for his shout with a $20 note, got change for a $50 note. Jack was the bloke who *always* managed to return from the races not just with a profit *and* a skinful of beer, but also three or four phone numbers from some of the lovely ladies he'd met during the day, *and* get let off with a warning from the random breath-testing van parked outside.

Jack was one lucky bastard.

Anyway, one day a couple of months ago, Jack got a call from a lawyer in one of those little wheat-belt towns halfway between Perth and Kalgoorlie. Apparently some distant relative of his had died, and in his will had left his farm ute to Jack. Well, Jack had nothing specific planned for that weekend, so I gave him a lift up to check out the ute. We figured that, if worst came to worst, we could go back up the following weekend with a trailer and take it back. Either that or just tow it out to the local tip.

We followed the directions supplied by the lawyer, and found the shed behind the run-down old shack that passed for the farmhouse. Jack opened the shed and there it was. Under a sheet covered in red dust was a 1966 HR Holden ute. And she was immaculate. The blue duco was virginal, the chrome polished, the upholstery unblemished. And when I peeked under the tonneau cover, I had the feeling that I was the first person to do so since she'd left the factory all those years ago. Only a thin covering of what dust had filtered through the covering sheet, and a few spider webs in the grille. I only pretended to be surprised, because deep down I think I kind of expected this.

Jack was one lucky bastard.

Jack poked his head in the cab, and read out the odometer reading.

'Twenty thousand miles – not too bad for a thirty-five-year-old farm ute, I guess – wonder if it runs?' he asked hypothetically – sort of as if there was a chance that it might not. This is, after all, Jack that we're talking about.

Jack flipped down the sun visor, and of course the keys were there waiting for him. After checking the radiator, brake fluid, tyre pressure and all the other things that you'd hate to go wrong during a test drive, Jack hit the starter. The ute started on the first kick, almost as if she was getting impatient about stretching her legs.

A couple of laps around the yard and Jack reported back.

'No funny noises from the diff or gearbox, brakes work all right – are the headlights on? Right – I'll see ya back in town!' called Jack.

'Don't want me to follow?' I asked. I think I was more worried about *my* ute making it back than I was about Jack.

'Nah – she's right. Catch ya at the pub later tonight, all right?'

'No worries,' I replied, and headed off back to Perth.

That night at the pub, there was no Jack.

'Probably picked up a sheila at the servo while he was topping up the tank,' quipped Tommo, only half joking. He knew, after all, that Jack was one lucky bastard. Of course, the story about the HR only reinforced his thinking.

'Hope he hasn't broken down,' mused Chuckles, the resident pessimist. 'There's a lot of nothing between towns out there. A bloke could get into some real trouble.'

'Whatever you reckon, Chuckles,' Tommo and I said in chorus for about the twentieth time that evening. He'd been in fine form, forecasting anything between the End of Civilisation As We Know It and the impending crash of the Aussie cricket team (which, when you think about it, are pretty close to being one and the same thing).

By mid-week, no one had heard from Jack. It was as if he'd disappeared from the face of the earth. He wasn't at home, he hadn't showed up at work (which wasn't *that* unusual), and his mum hadn't heard from him for about three months (again, not unusual).

By the following Friday night, news of Jack's mysterious disappearance had filtered through the pub crowd. The last time he'd gone missing for this long was when he was told that Murph's wife was pregnant, and that Murph's two-year-old vasectomy had given rise to some pertinent questions. Jack was one lucky bastard. He was also pretty gullible.

Anyway, late in the Friday night session, a bloke approached us from the other end of the bar. He had evidently heard the story of Jack, his new/old ute, and how he'd disappeared. It seemed this guy was a truck driver who was down from the very same wheat-belt town where I had delivered Jack the weekend before.

During the week his mate, who happened to be the local wrecker, had mentioned in passing that he'd come across the wreck of a very recently immaculate HR ute. The odometer reportedly showed only about 20,000 miles.

My ears pricked up, and the beer-induced fog started to clear away. Tommo was first with the pertinent questions. What happened? Where was it? How bad? Any idea about the driver? It had to be the same ute, didn't it? There can't be too many like that around, can there?

'I knew it,' said Chuckles, wearing a look that somehow made him look both worried and smug at the same time – I don't know quite how he managed to do *that.*

'Sorry, mate, that's all I know,' said the truckie. 'Hope your mate's OK. Sounded like the ute was a bit of a mess, but.'

So what to do? Call Jack's mum? Call his boss? Tommo, who, it became obvious, was far more sober than the rest of us, came up with the idea of calling the hospital or ambos in the wheat-belt town. He disappeared with a pile of change to the back of the pub where the public phone was.

After about a half-hour on the phone he returned. No ambulance call-outs last Saturday afternoon, no mysterious coma victims at the hospital. It was as if Jack had disappeared from the face of the earth. Just at that point, the new barmaid – sorry, bar attendant – came up to us.

'You blokes are Jack's mates, aren't you?'

'Yeah,' said Tommo, a gleam of hope in his eye. 'You've seen him?'

'No,' she replied, 'but this came in the post yesterday.'

It was a postcard.

From Sydney.

From Jack.

In short, sparing you the gory details, this is what happened.

Jack crashed the ute. A combination of glare from the setting sun, a kamikaze kangaroo and curiosity regarding the top speed of a mint-condition HR ute led to its untimely demise.

Jack suffered minor abrasions and cuts, and bleeding from a cut on his scalp made him look a fair bit worse than he really was.

This was when the minibus arrived.

I can just picture Jack, face covered in claret, next to a burning HR ute wrapped around a tree, when a minibus carrying the Western Australian Women's Volleyball Team on their way to the National Championships in Sydney stops to offer assistance.

Jack is one lucky bastard.

Sole Remaining Asset

Steve Bloomfield
Peak Hill, NSW

In September 2000, I finally found the ultimate one-owner WB ute.

A real Grandad Special, right down to the factory-option sun visor. After some terrible crawling to the wife, I became the new owner and it became my eighteenth Holden ute. I lavished attention upon that ute; it was my pride and joy.

Well, I came home on Christmas Day to be informed by my wife that she was leaving me. I laughed at what I thought was a fairly funny joke. I nearly died when she told me she was serious. Even more so when she blamed my WB ute obsession over the preceding twelve years as part of the problem ...

Anyway, she took the kids and the furniture and I was left with the WB, a red cattle dog and a toasted-sandwich maker. After some correspondence, I christened the ute 'Sole Remaining Asset'.

Since I was miserable and despondent, my younger sister suggested that I travel to Sydney to try my luck at the Desperate and Dateless Ball. Reluctantly, I agreed.

Travelling through the Blue Mountains en route to the big event, I got hit from behind by a tourist coach. The ute then speared across the road and was T-boned by a Hyundai ...

'Well, I came home on Christmas Day to be informed by my wife that she was leaving me . . . she blamed my WB ute obsession as part of the problem.'

I eventually got home and had the insurance assessor look at the ute. He totalled the damage at $5,900, but the insurance company only valued the ute at $4,200. This was despite the fact that I had paid $6,000 for it in September AND spent nearly $2,000 on it since ...

After much haggling, I convinced them to let me retain the ute to allow me to have a mate repair it. They told me that a cheque for the difference would be forthcoming.

Hearing nothing for several weeks, I started to make a few enquiries. I found out last week that my insurance company is one of those that have gone broke ...

What a bloody year!

Ute Power

Peter Peterson
Kellyville, NSW

My old man has the most powerful ute in Australia.

He started out in life as an electrician, running in and out of farmhouses, up and down power poles and sticking fuses in boxes. He stuck an un-insulated screwdriver in a fuse hole once and he swore he'd never do that ever again.

Being a sparky paid the bills, but didn't give him much of a challenge. After a few years of being bored out of his brain, he decided to become an 'electrical expert'. He bought himself a laptop computer and developed some programs, which he used to check on other contractors' electrical installations.

He loved this new slant on being a sparky, because it allowed him to solve the problems others couldn't. He developed his programs to such an extent that big organisations started calling on him when their electrical systems went down, or when they couldn't work out why things didn't work. He'd just hook up his computer to the network and pretty soon he could suss out where the problems were.

His customers grew to love him as much as the other contractors started to hate him, because he could always detect shoddy workmanship quick-smart.

During all of his electrical travels he'd always drive his Ford ute. Dad always reckoned any other brand was crap. When the new AU Falcon utes came out he just had to have one, and sure enough one day he turned up at home in an XLS eight-cylinder model with New South Wales numberplates (1 AU UTE).

One day Dad discovered that with new software he could hook up his mobile phone to his laptop computer and suss out all his electrical programs from the cabin of his beloved AU ute. This meant he could dial up a customer anywhere in Australia, and sitting there in his ute he could access all their electrical systems. He was in heaven, being able to do what he loved most from his favourite location: his ute! 'And people pay me money to do all this, too!' he used to tell Mum, who was always vaguely suspicious of how all this techno stuff hung together.

Some of Dad's larger customers used to pay him a retainer to look after their lighting systems. This meant that he performed regular maintenance on their systems, all via his laptop computer and within his mobile office.

One night several years ago I went to the movies with a few mates and Dad had arranged to meet me outside and drive me home after the movie was over. Dad arrived a bit early, and was sitting parked in his beloved Ford ute with about thirty minutes to kill.

As he sat there in his ute in the dark, it occurred to him that he could use the time to crank up his laptop and undertake a little 'routine maintenance' on a couple of his interstate customers' systems. The economics appealed to him greatly; turning dead time into a productive opportunity. First off, Dad decided to test the emergency lighting at the University of Canberra, which was one of the prestige customers that always received Red Carpet treatment.

It was about 10.30 pm, and Dad was confident that the building would be empty and locked up. So there Dad was, sitting outside a movie theatre in Sydney in his Ford ute, tickling the keys of his laptop and merrily turning the lights on and off in Canberra.

He was just finishing this little maintenance exercise as I got into the ute. I was careful not to sit on the laptop, which would have earned me the death penalty. Dad was still chuckling to himself as he fired up the ute; after all, he'd done some powerfully valuable work while just killing time.

Just then the mobile phone rang. Since it was still sitting on the dash, I picked it up.

'Hello!' I chirped.

The voice on the other end sounded angry and very irritated. 'Can I speak to Trevor?'

'Actually Dad's driving at the moment, can I give him a message?' I enquired.

'Yeah, it's the Venue Manager from Canberra University here. Tell him that we've had a late night lecture series tonight, and some jerk must have broken into the building. He's been running round turning the emergency lighting on and off. I've had three blokes chasing all over the buildings trying to catch him, but he moves like greased lightning. We haven't been able to catch him yet, but when we do we'll skin the bugger alive. I need to talk to your dad about installing a security program to stop idiots like this interrupting our activities.'

Onya Dad, another satisfied customer!

Pickup Confusion

As told to John Bryant by Vincent Bowyer
Larnook, NSW

This mate of mine started a company called 'Pickup Solutions Pty Ltd', which sold a spray-on product that protected the backs of utes. They sprayed this chemical goo about eight millimetres thick onto the load area, and this was said to prevent damage. After racking his brain for a gimmicky name, he ended up marketing the spray-on chemical under the name of 'HardWrap'. His advertising blurb read 'Let us HardWrap the back of your ute in the world's hardest protective coating'.

Pickup Solutions, like any business, was always hotly promoting its products, and a lot of the communication with its customers took place on the phone. If you ever called Pickup Solutions, chances are a bloke called Eric Munns would answer. Eric came out of retirement to work at Pickup Solutions and he'd had many years' experience in marketing, selling and customer relations. He presented an easy-going, friendly approach to anyone who called up; a real old-time gentleman! He was also a pretty keen salesman, and wasn't adverse to bulldogging the occasional customer order.

Well, business was enough of a challenge without getting involved in misunderstandings, but unfortunately everything isn't always as straightforward as it seems. One day Eric was working away at Pickup Solutions, plotting on how he could sell a few more orders of

HardWrap and beat his sales target for the month, when his phone rang.

'Pickup Solutions, Eric speaking,' he enthusiastically chirped.

'Is dat da pickup place?' asked a swarthy voice with a heavy accent.

'Yes, this is Pickup Solutions, how may I help you?' replied Eric, sensing another order to add towards his monthly target.

'What sort of girls you got?' asked the voice.

'Girls? What difference does that make? All our staff are well trained and experienced and we have an excellent reputation for quality. In fact, everything is covered by a twelve-month warranty,' said Eric, a bit puzzled by such a weird question.

'No, I wanna know what sort of girls. I don't care about warranty, just girls.'

'I think perhaps you may have the wrong number,' responded Eric. He was now totally confused and wondering why anyone would care about the background of any of the staff in the factory.

'Wrong number? You said dat was da pickup place!' complained the voice, getting a bit edgy. 'What business you in?'

'We sell HardWraps,' said Eric proudly, feeling that at last he was getting the customer back on the right track.

'Hard wrap? You just sell da hard wrap? How can you make da money out of just selling da hard wraps?' asked the voice in amazement.

'I'll have you know that Pickup Solutions is the exclusive supplier of HardWrap in Australia and that we are a very successful company. Every ute needs HardWrap protection!'

'Sure, everyone needs a hard wrap for da protection, but you gotta be crazy if you think I'm gonna buy just a hard wrap without da bonk!'

Now, Eric had never heard of anyone fitting a 'bonk' to a ute. In fact he wasn't sure, but he somehow vaguely assumed that a 'bonk' was a four-wheel drive product and certainly not something sold by Pickup Solutions.

'Can I send you out a brochure? What's your address?' Eric asked. This was always his last line of defence. Whenever he felt a deal slipping away he'd try and get a name and address so he could continue the sales pitch via Her Majesty's mail.

'I don't need da bloody brochure. I use plenty of hard wraps before.'

Eric felt a glimmer of hope; he now knew he was talking to a repeat customer, the easiest of all to sell to. He started to get excited; he felt the sale was almost in the bag.

'Great, you've used HardWrap before! How did you use it? Were you satisfied with its performance? Did it provide the protection that you needed?' he asked with expectancy.

'What? You a filthy perv or sumfink? You guys must be &$#&^& crazy!'

The line went dead.

'Geez, maybe I'm slipping,' thought Eric, as he stirred his white tea with two sugars. 'It's not often I can't get a brochure into the mail.'

Wal and Les's Fishy Tale

David Mayo
Bellingen, NSW

There aren't too many people who can claim to know Wal Piggott and Les Atkinson.

Those who do don't get five minutes of peace before hearing about the whopping great cod Wal and Les pulled from the mighty Murray back in '76. Until this very day in pubs around the country the story can be heard, and goes something like this:

The October of '76 saw the Murray run pretty high with some good rains, which not only made the cotton cockies happy, but also put a smile on the faces of Wal and his good mate Les. Wal and Les had been dreaming of catching a monster cod, but from all reports the days of these whoppers had long since passed. No such rumours were about to stop these two, however, especially since both their old ladies were busily cooking pumpkin scones for the upcoming show. Wal and Les weren't about to let a weekend of freedom slide away.

So off they set after loading up Les's FJ ute. Les loved his ute, but Wal wished he'd drop a new donk in it. Sitting on 40 miles an hour down the Newell was not Wal's idea of a good time. To ease the boredom Wal started to talk baits and rigs, which pretty much fell on deaf ears as Les had a habit of astutely listening to the chug of his beloved ute no matter how long the journey. Les used to do this with his head leaning slightly forward and tilted to the side as if the offer of his ear was comforting the old girl.

This must have gone on for about two or three hours, Wal's idle chit chat, Les's familiar pose, until a whopping great thud and flash of yellow and white bouncing off the windscreen threw Les back against the back rest and jammed his foot on the brake.

To his left was Wal, in the same position but looking markedly whiter and more shaken than his mate. A few seconds passed before Wal broke the silence. 'Cripes, Les, I think I've shat myself. What the hell was that?'

'Well, Wal, that was a sulphur-crested cockatoo,' Les stated as he anxiously struggled to find reverse gear, 'and those buggers make the best cod bait known to man!'

Wal couldn't believe what happened next. Not thirty seconds after taking this poor bird's life, Les was down on his haunches with a gleaming smile, scraping up the road kill to use for bait. At the least he could have shown a little remorse!

About four hours later, they both sat on the bank of the Murray with not a worry in the world, except for the twelve carp sitting beside them which seemed to be the only things taking a liking to the feast of earthworms and bardi grubs on offer. Wal was a good fisherman, but a slightly impatient one. These characteristics meant that he very rarely let pride get in the way of catching a fish.

'Hey, Les, how 'bout we give that galah of yours a go?'

To which Les replied, 'It's not a galah, Wal, it's a bloody white cockatoo. Big cod get spooked by any bright colours, especially pink!'

Les unwrapped the cockatoo and passed it to Wal, who proceeded to shield the bird from Les's vision as he plucked the bright yellow crest from its head. After feeding a hook through the bird he quickly tossed it into the river.

Well, this darn bird must have floated right down into the mouth of a big green cod no less than sixty pounds. Wal got the fright of his life as the monster stripped the line from him quicker than a Bemborough finish. This giant of the river struggled to carry her huge weight, however, and an experienced Wal played her out until she was too tired to lift a fin. Both Les and Wal were quivering with excitement as they struggled to drag the beast up the bank. Out of the water she was just as big as they had imagined.

Surely no one could deny them this fishing tale; the proof was right in front of them this time, and there could be no talk of the one that got away. In their haste to get to the local to show off their catch, the two proud anglers decided to head off directly, despite the beast still having a little kick left in her. Les got into action quickly after recovering his breath. He hopped in his ute and backed her as close to the fish as possible to hoist it in, without allowing the angle of the bank to hinder the FJ's take-off.

What Les had not accounted for was the fact that the slime from a sixty-pound cod greatly reduced the coefficient of friction against the tray of an FJ Holden ute. With the fish in the back and a foot on the pedal, Les and Wal started to labour up the mounds and hollows of the bank. With each little bump that big fish slid closer and closer to the tailgate, before it eventually sprang the latches and hit the turf. Wal and Les heard the big thud and had just enough time to see their fish of a lifetime slide towards the water. With a weary flick of the tail, the big green beast slid gracefully into the depths of the Murray.

The tears started to well in both their eyes. Wal even desperately looked around on the off-chance that someone had witnessed their awful plight, but there was no one within cooee, and surely no one was going to believe their story.

Les's shoulders couldn't slump any lower as he got out of the ute and walked towards the back. Just as he went to shut the tailgate he noticed a huge scale about the size of a beer coaster caught up in the hinge. Les let out a little chuckle at the reminder of the beast. He picked it up and off they headed. In contrast to the drive down, Wal didn't say anything on the way home, and Les couldn't have cared less about the chug of his FJ.

It took many a year for Wal and Les to get over their loss, but if you ever bump into them at the local down the Riverina way, I'm sure they'll spin you the yarn till they're blue in the face.

And before Les makes his way from the pub, just be sure to get a glimpse of what dangles from the end of his FJ's car keys. I'm sure you'll agree that huge cod scale makes a darn fine key ring and, for Les, an enduring reminder of that fateful day and of the one that got away.

John and Liz

As told to John Bryant by John Rottenbury
Glossodia, NSW

John Rottenbury (real name) from Fair & Square Bricklaying (real company west of Sydney) drove a Holden HQ (real Aussie ute) with a Chev 351 motor (real fast) in his younger years. Although he's over thirty now and much wiser, he admits to being Young and Naive when he first started slapping mud around building sites.

Young John became infamous fairly early in his career. It started when he was working on a city building site and the concreters had just finished a big pour. The concrete had just gone off when Young John decided it was time for Lizard, his shar pei–blue heeler cross, to take a break from guarding his ute.

Lizard was some dog. He had blue eyes, blue lips, blue fur and even a blue tongue; in fact if ever a dog should have been called 'Bluey' it was this one, but Young John named him Lizard in celebration of his unique tongue.

Anyway, in his enthusiastic response to being freed from the chain in the back of Young John's HQ, Liz dashed straight through the fresh wet concrete. Young John went berserk, shouting and frothing at the mouth. Poor dog thought John wanted to play so he dashed straight back through the concrete, wrecking yet another area of the slab!

Young John's most famous exploit was at The Big Party, when a newly arrived neighbour threw a house-warming party and invited the whole district, including Young John and partner. The new neighbours were apparently incredibly wealthy (or very corrupt?), because they arranged a *pallet* of Jack Daniels, which meant The Big Party lasted several days.

During the course of The Big Party many people became somewhat extroverted, performing with the karaoke machine and doing their favourite party tricks. Young John was a quiet lad, so when it came to be his turn he just grabbed Liz and let everyone stare down his blue throat. The amazement didn't last all that long and there were suggestions that Young John needed to do a bit more to entertain the group. Liz slunk off to sleep in the back of the HQ while Young John struggled for ideas.

'OK,' said John, 'I'll jump me ute over that dam,' pointing at a small, muddy lake about half a kilometre down the back paddock.

There were wild Indian whoops and cries of 'Go Johnno!' as the HQ belched smoke and spat turf. After a few hoops, accelerating as hard as he could, Young John hit the dam wall at somewhere between 30 and 100 kilometres an hour. Eyewitnesses just couldn't agree on the speed, but they all agreed on what happened next. The HQ ramped up and flew into the air at the same angle as the dam wall: front pointing moon-ward, rear pointing ground-ward, sort of like a Cape Canaveral rocket stalling at the launch. The engine screamed, because Young John forgot to take his foot off the accelerator when the wheels left the ground. The HQ seemed to defy gravity and just hang there in space for a few seconds, before coming down fair in the middle of the dam. There was a huge tidal wave and lots of steam, as the HQ sank slowly to the bottom. As the wash subsided Liz was seen dog-paddling to the shore, blinking his blue eyes, with his blue tongue licking his very wet blue lips.

The crowd screamed and applauded, mostly in amazement that anyone could be stupid enough to think of such a stunt, let alone try it in his OWN ute.

In all the excitement it occurred to only one person that Young John was nowhere to be seen. A local man, who was the best horse rider in the district, sprinted to the dam and dived in, boots, clothes, hat and all. After a lot of froth and kicking he emerged next to a dazed but smiling Young John, who had his right thumb raised heavenward. The crowd went berserk, and for years afterwards everyone in the district stood in awe of Young John's breathtakingly brave but extremely stupid stunt.

When telling the story, though, Young John rarely mentions what happened *after* The Big Party. When the party cobwebs cleared, the neighbour realised that there was a rotting HQ still in the dam under water level. There was an oil slick as well. 'Pollution,' thought the neighbour. All pretence of friendliness vanished, as the neighbour demanded that Young John remove his HQ or suffer the legal consequences. After a lot of sweating Young John finally was forced to get a professional diver to come and attach chains, plus hire a crane, to remove it.

She's My ...

Pete Hocke
Flynn, ACT

I've had my share of fast cars,
Some shiny ones at that;
I've also had some other ones
That were just heaps of scrap.
I've knocked around the city
And around the bush as well,
But I was missing something,
Just what I couldn't tell;
Until one day I saw it,
Then yelled out, 'You beaut!'
For standing right before me
Was a beat-up Holden ute,
With multicoloured panels
And scratches everywhere:
Just the sort of thing you need
To take you anywhere.
I didn't show much interest –
That just isn't how it's done,
'Cos negotiatin' the better deal
Is all just part of the fun.
So we talked of fishing and football
And then I took the plunge:
I asked how much he wanted
For that heap of mobile grunge.
One thousand dollars poorer,
But gee, I'm feeling great,
'Cos I know I have found

My best and truest mate.
She's had her share of hard knocks
And got some scars to show
And heaps and heaps of rattles,
But strike me, can she go!
She uses oil like a sieve
And guzzles petrol too,
But if someone ever stole that ute
I don't know what I'd do.
We've had a lot of fun together
And our share of problems too,
But together me and that old ute
Will always see it through.
You see, she's more than just a car,
She's as tough as an old boot.
Thirty years on and still going strong:
She's my Holden ute!

Dad's You-Beaut-Ute

Glenny Palmer
Cedar Vale, QLD

My old dad was a real bushie. He reckoned it was better to keep your mouth shut and be thought a fool than to open it and confirm the fact. When he did have something to say, it was short and to the point. I remember a bloke asking him, 'What do you call your dog, Bob?' and Dad said, 'I don't call him nuthin', he follers me.'

It was this quirk in Dad's personality that made it bloody near impossible to argue with him. But that didn't mean he wasn't disagreeable or, for that matter, crafty, shrewd and devious.

There were several things that Dad always held sacred. One was his old LandCruiser ute, and another was his cattle dogs. The closest I ever saw Dad come to outright argument involved these hallowed two.

Dad was cursing because his cattle dog Blue was once again nowhere to be found. Dad was half a mile from his camp, searching and calling for him, when his mate Jack drove up in his Ford ute. He stuck his head out of the window and said, 'Lost something, Bob?' Dad snarled.

Next thing Blue jumped out of Jack's ute and joyfully bounded around Dad's legs. 'I picked him up at the Nine Mile,' said Jack. Dad snarled again, as he and Blue climbed into Jack's ute and headed back to camp.

'Nothin' worse than a mongrel that wanders,' Dad muttered.

'Wanders be buggered,' said Jack, 'he keeps falling off that rustbucket of yours. This is the sixth time I've picked him up in a month. If a bloke could talk sense into you, you'd get yourself a new Ford ...'

Dad gritted his teeth and said, 'A new dog's what I'm getting.'

Mrs Mavis Thwaites from Burnie Downs had pups for sale, and Dad would not be shifted from his resolve to buy one to replace Blue, there and then. Jack tried valiantly to dissuade Dad, as he quite enjoyed the established routine of picking up Blue. It had provided him with many happy hours of tormenting Dad.

'Look, Bob', said Jack, 'there's a helluva storm brewing behind Burnie Downs, and you'll kill yourself if you try and outrun it in that bloody old heap of yours.'

Dad said, 'I'm getting a dog. I'm going in me ute. She'll outrun any storm, and any bloody Ford!'

'You're on!' said Jack, waving a £20 note.

Business was never officially sealed at Mrs Mavis Thwaites' place until a nice hot cup of tea and some pumpkin scones had cemented the deal. But such was the weight of pride and competition upon Dad and Jack that good manners and the pumpkin scones were waived, and the pup was tossed into the back of Dad's ute and they bolted.

The storm was in full force as Dad streaked towards his camp, with Jack behind him at times, beside him at others, and occasionally disappearing down so-called short cuts.

Dad and Jack were neck and neck as they hurtled into the camp. Lightning split the air and lit up their eager faces. 'Ah ha,' cried Jack, triumphantly pointing to the three spots of rain on his windscreen. ' ... The Ford wins. She outran the storm by the leanest margin.'

Dad said, 'Pull the other one, mate. There's no rain on the Cruiser's windscreen, and look here, the puppy's drowned in the back of the ute!'

The Promise

Dianne Keller
Cooktown, QLD

Cooktown is a drinking man's town, par excellence. My husband and his brothers have honed this skill to a level equalling the finest neurosurgery. They are decent, hardworking Aussie blokes so I had learnt to accept the Saturday Night Charade. Besides, they were cheerful drunks and entertaining in a beery, nonsensical sort of way.

This particular Saturday night promised to be quiet and domesticated until the spouse, Brother Number One, received a phone call. Brothers Two and Three were flying in for a quick visit to our frontier town in the rugged Far North and could we all meet at Brother Number Four's place for celebrating the reunion of the clan? The only other passenger on the tiny plane was the largest bottle of rum ever made at the Bundaberg Distillery.

The evening was inebriated but happy. I dispensed food, laughter and affection and, at midnight, I commenced my strategy for getting the husband home and bedded before the dawn.

We were finally mobile with myself doing the driving; another wifely duty found only in the fine print of The Contract. I congratulated myself on a successful getaway, naively relaxing as the cooling night breeze drifted through the broken window of our little utility. Then I made The Big Mistake!

'Look, honey! There's a huge carpet snake crossing the road. He's the biggest I've seen for a while around here.'

'Pull up! I want to look at him.'

'No, let's leave him be. He's probably going to visit his girlfriend in the scrub over there.' Even snakes might look forward to romantic Saturday evenings, I thought.

After the insistent demands of the husband, 'Stop the car! Pull over, pull over!', I acquiesced, but the person who instilled in me the virtues of being an obedient wife has much to explain.

To be fair, the husband is widely experienced in the handling of snakes, having dabbled in this domain since childhood. He does not behave foolishly even when alcoholically pickled and is very caring of the animal populace. The giant python was soon expertly loaded onto the ute. I did win one concession, in that The Beloved and The Reptile were to travel on the back, not in the cabin as initially suggested. No one chooses to vie with a cousin to the anaconda for possession of a utility's gear lever.

We pottered along towards our camp in the bush. All was fine until I chose to strike up a conversation.

'You all right, honey?' No answer.

'Honey, are you OK back there?' Silence.

Me, a tiny bit worried now: 'Don, answer me, please.'

'This [rude epithet] snake is trying to strangle me!'

Me, confident of husband's supreme reptile-handling ability, 'Oh, don't be silly. It's only a carpet snake.'

Silence again.

'Don?' Worried enough now, I risk taking my eyes off the bush track and glance behind. Silence. 'Don!' very loudly.

'Aaargh!'

Never in real life have I heard anyone seriously choking, but all the horror films containing sinister strangulations have sounds just like this one.

I urged the little ute to lurch along the remaining stretch of track to our camp. This was a time for speed, not finesse. Stalled it, but dashed from cabin to tray in a twinkling.

Murder rose in my heart. The foolishness of anti-climax is apt to provoke this reaction, it seems. The Beloved slumbered, all innocence except for the vice-like grip of his hand on the snake. The Reptile had not enveloped The Spouse; The Spouse had enveloped The Reptile!

I flounced off – with some difficulty, as the track to our caravan home was uphill and over pure sand. But anger can lend dignity and menace to the lowliest action. Inside, I savagely pulled on my least sexy nightie, the lavender-with-white-flowers, neck-to-knee creation that I had bought for emergency trips to hospital, and viciously kicked the flimsy black lace number along the floor so that it slid into the far corner in a sulking heap. Romance was definitely off the menu for this little wifey on this particular evening in paradise.

Sleep also was as elusive as the winning numbers for my Saturday night Lotto ticket. The marital promises, 'From this day forward; In sickness and in health; For better, for worse', marched as if by teleprinter across my brain and back again, across my brain and back again.

I got out of bed intent on action. There they still were, seemingly glued to the tray of the utility. They resembled a pair of lovers ardently entwined, excepting that one was blissfully snoring, though not relinquishing his hold on his mate, while the other bore the saddest look of reptilian resignation I have ever seen.

Of spousely sympathy, I had none. My concerns were for the lady snake. I knew instinctively that this long-suffering reptile was female. What is more, she was a sweet-tempered female, or why did she not simply bite the fiend and be done with it?

She seemed to be weaving her upper body about, as if seeking something. I followed the pattern of the movements until I realised that she needed some type of stepping-stone between the level of the ute and the safety of the nearest scrub. Her strategy was now clear. She would lower her upper body to the stepping-stone, grip it tightly and hang on doggedly until, hopefully, her captor lost interest in retaining her and released his hold.

I must provide the means to freedom.

There are no manuals on etiquette for this type of snaky dilemma, but I decided that an old iron kitchen chair would fit the bill nicely. I dashed back to camp, the slippery sand no longer a problem. The chair was placed just below the level of the ute. My sister snake launched her skinny shoulders into space and grasped the metal backing of the chair. The test of wills began with my barracking, 'You can do it, girl!'

The Spouse snuffled, squirmed and released his grip. I cheered in delight. Mrs Snake paused halfway down the leg of the chair, gave me what I could swear was a reptilian 'Thank you' look and then slithered gratefully away into the tropical night. My duty done by man and beast, I slept.

Hours later, a rum-smelling spouse bumbled his way into our caravan kingdom. The apparition aimed a sloppy kiss in my direction, patted me distractedly on the bottom and fell into the sleep of the innocent in a diagonal axis across the bed. I curled into the foetal position in the only tiny corner left for wives and began the religious chanting that would eventually lull me into blissful slumber: 'I promised for better or worse; I promised for better or worse ...'

The Pride of Coochie Flats

J.M. Sandhu
Terranora, NSW

The wail took us all by surprise. It rose up on the air like a thousand banshees. The windows shivered and Aunt Ethel's hideous vase ('It's a genuine heirloom, you ungrateful sod!') wobbled and teetered before settling firmly back on the mantel and grinning smugly at me.

'Strewth, Ruth!' I exclaimed, bouncing out of my chair. The *Coochie Flats Gazette* went flying, and as the pages rained down on me Em appeared in the doorway, her eyes as large as saucers. We were staring at each other like a pair of loons when off it went again. This time it sounded like someone had struck a pig with something particularly nasty.

Now, there's only one thing in Coochie Flats that makes a racket like that, and sure enough, there on the front lawn was our daughter Lizzy. A determined kind of girl is our Lizzy, never afraid to speak her mind, and she was sure speaking it now. Got it from her mother. So there she was, all five-foot-nothing of her, and she was laying into her fiancé, Josh, something fierce. Her pretty little face was all screwed up and red, and the language! Didn't know the meaning of half of it, but I sure got the message. She was plenty mad! Spotting her ma, she collapsed with a final shriek and wept like her little heart was going to break. Em just gave me 'The Look' as she helped the prostrated Lizzy back to the house.

Now, thirty-odd years of marriage can teach a bloke a thing or two. One thing I've learnt is 'The Look' is not good. It's trouble, big time. It means 'Joe Phillips, you do something about this, and I mean right now!'

So there you have it. That's why I'm standing here with this hulking great future son-in-law of mine and asking him why my girl saw fit to ring a peal over him just the day before the wedding, and won't I be needing my monkey suit after all? He just stood there like a mooning calf, which wasn't anything too out of the ordinary, then moved aside to expose the bent and crumpled bonnet of Viv the Valiant.

Now, some folks say I'm a bit slow. Myself, I like to think I'm just thorough, but even I could see at a glance that Viv the Valiant wasn't going anywhere for a while, and she certainly wouldn't be carrying the blushing bride to the church on the morrow. I scratched my chin and looked over to the house, where the sounds of caterwauling could still be heard coming from the front parlour. Now, Em's the expert on such matters. She should be after raising five daughters.

'There, there, love,' I could hear her say, 'Pa will sort it, you'll see.'

Well, what's a bloke to do? I hightailed it off to the shed like I had one of those banshees after me. Like I said, I'm no fool.

Ah, bliss. I grinned at Blue the cattle dog, and he grinned back at me, all teeth and lolloping tongue. 'Bloke's Heaven', we call this, home of the Beautest Yoot this side of the Wondalilly. There he was, as basic as dirt, but this baby could rumble! A lusty V8 heart that would give you chills; 165 kilowatts and torque as thick as concrete. And no poncy automatic either, like that milk crate on wheels

Em had wanted. No, sir! Five on the floor with a 3.45:1 diff. The Beast works hard, plays hard, and when you lean on the throttle, makes every other drive you've ever had fade in comparison. So there we were, The Beast, Bluey and myself, all sitting grinning at each other, when I remembered what had sent me scuttling out here in the first place. Blue woofed sympathetically and laid a cold, wet nose on my slipper.

You know, from the very first time I ever beheld the blotchy red prune that was my little girl and she grabbed hold of my nose, I've been her slave, and I wasn't about to change now. If I had to carry her to the church on my back, so be it. And by crikey, if it didn't hit me in a blinding flash of white light! The greatest idea since Noah's missus told him to get the sheets off the line! Blue whined suspiciously and The Beast scowled.

'Now, boys,' I told them, 'we've all got sacrifices to make, and if I have to get all dolled up in that damn monkey suit, then you two can lend a hand as well!' Blue sneezed in disgust, but a man's gotta do what a man's gotta do.

I worked all night, washing and polishing The Beast till he shone. I put one of Em's nice chairs up on the tray and covered it with one of the 'good' bedspreads, then I set to work in the garden. Em's pride and joy, this flower garden, and by heaven there wasn't a bloom left to be seen by the time I had finished with it!

I met my red-eyed, sniffling princess at breakfast and led her out the front door. There was The Beast in all his glory! Transformed into a veritable bower of roses and daisies and goodness knows what else. Em gasped and dropped the teapot as she eyed the chicken-wire arch dubiously. Not that any wire could be seen for the riot of blooms and fernery. Blue whimpered and hid his face, but Lizzy ... Lizzy, for once in her life, was speechless! Her blue eyes opened wide and her jaw fell. She couldn't believe what she was seeing!

Then the giggle started. It started somewhere in her belly, and rose like a tickle up through her throat, till she could stop it no longer and it burst forth. She threw her head back and laughed and laughed and laughed. Blue hung his head even lower.

'I'll ... be ... just ... like ... a ... fairy ... princess!' she gasped through her tears. 'Oh, Pa, thanks!'

And I got the biggest hug and kiss a proud dad could ever hope for. She looked again at the canopy of flowers and the 'throne' and collapsed in giggles once more. I don't know what Em quite meant when she said it was a good thing our girl was blessed with a sense of the ridiculous.

Anyway, they both did me proud that day. Even Blue condescended to ride along with Lizzy as Best Man. He said it was to keep The Beast company. I'll always remember the look on young Josh's face when his fairy princess arrived.

'Good onya, love,' Em whispered to me, and squeezed my arm. She would have given me a big kiss, but the bunch of cherries on her hat kept slipping to one side if she moved too much. So, in the end, that's how the Pride of Coochie Flats made it to the church on time!

Buck's Night at the Bay

David Cameron
Merredin, WA

Two of my mates were getting married, and decided to have a combined buck's night. It was safety-in-numbers type of thinking. It didn't work, but that's another story.

A weekend up at Jurien Bay was organised.

Now, most of the guys that came were from the city, so they were straight into it. Yahooing as we drove through the Pinnacles. Riding on roo bars, bonnets, side rails, roofs. You name it, they hung off it.

With an afternoon of this under their belts you would have thought they'd be right to stay in the vehicles as we hit the dunes that night for some serious four-wheel driving.

This, however, was not the case, and while we were letting down our tyres Dames and Dunny (one of the bucks) were working out how they could ride on the back of my ute. This took a bit of thought, because it was a dual cab with a canopy. In the end they dropped the tailgate. They were going to stand on this and hold on to not a lot. Also, the other buck wasn't prepared to give up his front seat.

We set off, my vehicle in front, the other following closely behind.

We couldn't hear much from the cab, but those who remained up front were looking back and saw the groom-to-be banging and screaming that he wanted to get off. He obviously had something to live for.

Dames, on the other hand, had already been married for twelve months, and he was going to keep on riding. While Dunny made his way off the tailgate, Dames managed to talk James, a friendly Indian dentist, into riding with him. Dames assured James that if they bent their knees they would be able to stay on while the tailgate bounced up and down beneath them. He was convinced. We took off again.

This time we had to gun it straightaway to try and make it up a big dune which lay directly ahead of us.

We made it up the steep dune remarkably easily, and were still travelling at pace when we hit the top. My eyes opened wide and my heart hit my mouth. We were confronted with a landscape that was cratered like the surface of the moon. I hit the brakes, trying to slow down before we started on the dips. I knew we were going to get bounced around a fair bit in the cab, let alone what might happen to the tailgate.

We ended up going through three of these dips and ridges. Each of these was deeper than the one before it. We jerked to a stop in the sand. The other vehicle got to the top just in time to see it all happen. I didn't know what had happened to the tailgate riders, but I feared the worst. I jumped out of the cab, slamming the door on my way out.

Dames had been thrown off to one side. He had been face-planted into the dune and his foot was just centimetres from the back wheel. He was getting up by the time I got there. He was covered in sand and busy trying to spit some of it out of his mouth. If Dames was thrown this far, then where was James?

I was shouting out, 'James! James!' while looking out into the darkness. Now, James had a better tan than the rest of us, so I didn't think he would be too easy to find. I heard a quiet voice when I stopped shouting.

'David! David!' Where was he?

He was on the roof. Up the front of the cab, and he had knocked my aerials over on the way there!

'Are you OK?' I asked with great concern, not knowing what sort of condition he was going to be in.

All he said was, 'David, David, I'm all right, but could you please open your door?'

'What? Why's that, James?' I couldn't figure him out.

'Because my fingers are stuck in there,' he said.

He hadn't suffered any injuries until I slammed his fingers in the door of the dual cab ute!

A Few Cones in the Back of a Ute

Mark Braeckmans
South Penrith, NSW

This one will definitely make the pot-heads sit up and think seriously about joining the army.

It's about February '93, I'm the section commander of a platoon in the army. Together with my men, I'm running a VCP (vehicle check point) about 40 kilometres east of Baidoa, in Somalia. We've been sitting there checking vehicles using the MSR (main supply route) for a couple of days now, and if you have ever done this sort of work you'll know it can get pretty tedious to say the least.

Anyway, along comes this old LandCruiser ute – it doesn't look much different from any of the other vehicles that we've searched, except from about 100 metres out you could see that the occupants had a pretty worried look about them. Naturally anything like that tends to put one on the lookout for trouble, and by the looks of these guys something was definitely going on.

Now, due to all our previous contacts having been with young blokes between eighteen and thirty-five years old, as these clowns were as well, we were really suspicious. Approximately ten seconds pass, these guys pull up and the search begins. First we get them to switch off the vehicle. They pretend not to understand. A rifle point's at the driver's head and he suddenly speaks Oxford

English. Next we unload the passengers and driver, and they are all taken to the side of the road and searched for any concealed goodies.

Nothing, not a single thing is found. So we turn our attention to the vehicle, and with the aid of the driver we start at the front: bonnet up, and searched, nothing; cabin doors opened, cabin searched, still naught. Now, this guy can see we are getting pretty pissed off and he starts to giggle. I turn around and his mates are off to the side of the road and they're in hysterics. Now I'm startin' to think these characters are having a lend of us, when suddenly the whole Section is hit by this smell.

For about ten seconds we sit there staring at each other in disbelief, then one of my blokes starts to laugh and dives into the back tray. He proceeds to throw these big potato sacks over the side. The rest of the search team make short work of these sacks.

Inside are over 250 parcels a bit bigger than a Coke can, and each is chockers full of compressed heads of marijuana! Now, we are in an Active Service Zone, and I'm buggered if they mentioned anything about what we should do if we come across a ute full of cannabis. So I'm on the radio to a higher authority. 'Let them and their property go,' they say. So after consoling my men, who are near to tears, I send them on their way.

Now, these geezers think we are the tops for allowing them to keep their pot, and as a goodwill gesture offer to sell us a couple of parcels, which were about four ounces each, at two dollars a shot. Needless to say we, being good Aussie soldiers representing our beloved nation and all, refused their generosity. (Bad luck, pot-heads!)

A few days later we were tasked with more pressing matters, and whilst being briefed I was informed that marijuana was now illegal in Somalia and any found was to be confiscated and handed in to be destroyed. By burning no doubt!

Johnny's Beaut Ute

Yolanda Rogers
Hamilton, VIC

It was funny the day I saw my husband's pathetic figure climb out of the car as he unloaded the old, battered ute that was sitting on the trailer. He was looking pretty grotty and his hair was tousled after that big hunt.

I stood in the driveway trying to stifle a giggle. 'What are you gunna do with that rusty-looking thing? We've got enough rubbish around here,' I remarked. John looked at me as if I had done him a grave injustice. 'Just wait and see, dear ... I bet she'll turn out like you wouldn't believe,' John replied, narrowing his eyes with an air of unmistakable optimism.

He was fair dinkum about it. He was being ambitious, I thought. I was quite sceptical at the prospect. I found it hard to believe then that a dud-looking machine like that ute could ever be restored to its original beauty.

John worked as a boilermaker and had an extraordinary love for engines, his boss had once said. Motor-mad person, I reckon. He had this great big shed jam-packed with his collection of car parts, some of which he fished out from the tip. Young chaps building an old bomb knew where to go when hunting for some parts. 'Go and see Johnny' was the word of mouth.

John battled with the ute for a week after he towed it home. He knew it would involve a helluva lot of hard yakka, hundreds of cuppas (to keep him awake while restoring it) and heaps of engineering smarts. He was obsessed with the ute. His aim was to create a Euro sports ute. Piece by piece he laboriously flicked all the parts apart except for the body. Everything had been smoothed out, and all baddies changed into goodies, and the six-potter converted into a V8 predator. A real predator, 'cos it could roar all right! I was not that well-versed in car parts; I only knew a bit about it because I had often heard my husband yakking about his endless tales to his mates. I had gotten sick of listening to his 'yoot yarns' after a while, you see.

Our shed was always neck-deep in creepy-looking fellas checking out John's ute. Blokes of all sorts, heavily tattooed, pierced and long-haired, who would greet me, 'How are yer doin'?' if they happened to see me. They would open the bonnet up and shove their heads under it, examining the engine as though they had never seen one before. A good peek under the ute like they thought they knew what they were looking at.

John's projects really cheesed me off, since he spent many a late night in the shed. I consider my husband a real work addict – which means that he plunges himself into work like someone hurling himself off a hangar.

One night I rushed into the shed, since he wouldn't come in to have his tea after I'd called him a dozen times. 'You could've married that clunker instead of me,' I hissed as I put my hands on my waist.

My annoyance suddenly changed into laughter as I saw that white-faced John had black marks all over his face and a generous smudge of grease on it too. Still, he managed to say his all-too-familiar line: 'You know I love you, dear, I wouldn't have married you if I didn't love you.' He wiped his greasy hands, sat me down on the chair and gave me a gentle kiss. End of blue.

We had a bit of a disagreement about the colour. 'I'd like to see that ute hot pink,' I suggested, imagining the pretty colour from what I'd seen in a car magazine.

'Hmmm ... pink is a bit common, I reckon. I'll paint it black and blue,' he said, as he ambled off to test the engine.

John revved the engine so hard that it produced a thundering loud noise, which startled the little old lady next door who was having her afternoon nap at the time. The noise sent her out of the house whingeing and her dog charged out behind her. She looked mortified as she sticky-beaked over the fence and sounded peppery. 'I shan't put up with that – that cranky old John shouldn't be allowed to go revving that noisy motor at this time of the day. He'd be better doing that out in the paddock instead. I'll be forced to notify the police if he does it again. Mark my word.' Then she stomped inside.

I sort of agreed with her, really. I was only young then but I could not stand the deafening noise pollution either. I felt as though the ground quaked whenever John did that revving, not to mention the terrible black smoke it produced.

After twelve months John's mission was finally over. The yucky yoot grew into a real beauty. The motor was a GT 351. The bodywork was splashed with black and blue paint, with striking yellow fire stickers slanted across the body, the inscription 'Falcon' obliquely stuck in the middle part and a personalised plate that read 'Johnny'. Quite impressive.

But there was this lumpy contraption protruding on top of the bonnet. I asked my hubby what it was.

'It's a scoop, woman!' he said ingratiatingly.

'And what does it do there?' I queried.

'It covers two carburettors.'

Needless to say, we were rapt with the finished product. That was John's first serious build-up, and he received quite a lot of praise, which made him put on his big watermelon smile. Now and again he would take the rocket for a test drive, but never when the weather looked iffy.

He decided to enter the ute in a South Australia 'Show 'n' Shine' car show. I had even grown to like John's ute, 'cos it was immaculate, cool and dazzling – not something I'd drive to go shopping, though. He paid 500 smackers for the gawky refuse that had metamorphosed into one fine-looking machine.

One day an American friend visited us, and after we had had our dinner John said to the Yankee: 'C'mon into the shed and have a look at my ute.'

'Ute? What's a ute?' He looked at John as though waiting for him to explain the never-heard word.

So John said, 'Utility car, ute for short.'

Then he said, 'Ow, that's right, a pickup or a truck!'

The day of the car show had finally arrived. I smiled smugly that morning as John left for the show. I gazed at the used-to-be-an-eyesore package, its paint shining brilliantly in the morning sun. Even John seemed to sparkle, looking nicely scrubbed in his crisp white shirt. He cuddled me ta-ta and then hit the road towing his pride and joy.

Just One of the Boys

Cathy O'Keeffe
Bowraville, NSW

The class of '79 school reunion was that night. We still knew most of them. After all, even if we didn't exactly see them every day, we'd see them every week or so when they came into town for groceries, rat bait, cattle wormers or economy-sized sacks of dog tucker. A two-pub town: if you didn't stop in at the top pub, you'd be at the bottom one. The old blokes usually took the bottom one 'cos they let your dog in, long as it'd stay under your chair and behave itself.

You could pick the locals at a glance. Working men in working men's elastic-sided boots, a bit down at heel and coated in cow shit and mud. But even before you had a chance to see their boots, you could pick them when they drove up. If their ute wasn't a Holden, it was a Ford. Only the hobby farmers and wives drove sedans or station wagons.

So, when the boys and me were sculling the compulsory New or Old and pondering the relative merits of pour-on over dipping, we knew, without thinking, that the bloke parking the BMW behind the wired-on tailgate of Pete's rusty HK was a city boy. Even before we caught a waft of chilled air from the air conditioning and he locked the doors with one of those remote control thingees. You could have run a solar generator off the polish on his hood, used it to power a neon sign with the message 'Urban Professional' and stuck it on his back with duct tape. He couldn't have been more conspicuous. Like a snowdrift in a sheep-dagging yard.

But there was something familiar about him. I just couldn't put me finger on it.

He nodded to us on the way in, his shirt disturbingly white and crisp, trousers pressed, gold watch gleaming. Pete half turned his head in that slow way Pete's always had, then commented as he went back to leaning on the rail, staring blankly at the familiar main street, 'Geez. The things ya see when ya ain't got a gun.'

It was my round. Ellen had them half pulled before I got to the bar. 'How's Suzie?' she asked as I slapped a twenty down on the slop towel.

'Better. The little bugger's a good looker, like his dad. Might even keep him.'

Mr White-and-Wrinkle-free twisted in his seat to face us. 'Congratulations.'

'What fer?'

'On your son?'

'What the hell d'ya mean?' Was this some lawyer bloke on a mission to prove the paternity of some city kid?

'You just said ... you know, about your wife ...'

'Either you drink a shitload faster than me, mate, or yer hearin' things.' Then the dead koala dropped. 'Suzie's me dog, mate. Just littered.'

'Oh.'

'Yeah, six pups and lost all but one, and he was about as pretty as road kill fer a while. She was crook, but she's OK now.'

'I see. Kevin,' he introduced himself.

A second deceased marsupial descended. I knew this bloke.

'Class of '79?'

'Same.'

'Well, just give us a sec while I get rid of these, and I'll buy you a beer.' I delivered the boys their schooners. 'What took ya so long? Could've died of bloody dehydration.'

'Kevin. Bloke in the Beamer.'

'Not Kev from school?'

'Yeah.'

He decided to come with me. If you were looking for two blokes more different, you couldn't have gone past Pete and Kev. Pete, if you could get him to talk at all, kept it short and simple, and only did it when absolutely necessary. Put a beer in his hand, and the only way you'd know he was breathing was because he'd bend the elbow from time to time.

Kevin was all shiny exterior, movement and noise. He threw his arms about like a blue heeler at a cat show and, within thirty seconds of hitting the bar stool beside us, he was bragging about his big city business, his collection of sports cars, his model wife and two football hero sons. Pete raised his head once during Kev's marathon bull-shitting bout to glance over the bar. Maybe he was looking for something big enough to block up the hole in Kev's face.

We left early and headed for the reunion. Pete always left the pub a half-hour before dark 'cos his headlights had died in '82 and he'd never got around to fixing them. Buggered if I knew how he'd get the old girl through rego when his dad retired and sold the garage/general store/truck stop. He had parts in there that you couldn't get from a collector, and could pull a gearbox faster than any three other blokes.

I took the Esky out of the front seat before I picked Pete up. There were two advantages in this. First, if Pete came with me, he wouldn't have to drive home in his beast with his Dolphin torch on the dash. Second, if I was driving, Pete could make an attempt at breaking the tinnie record set at the last reunion back in '94. I didn't want him to get a head start, so I stuck the Esky in the shed.

I'd forgotten about Kev. The Beamer had pulled in just behind us, a bit dustier now but still as glaringly conspicuous as tits on a bull. Without a conspiring word, Pete and I were out of the ute and away before Kev had a chance to talk to us. By the time he got inside, we were buried as far away from the door as humanly possible without going through the rear wall and falling the ten feet into the paddock out back. Two minutes later you could hear his voice, despite the crowd, giving the same speech he'd practised on us in the pub.

Pete stood, contemplatively, for a few seconds before he spoke. 'Did ya leave yer toolbox in?'

'Ya had yer feet on it the whole way in, yer stupid bastard. Why?'

'I think I'm going to have to wire his gob shut.'

By eleven o'clock there wasn't a soul in the class of '79 who hadn't heard that speech, but most of them were too written off to care. Pete was within three tinnies of breaking the record, and was still upright. I knew that he had at least four more cans in him once he went in the legs, so I thought the new record was pretty securely in hand. The noise level had risen as the keg levels had fallen, so at least we couldn't hear Kev any more.

That was when Sergeant Bob arrived. I didn't think much of it at first, 'cos we'd invited him along for a few drinks when we'd spotted him sticking fines on tourists' cars for parking infringements a few days back. Even though he was class of '77 we knew he was keen on Ellen, the only single girl over thirty in town, and we felt it was our duty to get them together.

But Bob was in uniform. When he strolled over to Kev, the conversation died like a bug on a windscreen.

'Kevin?'

'Err … yeah.'

'We just got a call down at the station. You have a son, Gregory? Aged eighteen, unemployed, living at your rented address in Dubbo?'

'Ummm … yeah.' Dubbo?

'Unfortunately, he's just wrapped a utility, rego CUR 020, around a tree in the front yard of a residence in High Street.'

'Me ute!'

'He's uninjured, but it seems that he was running from police at the time.'

'Why? He's got a licence.'

'Actually, he doesn't. He lost it after that culpable driving incident earlier this year.'

'What incident?'

'When he stole a car to visit his mother in gaol. You'd better come with me. We'll drive over, but this could take some time.'

'But I have to return the car! It'll cost me a week's wages at the meatworks if I don't get it back before ten o'clock tomorrow.'

We drove the car back for him. It was the least we could do for an old mate. I couldn't hardly blame Suzie when she puked all over the velour upholstery in the back. After all, she'd never been in a sedan. She was a ute dog.

Ute Surfin'

Jackie Brennan
Runaway Bay, QLD

Some of us got 'em and some of us ain't. Me, I've got 'em
– fleas, that is; but then, so do most dogs. Not to worry …
kinda sorts us streetwise mongrels from them prissy,
pedigree couch potatoes.

For me, with my shaggy, brittle fur, every day is a
bad hair day. And for a touch of feral contrast there's a
patch of mange on my rump – a bit like a mohawk. But
I still have a thick head of brindle hair – which is more
than I can say for my boss, Bluey. And just 'cos ya can't
see my peepers, doesn't mean I have a problem with my
eyesight. From in here it's a bit like lookin' through a
slim-line, tan and grey, vertical blind – custom-made
sunnies, ya might say.

Smell! … What smell? That's honest sweat, I'll have
ya know. I'm a workin' dog. No, I don't mean one of them
intellectual types like yer kelpies or border collies who
lecture to a bunch of sheep for a livin', or that poser
Kane, TV's hunky stunt pin-up. And ya wouldn't catch
me struttin' me stuff on the big screen either, not with
them egotistical tree-sniffers Lassie and Beethoven in the
business. In my opinion, Benji's the only one's got any
real talent in that snooty crowd. Did ya know they spend
at least half their day in one of them poochy parlours?
Bloody K9 torture, that is!

You try keepin' yer coat glossy and manageable when yer ridin' shotgun in the back of a rustin' ute with a concrete mixer and a dag-encrusted load of scaffoldin' for company. Ya see, I'm a brickie's labourer.

Me and Bluey, we were doin' this job out the back of Woop Woop ... wanted to get it finished before dark ... save us comin' all the way back for an hour's work the next day. Got it all done, too – just don't look too closely at the top three courses ... gets a bit skew-whiff when he's pushed for time, the ol' Blue.

It was a Friday afternoon, middle of winter, and damn cold in the back of the old ute, too, let me tell ya. As we wound our way down the narrow mountain road, Bluey turned on the headlights, although at that eerie time of dusk they never do much to light the way.

There's me in the back, legs splayed, expertly shiftin' my weight as I surf my way through each new curve. But with the promise of a coldie in his nostrils, Bluey couldn't resist nudgin' the accelerator out of each turn.

Mind you, he's a good driver, but I wish he'd try, just once, ridin' in the back when he's doin' his Dick Johnson impersonation. The rear end started to swing wider. I could hear the tie-down ropes strainin' against the concrete mixer as it jolted and lurched with each whiplash.

'Struth, Blue, are you deaf?' I barked frantically. 'The mixer's chuckin' an atomic wobbly back here!'

The rear tyres were skiddin' into the gravel shoulders and I realised there was no way Bluey could see me through the clouds of dust the ute was spewin' up. I could feel my cement-crudded paws losin' their grip. Now, for those of you who aren't familiar with ute surfin', let me explain. Once ya lose the plot, yer a goner – that is, until ya hit another straight, then ya can usually snatch the chance to plant yerself on all fours again.

So there I was, bein' hurled from side to side, not to mention coppin' a clobberin' from the floats and trowels that were flyin' across the open cab. I panicked when I saw the spirit level cartwheelin' towards me and tucked my tail in for protection. Just as well – damn thing nearly jabbed me in the jollies!

'Eh, Blue, steady on, mate! The beer'll still be cold when we get to the local.' I skidded on the plumb-bob and went crashin' against the gyratin' mixer. The boss obviously hadn't heard me over Martin/Molloy blarin' on the radio. I barked louder, addin' a few familiar adjectives sure to grab his attention.

'You try keepin' yer coat glossy and manageable when yer ridin' shotgun in the back of a rustin' ute!'

I woke up in complete darkness at the bottom of a gully to the creepy sound of the nocturnal locals scavengin' for a feed in the scrub. I just lay there with a terrible pain in my left hip and thought of Bluey ... probably settled in at the pub, guzzlin' down his third schooner.

By dawn my mangy leg was swollen to more than twice its normal size, and I'd lost count of how many times I'd heard the familiar rumble of the ute cruisin' past. There it was again. It was slowin' down. Shh ... wait for it, wait for it ... yep, there she goes, that familiar crunch of the mixer as the ute comes to a stop. I'd know that sweet sound anywhere.

I barked – or was it a yelp? No, I'm no sook – it was definitely a bark.

'Hey Bluey, down here mate!'

Four weeks later and I'm back to ute surfin' again, only now I'm shackled in my flashy new harness. This is great – no more wipeouts! And ya should see the fancy tricks this gizmo lets me do. Abseilin' off the mixer, hangin' ten from the gunnels an' bungy jumpin' off the roof. Reckon I should ask Bluey for a helmet and shin pads, then you'd really see some action!

Big Spenders

Steve Turner
Oatley, NSW

I've still got the FJ ute that we got married in twenty-six years ago this December.

What a knees-up the wedding was! We decided to give everyone a real treat and have the do on a ferry on Sydney Harbour. We hired the *Prolong*, which was the ferry that sank in the harbour a few years later, but thankfully we stayed afloat. Me mate and I filled the ute up with three 18-gallon kegs and a nine-gallon so that the guests wouldn't get thirsty during the four hours on the boat on a hot December arvo.

My wife came in a hire car, but I didn't see much of that because we were still getting the grog started without a regulator on the beer plant.

It was a good turn-out. My uncle fell down the stairs head-first; the ladies got photos taken with their dresses blowing up; my dad and my uncles all had squinty eyes. When we pulled up to the wharf next to where the Water Police were then, we thought they were going to arrest us all.

So me and me new missus got into the ute with all the ribbons and tin cans and drove off under the Harbour Bridge heading for the North Coast. Well, I was so buggered that we could only make the motel at Mt Colah about twenty miles out of Sydney (miles, because that's what the ute's speedo reads).

*The FJ ute that we got married in twenty-six years ago this December —
with my surfboard on the top.*

The next night we made it to Scotts Head, some 350
miles north, and we pitched a tent that my best man lent
me. By the time we got to Coffs Harbour the next day I'd
had it with driving, and since I only had a week off and
the wedding took up one day, we didn't have much time
left. I'd put a rack on the top of the ute the week before
so that I could go surf skiing, and it worked real fine.

We stayed in a motel on the corner into Coffs, where
someone was killed during its construction.

On the way back we sort of ran out of time and couldn't
decide where to stay, so we pulled up under the railway
bridge at Wyong, moved a bit of gear around in the back
of the ute and slept in there. The only trouble with that
was that my wife didn't wear shoes and socks to bed and
her feet got bitten by mozzies.

We are pretty sure that the ute had something to do
with our daughter Claire, because she was born nine
months later.

To celebrate the good service the old girl's given me

I have done her up. So far when I divide the cost by the number of years I've had her, it works out at about $450 a year. Because it's our twenty-sixth anniversary this year I plan to take both girls away again. We plan to do the same trip in December 2001. But it will be four-star all the way and maybe for more than six days.

So if you see my brown FJ ute heading up the North Coast in December 2001, say hello. You will know it; it'll have my surfboard on the top. See ya.

Thank Heavens for Utes!

Callum Jones
Spring Hill, QLD

I was riding my pushie home from school one day when I had a stack which broke my shoulder. To my surprise I was entitled to compo, so that was a bonus. Unfortunately, I still had to go to school. Bugger!

I was in the market for a paddock-basher to hoon around the property and practise my driving, as I was almost old enough to get my licence. The only requirements were that it could go, was a manual and was a ute (of course).

I was scouting the local *Trading Post* and my eyes lit up when it jumped from the page. A 1973 XA Ford Falcon ute for $400. I was on the blower quick-smart and sure enough, it was still there. My old man and I rocked up the next night in pitch black and all we had was a crappy torch. It turned out that the guy's missus had caught him driving the unregistered ute one night when he was pissed as a fart, so it was either him or the ute that went. The ute was rough, all right, and certainly not worth the price tag even if it was a ute, so I offered him $250. BUT, he said if it was out of his sight by the end of the week I could have it for $200. (I think he was feeling a little backed up.)

I handed over the cash and she was mine. Next day the towie dropped her to my place and she really was all mine. Now was time for the fun to begin, along with the discovery of rust, and lots of it. Driving her with a broken shoulder was going to be a challenge, but that wasn't going to stop me.

Later on I had to go to the doc for a check-up to keep the injury comp people happy, and it was suggested that I needed to do exercises using my shoulder, like stirring movements, up and down and so on. As the beast was column shift and drove like a tank, she was perfect for my exercises, so off I went with my mates to do some circle work.

We had this pumpkin patch that was overgrown with weeds, like six or seven feet tall. We'd go flying through it, with no visibility, and at the end of the day all that there was for tea was mashed pumpkin!

By that time the column shift had shat itself, so I cut a hole in the floor and, with a dog leash, I would pull the linkages up into gear. Sometimes it wouldn't work, so you'd have to hop out and change gear. That was interesting.

One night after a school function, me mates and I came home to take the beast for a spin. I'd managed to find a back seat from one of those luxury Jap cars for $5 at the markets, which was great for riding in the back. Anyway, with one headlight we were off fangin' around the bush trying to spot each other. Somehow we managed not to kill ourselves. Eventually it became light and, as we were all rooted, we admired our handiwork on the grass and drove to school, which is where we got to catch up on some sleep.

She was a great old ute. She taught many people how to drive, including my ten-year-old sister.

And now, when I look out the back shed and see her on blocks with a smile on her dial, I know the beast retired happy and well worn-out. Rest in peace, beast.

Riley's Wedding (Funeral?)

Rhonda Barthe
New Plymouth, NZ

Riley stood in front of the congregation and peered
from face to face. His bride's family, on one side, glared
darkly back. And there on the other side was his mother,
wringing her fingers like they were live snakes that needed
to be dead. And there was his father, whose hand she
held, head down and snoozing in the pew, regardless. And
there was his Shirl in her bridal kit in a chair by the altar,
where someone had kindly stuck her to stop her falling
over. She looked like a fried egg, he thought tenderly, all
the crinkly bits spread around the plate; almost like a roll
of dunny paper that had got wet on one end. He supposed
her legs had got tired from all that standing up.

'I know I'm late ...' he began. 'But it weren't my fault,
see?'

Shirl's family had done their best to talk her out of
getting wed; she was such an elegant cook, which he
figured came directly from being the ex-ex-girlfriend
of the manager of the greasy spoon in town. But now
that they were finally here, they'd changed their minds
completely. They looked very committed. Riley began
again, by apologising.

'I'm sorry. It were Bluey's fault I'm late ...'

'Bluey's bloody dead!' shouted someone from the
back. 'Dead as a bloody doorknob, so ya can't blame
him.'

'We wanna know why you kept our Shirley waiting. Yer should be bloody ashamed!' That came from Shirl's brother, who'd always been known as Muhammad Ali, and not for religious reasons.

The whole church shifted like a pie-bag full of blowies. Riley shuffled his feet.

'It weren't my fault, I'm telling ya,' he tried again.

'You'd better make this good,' warned Shirl's father, known far and wide as Rod for his inflexibility and the length of his one good arm. It was said that Bluey had been his only true friend. He'd tried to save his life that night when he tipped into the brewery vat, where he'd gone for a sly nog when he was thirsty. Rod had told him to try to drink the stuff, to save him. It was said he'd never recovered from the fact it hadn't worked.

Riley watched Ma try to wrench the heads off all of Pa's fingers.

'Well, you know how Bluey left his ute to Rod when he died?' He didn't really want to bring it up, but he knew he had no choice. It was another sore point. Rod had decided he seriously didn't desire it and had given it to Riley as a pre-nuptial present. Riley hadn't hungered for it either, but it had been impossible to refuse. ('Don't look a gift-horse in the mouth,' Rod had said. 'I WANT you to have it.')

'And you know how that mutt of Bluey's thought the ute was really his ...?'

They'd been inseparable, all three of them: Bluey, the ute, the dog. Riley looked around at eyes sharp as razors, especially on the bride's side of the church. 'That wasn't the worst of it. The worst of it was that the dog thought the new driver was really his as well.

'Perhaps I'd better start at the very beginning,' said Riley, solemnly. 'I met Shirl at the butcher's when I went in for sausages. Shirl came round and showed me how to do sausages and it went on from there. Then one day she reckoned we should get hitched,' Riley gulped.

'Anyway, she still had the frock, see, from when Harvey Wilson did his runner, and she still fits it, even after the first baby ...' He took a deep breath. 'Well, anyway, things were fine, things were just dandy, until that rotten Bluey up and *died*.'

'I tell you, Bluey was like a brother to me!' yelled a bloke from the second row. 'You blinkin' watch yerself, I blinkin' well miss him.'

'Of course you do,' Riley said hastily. 'We all do, mate. And that's where that moth-eaten, weather-beaten, rotten excuse for a huhu grub comes in.'

'Yer won't speak ill of the dead or I'll yank yer tonsils out!'

'I weren't speaking about Bluey,' Riley offered quickly. 'I were speaking about the dog.' His shoulders slumped. 'If you could call that slobbering hand-grenade a *dog*. He won't get off the ute, y'see. He's claimed that flatbed like it's a boat and he's captain of the ship. He thinks he's the admiral!' Riley's voice got high.

'He does his exercise like a prisoner going round and round the yard. The *execution* yard. He pees off the back whenever the urge takes him; never seen a dog do that before. I have to park that ute two foot from the kerb or else he *wees* on people's feet when they come up to pat him.

'Yes, well,' he shuddered, as though the memory made him truly distraught. 'Do you know, that dog can stick his tongue round the side of the vehicle and straight in the driver's ear? No? I think Bluey was bent if you ask me,' said Riley. He looked up guiltily, and continued when no one argued.

'Every night, round nine o'clock, he starts to howl. Stone the crows, you wouldn't believe it. Bluey'd be knackered, see, and just about to head to bed, and the wife, she'd be getting set for a quiet night, when the dog would start. Bluey would have to go shut the mongrel up, and by the time he got back his old girl would be snoring ... The dog kept 'em apart for years.

'You'd have thought a dog wouldn't mind a sheila like Shirl who could cook, now, wouldn't you? But, oh no. That rotten dog hates Shirl's bones. Don't he, love?'

The bride, sitting in the centre of the fried egg, nodded sagely. 'I've never known a dog to hate no one as much as he does my Shirl. He thinks you're about as presentable as a dead rat on a dinner-plate, don't he, darl?'

The bowed head bobbed again, with a little more vigour this time. Riley got ready to sum up for the jury.

'So. We can't get that dog off the ute and we can't take the ute anywhere *without* the ugly mongrel. And when the son-of-a-bitch swallowed the keys, just as I was coming here early,' Riley stressed, 'pulled them out of the ignition and swallowed the damn things whole, there was nothing I could do except leave the ute parked, and him in it ... At least I don't have to lock it – a man'd be a fool to take that dog ...' His voice petered right away to nothing.

'Anyway, I went to get my mobile out, to call up old Seesaw to come and get me, and I couldn't find it. Then it turns out that the dog found the phone on the ute seat, and ate it as well! I had no choice,' said Riley, sincerely. 'I had no flipping choice but to walk the whole way here, the whole twelve miles.'

A hush descended upon the congregation, and there was not a dry eye in the house as every man, woman and child, on both sides of the church, acknowledged poor Riley's pain. He'd won that mobile for breaking in the biggest bag of balls in the Walla Walla rodeo, the invincible Attila the Hun. Only the bull had got pretty feisty and broken his as well, and he'd had to take his steak and eggs standing for the next three months. Even the bride's rellies dropped their heads and gave Riley and his phone two minutes' respectful silence.

'And after the wedding,' he said loudly, to no one in particular, 'I intend to *give it back*.'

Rod with the long right arm leant miserably into his wife when he realised it was something with four wheels, four legs and no rechargeable batteries that Riley had referred to.

The bride rose to her feet and Riley proudly took his place beside her at the altar, while from far, far away, in the following tremulous quiet, came the unmistakable sound of a rapturous and magnificent howling. And after that a lesser one like the sound of a mobile phone ringing.

McEncrow's Hearse

Cathy O'Keeffe
Bowraville, NSW

When we'd bought her, she was nearly new.

'What's five thousand kilometres?' Dad had asked. 'To the front gate and back.'

It may have been a bit of an exaggeration. But the house *was* over a kilometre from the nearest road, and connected to it by a road so deeply rutted that it would mercilessly tear out the diffs of Townies stupid enough to brave the distance to attempt to sell us insurance or encyclopaedias. Once it ate the entire exhaust of an Avon lady, who then tried, unsuccessfully, to sue us for damages. We were saved by Dad's sign collection, which adorned the front gate. Mostly people didn't stop to read all of them. But Dad had once read about some meter man who sued a bloke because the bloke's blue heeler mistook him for a meat platter. Apparently the judge had ruled in the mauled man's favour, cautioning that a 'Beware of the Dog' sign would have saved the owner from litigation.

After that, Dad thought it prudent to err on the side of caution, and so our gate was festooned with a patchwork of warnings: 'Beware of the Dog, the Pig and the Wife', 'No Trespassing', 'Private road', and the 'No Hawkers or Canvassers' sign which had saved us from the Avon lady.

When the Council had finally straightened out Bent Back corner, Dad had acquired the 'Winding Road 3kms' sign and wired that on, too, by the holes left in it by twenty years of teenage target practice.

But my personal favourite was 'If we want religion, we'll come to you'.

So only the foolhardy or tenacious came to visit. Luckily our friends were both, and negotiated the perilous kilometre perched atop the ridges between the wheel ruts. You always heard the screaming of their gears before you saw them, as they worked the gearbox to slow their descent of the deceptively gentle-looking, but positively treacherous, hill above the house.

The ute had been a bargain, the likes of which are only found at deceased estate auctions. Dad reckoned you could halve a crowd and knock a quarter off the price of a house if the owner had died in it. But, in this case, the old bloke, McEncrow, had bundied off behind the wheel of the ute. The station hand had found the ute circling on full lock in the paddock. He'd seen some show, probably 'World's Most Stupid Stunts', and something retained from it by his less-than-sober brain had compelled him to jump, head-first, through the passenger window, thinking that the driver had just passed out and was in need of a bit of a hand. When he'd found McEncrow dead, he'd been so spooked he'd dived straight back out, leaving the vehicle circling while he hightailed it to the farmhouse to call the police. By the time they arrived three hours later, the ute was out of petrol and had stopped in the giant, doughnut-shaped wheel ruts.

Dad had stuck in heavy-duty springs to give her a bit of lift, and scraped a bit of road kill off from under the bumper. We'd been wondering why it smelled like a Pal dog fart in there, but hadn't wanted to think about it too much. After all, the coroner had said that McEncrow had been dead for about a day, and it had been a scorcher.

And so, for nearly a year, we'd never really thought about the ute's former owner. She went well, received the same basic maintenance and quarterly hose-down that all the farm vehicles before her had been given, and had become just 'the new ute'. The old one was allowed to run out of rego, and became 'the farm ute' and the general paddock-basher.

The only reminder that we had of the ute's morbid past was the moniker that the blokes down at the local had nailed her with: 'McEncrow's Hearse'. Dad didn't pay much attention to that. He'd never been superstitious or religious, or so he kept telling us. And to date, I had to admit, the ute had given him no cause to start.

It had been one of Mum's clean-up days. Every so often, she got up Dad to do some maintenance close to home, and this time it happened to fall on the anniversary of McEncrow's death, though we didn't figure that out till later. We'd hosed out the ute, fixed the hen house and the vegie-garden gate and mowed the house paddock. The grass had been brown on top where it had been scorched by the sun, but it was greener near the ground. Mum had an orphaned roo that she reckoned needed some green feed, so she got us to rake off the hay. In comparison with the hill paddocks, it looked like a bowling green when we'd finished. We sat on the verandah at dusk, smelling the new cut, watching the less-than-originally-baptised Skippy grazing contentedly, while we attempted to replace several of the litres of moisture that the sun had sucked out of us ...

* * *

'Bloody vandals!'

I shot out of bed, not knowing what to think. I found Dad in his Y-fronts, gesticulating incomprehensibly, foaming at the mouth, and gesturing wildly towards the house paddock.

'Bloody kids! Nothing better to do! Deserve a good kick up the arse! Bugger!'

I looked. Two neat concentric circles deeply engraved in the paddock by some vehicle which, somehow, had not woken us, twenty metres away. This was wrong. But it wasn't the only thing, though at first I couldn't put my finger on what else it was that didn't seem quite right.

As the sleep drained from my brain, I knew. First, the circle was a clean ring. No entry or exit paths. And second, I'd padlocked the gate the night before. And even from thirty feet away, I could see that it was still intact. A chill shot up my spine. I headed for the shed. The ute, which I'd hosed off myself before garaging it, was encrusted to the dress rims with mud. The wheel arches were packed with clay. But it was the smell that got me – the unmistakable stench of long-dead road kill.

Down at the pub, the locals were theorising.

'Crop circles.'

'Act of God.'

'McEncrow's ghost, mate.'

'Aliens.'

'Bloody big snails.'

'Mutant nematodes ... I'll lend ya me sprayer.'

Dad downed another cold one, and told them for the tenth time that they were all stupid buggers.

But that night, as he stopped so I could open the gate, the ute's headlights hit a bald spot where my favourite sign had once been.

Hot Rod

Hugh Macdougall
Bowen, QLD

G'day. I'm a fisherman. Well, I used to be a fisherman, but I kind of lost interest after I caught the biggest fish ever caught in Australia. I used to fish off the cliffs near here. When you're cliff fishing you use a rod to catch them, but when you get them to the base of the cliff you have to use a gaff on the end of a rope to bring them up. That's where my ute comes in.

You see, I'm a ute nut. I've been working on utes in my spare time since I was ten and couldn't undo the nuts on the tyres without jumping on the wheel brace. Well, my ute and me often used to go fishing. It's great to have the mates around to work on cars, but when I'm fishing I only need my car for company. I used to pretend she helped me land them because I tied the gaff rope to her tow bar. Well, one day she did help me.

I had hauled up two or three fish, dragging them up the cliff with a three-hooked gaff on the end of a rope. Call me a perfectionist if you want to for using a seventy-metre rope that could lift a bus, but I never wanted to lose a fish because a rope broke. The fourth fish I caught was a Spanish mackerel, good one, maybe twenty kilos. He fought but I finally hauled him to the base of the cliff and snagged him with the gaff. Then it happened.

Lifting the mackerel clear of the water I caught a movement off to the left, fast and gleaming like a mirror just below the surface, churning up the water like a speedboat and as long as a Jap mini-sub at the War Memorial. With a tail thrash that would have sunk a tinny it leapt out of the water and swallowed mackerel and gaff in one bite, landed with a splash that wet my boots ten metres up and headed for the open ocean.

It's hard to keep a clear head in a situation like that but I managed. I turned and ran for the ute, jumped in, rammed my foot on the brake, checked it was in first gear and the handbrake was on, and waited. I didn't have to wait long. That fish ran out of rope with a jerk that pulled the ute back a metre and nearly gave me whiplash. Thank God the chassis was as strong as a tank's, or the tow bar would have ripped clean off.

Anyway, I sat there expecting the rope to break and pushing down on the foot brake as hard as I could. The fish ran to the left and ran to the right and on the end of each run the jerk would pull the back end round but still that rope held.

After about three hours of this I was getting worried. My foot was aching, my legs were beginning to tremble and if I hadn't blown up my ex-girlfriend's inflatable neck collar and stuck it on I would have had a crook neck for months. The thing that was really pushing my panic buttons was that the fish had worked the ute back fifteen metres till there was only a metre and a half left between the tailgate and the edge of the cliff.

I had a real problem. If I jumped clear I would save my life, but my ute would be smashed to pieces at the bottom of the cliff and the fish would get away. Even if my insurance company believed my story, I would never get back all the hours of work me and my mates had put into that ute. She was the shiniest, glossiest piece of mobile art from Perth to Cairns and she had the best-tuned, most powerful legal donk in the country. She had cost me thousands of dollars and two relationships but she was worth it. I had to stay with her to the end if that was the way it had to be.

I knew the fish was tiring, because the time between runs was getting longer. Bang! Another jerk and I was half a metre closer to the cliff. Two more of those and I would be a goner. I waited ... and waited ... Nothing. It was time to act.

Carefully I started the engine and waited for a response from the other end of the rope, but my baby snored so peacefully the fish didn't have any idea what it was up against. I eased off the handbrake, ready to haul it on again instantly. I eased off the foot brake, let the clutch out and gently moved forward. I could imagine that fish, half-asleep, too tired to feel the pain, drifting along slowly flapping its fins. Suddenly it noticed.

I had pulled slowly forward four metres when it started. The fight was on! That fish was awake and full of adrenaline. It tried to take off and it dragged me back a metre. I increased the pressure on the accelerator and held it with the tyres spinning and smoking and dirt and turf flying out from under me and over the cliff. The fish headed right, but the ruts I was making came in handy and at the end of this run I held my position.

When the fish stopped I increased the power again. The soil was shallow and I was down to the rock, so the tyres gripped and I began to haul the fish forward. I won't bore you with the details of how my ute, that fish and me struggled back and forth for another hour, but the fish really didn't have a chance against my baby. Eventually that giant head slid over the top of the cliff and into the history books.

When I had dragged it far enough over to make sure it couldn't flap back into the sea, I grabbed a baseball bat from the back of the ute and stunned it. Then I rang my mate Jeppa on the mobile and he came with his crane. When he saw the fish he called a television station, and soon there were helicopters landing all over the place with camera crews and pretty little reporters asking questions.

I was famous for a time and an American museum eventually bought the fish. It's amazing what people will pay for a 'freak of nature'. That's how I was able to set up my own museum, 'Newt's Classic Utes'. Most people who come in see the picture of the fish and me and think it's a fake. I see them laugh.

But some people remember the headlines, and if they're fishermen they ask, 'What kind of tackle did you use?' I just look at them and say, 'A climbing rope, a gaff, and that ute over there.'

Marty's Long Sleep

Peter Sinclair
Goulburn, NSW

Bloody good fun at them B & S balls. Isn't it, eh?

You can get blotto, and you usually do, and you can get tired and want to sleep, and you usually do, and if you get lucky you can get a sheila, and you usually do!

Not Marty. Marty wasn't a lucky bastard. Marty was just a boozer, and an aggravating one at that. He drove an old HQ ute with a ratty old interior and 400 kilos of rubbish in the cabin.

A few years ago at the local B & S ball we were all there and in comes the mouth from the west clutching a stubby, and already he's talking crap. Well, what were we to do? This bloke would wind himself up on whatever he could find and latch on to your ear and hold on like a Jack Russell. Then he'd get stroppy and then get tired and want to go to sleep.

Well, this time he did it again, didn't he? And we were ready for him, weren't we?

At about half twelve he staggered off to his heap of rubbish and fell onto the seat and went to sleep. He slept and slept and slept and still had not surfaced at four the next day!

We had all been to the recovery party, dropped down a few cold ones and generally slouched around the place for a couple of hours and had a bit of a sleep, but still no Marty.

'I suppose we'd better go and see if he's still up at the recreation area where we left him. He could have choked or anything.' So off we goes. We opened the door of the ute and he was lying there awake, propped up on one elbow on the seat, his strides all wet from where he must have had a dream of going to the toilet and gone!

'Geez, it's been a long night, mate!' he said. 'I could have swore that I seen three o'clock go round twice!'

Well, he had, and by crikey, we'd got him a beauty, hadn't we?

When he arrived the day before and had started on his verbal diarrhoea, a couple of the mates had gone and painted all the windows of his ute MATT BLACK!! Marty hadn't noticed when he passed out in the front seat after midnight ... sucked in, Marty! Serves you right, you noisy bastard!

'Bloody good fun at them B & S balls. Isn't it, eh?'

Big Al

As told to John Bryant by Michael Woof
Port Macquarie, NSW

Big Al was a qualified plumber, as well as a qualified accountant, as well as a qualified electrician. All his life he suffered an addiction to studying. Whereas most blokes hated the thought of bending over the books, he just loved it. Maybe study was a way to escape from his wife, or maybe Big Al just had a Big Brain ...

Anyway, Big Al decided to become the Most Complete Tradesman on planet earth. With all his qualifications he could clear a blocked toilet, rewire his electric eel, and take on the Tax Office when they disputed his depreciation allowance. He was a bit like the Cisco Kid, brandishing a variety of guns and ready to take on anyone, any time, any place.

Big Al was an orphan who desperately wanted to make good. Why, he hadn't even worn shoes until he was seventeen! To his delight his business flourished, but that was mainly because he was a hard worker. Even though he was studying law at night, he still put in his fifty hours a week bringing joy to the world as the best odd job tradesman in his town. His only limitation was that he was colourblind, so he tended to steer away from electrical jobs that involved high voltage.

He wasn't very image-conscious, so he didn't care where he lived or what he drove. His accountant mates used to look down their snotty noses at Big Al as they streaked past in their Volvos and Saabs, because Big Al drove a cranky, smoky Valiant Wayfarer ute, painted red, with pretty large rust holes along the doors and sills. He consciously chose red when he bought the Wayfarer from the wrecker, because he knew that one day all the paint would match all the rust. His large brain was always looking years ahead, a fact that annoyed his wife and all his mates.

Another fact that annoyed his wife was that Big Al had off-road tyres fitted to the two passenger-side wheels of the ute, whereas he ran standard on-road tyres on the two driver-side wheels. He did this to make a subtle point to his wife, because she tended to drive a long way over on the left-hand side of the road, with the passenger-side wheels constantly running off the bitumen and into the gravel and dirt. It annoyed the heck out of Big Al, but he never actually mentioned it to her. He just gloated that he had solved yet another problem using that large brain that he was sure he had.

Big Al kept the Wayfarer a few kilometres ahead of a major breakdown, because he was also a pretty smick mechanic. He completed numerous mechanical short courses during the uni Christmas holidays each year, so he knew which end of a wrench to hold.

To the delight of his mates, Big Al had some weird habits. Like the day he bought the Wayfarer he chucked the keys out the window and into the bush while driving home. He then rigged up under the dash so he could quickly hot-wire the ute any time he wanted to start it. 'Keys wear holes in yer pockets, don't believe in 'em,' he'd tell the occasional cop who thought he was stealing the ute.

Another intriguing habit was Big Al's method of waking up in the morning. Between five and five-thirty every morning, Big Al would suddenly break wind. It was usually one sharp 'crack' that sounded like a .303 rifle shot. Almost simultaneous with his mega-fart, Big Al would sit bolt upright and scream, 'What was that?' He'd then climb into the shower as though this was normal behaviour. It scared the daylights out of Big Al's mates when they went camping.

All the Wayfarer's accessories were products of Big Al's fertile imagination. His large brain, coupled with his mechanical brilliance, had created a manic desire to make his working life as efficient as possible. He'd made a pair of steel ladder racks which, when the horizontal bars were unclipped, telescoped out to become the jibs of a pair of cranes. The jib cables ran to an electric yacht winch bolted to the tray just behind the cabin. A bank of batteries, which were fed by a Honda generator that sat in the tray, fed the electric winch. With the flick of a switch and a bit of juggling, Big Al used to boast to his mates that he could lift a year-old heifer off the ground and into his ute. This incredible set-up was actually what fuelled Big Al's 'agricultural disaster'.

It happened like this.

One time, when uni was in recess and there were no short courses available, Al decided to pack up his Wayfarer and go and do 'work experience' at a Taree dairy farm. While he was there he asked Farmer Bill heaps of intelligent questions, like: 'When a cow laughs does milk come out its nose?' and 'Is it hard to train the cows to run through the gate when the blue heeler barks?'

It had been raining a fair bit and it was really boggy around the milking sheds. A large, nasty-looking

Friesian cow had wandered into the mud hole halfway down the paddock above the main shed, and got stuck up to her belly in the slop. Farmer Bill was about to get his Kubota tractor to try and pull her free, when Big Al said that he could do it quicker and easier with his ute.

Well, Big Al edged his way as close as he could to the bog hole, and swung his crane jibs towards the cow. With a lot of effort he got a wide sling around the cow, and tethered each end to a jib. With his Honda generator roaring flat-out, the winch grinding, both jibs straining, and the ute spinning its wheels, he started to pull the bellowing beast out of the mud. 'Leverage,' muttered Big Al as he sensed victory. To the amazement of Farmer Bill, his wife and their eight kids, it started to look like it was going to work, that the Wayfarer ute was going to win – the cow would be free!

However, just when all the forces were at 'max', the two on-road tyres on the driver's side of the ute let go, causing the ute to skew sideways. The Wayfarer started to slowly slide in an arc downhill around the cow, and as it did the strap went slack. The yacht winch sensed the slack and sped up, causing the sling to reel in faster, which in turn accelerated the ute's slide. With the anchored cow acting as the fulcrum, the ute gathered speed and shot off at a tangent, like a comet escaping the gravitational pull of the earth.

Farmer and Mrs Bill gasped in horror as Big Al, crouching in the back of the ute at the controls of his winch and dual cranes, stared bug-eyed at the milking shed, which was approaching at the speed of light.

Big Al threw himself onto the floor of the ute just as the Wayfarer broadsided into the milking shed. The ute cleared away the first row of milking machines like ten pins, and then smashed side-on into the two-hundred-thousand-litre milk storage vat. The impact was so great that the stainless steel vat was rocked off its concrete legs, went through the wall, and started off down the rain-soaked hill. Two hundred thousand litres of warm, high-fat, containerised milk headed straight for the main road, followed closely by one very bent Wayfarer ute. Big Al's teeth were clenched so tight a termite wouldn't have been able to fight its way into his gob!

To cut a painful story short, the vat hit the bitumen road and ruptured, sending a tidal wave of milk down Mrs Collis's hallway (she was a widow who lived opposite). Luckily, Mrs Collis was a good swimmer and liked milk.

Big Al woke up in John Hunter Hospital (without the sound of a .303) two days later, in traction, swathed in bandages and suffering from milk on the lungs. After Big Al had been lying there staring at the ceiling for half an hour, a nurse wandered in and saw he was conscious.

'How are we feeling today?' she asked with professional concern.

'Pretty bloody angry. The wife's never gonna drive me ute again. If she hadn't forced me to fit them mismatched tyres none of this would've happened ... By the way, do ya run any courses in this place?'

Dad's Folly

Gwen Leane
Port Augusta, SA

Mum was anxious. She kept going to the window, peering out into the dusk. No headlight beams pierced the gloom. The two elder boys were swinging on the gate. They too were waiting for Dad to come home.

With deferred pay from a stint in the RAAF during the war, Dad had gone to the big smoke to buy the family's first-ever car. We had seen him off early in the morning on the bus and now, as night fell, excitement knotted our stomachs. A family of six certainly needed a set of wheels, but cars were as scarce as hen's teeth in post-war 1945. It had been a long, tense day of wondering just what Dad would bring home.

It was just on dark when a set of twin lights left the main road and wound their way up the sandy track to our house. Mum and the four children were on the front lawn. Our first glimpse suggested that our dreams had come true: the car was big, black and shiny. Mum was silent. Then, staring, she cried, 'No! He wouldn't!' Her voice wobbled with unshed tears. Her dreams had been dashed, and so had her standing with her neighbours.

A Light Six wooden-spoked Studebaker hearse, complete with blinds, winches, false panels and glazed windows, slowly cruised to a standstill on the front lawn. Dad jumped out. With the proverbial Cheshire cat grin enveloping his face he asked, 'What do you think of her?'

'How could you bring home such a thing, Len?' Mum's voice rose to a screech in her disappointment. All those years of foot-slogging down to the store and to church while Dad was at the war rose up in her mind. How could he!

'It won't look so bad,' he consoled. 'It'll make a good ute. We need something to cart the vegies to market – it'll be good for that.'

The two older boys were swarming over the hearse, examining it with a fine-toothed comb. Their macabre imaginations were running riot, and as they wound the winches in and out they conjured up bodies, thought to be dead, suddenly sitting up and saying, 'How dare you interrupt my sleep,' or, 'What am I doing in here?'

Over dinner, Dad enumerated the vehicle's assets: a 199-inch wheel base (just right for turning it into a ute) ... A well base under the polished wood floor ... Hardly run in yet ... Hearses never get flogged ...

Dad was in love with his new toy. He might have squashed Mum's dreams, but his were billowing like clouds across the sky.

Next morning Dad manoeuvred the hearse into a stand of pines behind the cowshed and the metamorphosis began. Hammering, hacking and sawing accompanied the crunch of bending metal. The vehicle was reduced to a foot behind the front seat, then metal was fabricated to form a square cab and a long, sleek tray. The duco was as black as the ace of spades.

Mum leant on Dad. 'You paint it or else ...' Dad didn't think he should test the 'or else', so he painted the ute a respectable grey (which, when aged by rain and sun, began to peel. The kids assisted the process by picking off the loose bits, revealing the shiny black enamel underneath and adding to Mum's shame. Alas, once a hearse always a hearse).

The first official outing in Dad's hearse was a circus for Bruce and Peter. Mum sat in the front, chin high, face grim, trying not to notice the questioning looks and then hilarious smiles of passers-by as they realised the origins of the ute.

But it was my sister Clare who experienced the ultimate humiliation. While on the way to the funeral of an uncle, she, Bruce and Peter were sitting in the back of the ute and Mum, Dad and the other boys were in the front. Following behind was a dishy young bloke in a shiny red sports job. He was looking at Clare, and she was certainly enjoying the attention, when suddenly he burst out laughing and roared away. A blush of shame suffused Clare's face. Young men would always recognise the hearse but possibly never her charms.

To Mum, the ute was always a hearse. It has been, still is and always will be Dad's folly.

Hairy Tail

'Bluey, Son of a Bitch'
West Ryde, NSW

G'day, me name's Bluey. I'm a Hound and I get around in the back of the Boss's ute. A lot's been happening lately – but let me tell you about Phil.

I was riding through town in the back of the Boss's ute the other day when I first saw Phil. I was hanging out the side, wagging me tail and barking like ape. Phil had just picked up his brand new 1100-cc Suzuki rocket and was cruising through Sydney's five o'clock rat race in the next lane. Some people say Phil has a normal brain, but at the time I ran into him it was throbbing with joy from the feel and sound of his New Toy. In fact, it could be said that Phil wasn't paying a real lot of attention to the Rules of the Road as he gunned his bike.

I was in the middle of shaking a large blob of slobber off me whiskers and getting ready for more barking when suddenly I heard this loud thud. With great excitement I realised that our ute had sideswiped Phil's motorcycle. Shit, what fun!

Well, Phil's world went black. Funny thing, though; instead of hitting the tarmac, Phil was flipped into the back of our ute, leaving his bike lying in the gutter. As I looked down on the poor bugger, I could see that the impact of the prang had wrenched his helmet sideways, leaving his eyes staring into the helmet lining. Stunned,

Phil lay next to me in the back of the ute, trying to figure out if he was dead or what.

On the other hand, the Boss panicked. As soon as he realised he'd hit something he planted his foot and shot off, not realising his Victim was lying in the back of his ute.

I started barking like crazy, trying to warn the Boss that we had an Intruder on board. But all the noise did was alert the prostrate Phil to the fact that he wasn't dead, and that his main problem was that he just couldn't see. So he sat up, grabbed his helmet in both hands and gave it a big tug. As it came off his head sideways the buckle cut into the flesh above his eyes, causing the blood to run down his face. Geez that blood smelt good!

Peering through the trickles of blood, Phil checked me out with a dazed expression on his ugly face. As he lay there surveying his surroundings from the back of the speeding ute, he wondered where the @#$! his bike had gone. Finally he sat up and started banging on the ute's back window, shouting a long and impressive string of Rude-Man Talk. And they reckon I can bark!

The Boss, hearing the racket, glanced in his rear-vision mirror. It wasn't a pretty sight: a close-up of Phil's ugly blood-soaked skull mouthing off! On went the anchors, and after a heated exchange the Boss turned around and carted me and Phil back to the scene of the accident.

When we arrived we saw a huge crowd of people gathered in a reverent circle around Phil's dented Suzuki, staring into the sky, trying to figure out where the motorcycle had come from and where the rider had gone.

The Coppers came. Phil shouted, the Boss protested he was completely innocent, the crowd jeered and clapped, and I barked so hard I nearly coughed me liver onto the pavement. What a bloody fantastic day it was.

Phil later said that the moral of the story was this: if you ride a bike, keep an eye out for utes as well as Volvos.

Keep on barkin'!

Nin-on over None-on

C. Inglis
St Ives, NSW

'Hey, Lennie!' someone yelled. 'Tell us the one about the ute and the caravan!'

Lennie sits on his haunches, a bit of grass between his teeth.

'Yair. OK,' he says. He's wiry and tough, weathered by sun and hard times.

'Well,' he drawls, as everyone settles expectantly. Some of the men are grinning widely. They know what's coming. 'It's a few years back now. We'd been married ten years, had had five kids and a couple of good years. "You ought to do something nice for Val," says me sister Marg. "Take her on a holiday. We'll mind the kids."

'That's how it started. Next thing I know we're both getting a bit carried away. I'm lookin' at caravans and them little slide-on campers that go onto the back of utes. That bit of cash we'd saved – well, I blew most of it on a little beauty. Just sat there on the back of the ute like she was made for it.

'Marg took me missus shopping for a "second honeymoon trousseau". They came home with bits of lacy stuff and see-through nighties – what I called her "nin-on over none-on". Don't know why she needed all that stuff. Those things stayed in the suitcase first time 'round.

'Well, we farmed out the kids, put our stuff in the camper, climbed into the ute and we were off.

'We hit the Newell at West Wyalong and headed towards Queensland and the sun. By mid-afternoon Val had gone all droopy on me. Too much excitement with packing and all. She had a headache, so I says to her, "Why don't you climb into the camper and have a bit of a sleep? I'll drive real careful like. It'd do you the world of good."

'She argues the toss a bit, then says, "All right." We stop and she climbs out and into the back. I starts up again and off we go, driving real slow.

'It's a bit hot in the back, apparently, because unbeknown to me Val decides to strip off. She puts on the nin-on over none-on, stretches out and goes to sleep.

'After an hour or so I see this bit of bush just off the road and decide I'll pop in and answer the call of nature. I slow up as gently as I can, stop and nick out into the bush.

'Now Val wakes up 'round about now. She looks out the window just in time to see me disappearing into the bush. "Good idea," she thinks, "I'll go too." But of course I'm quicker than she is, aren't I? And when she comes out of the bushes here's the ute just beginning to roll away. Well, she yells and screams and jumps up and down and waves, but I don't hear her. I'm busy concentrating on a smooth take-off so as not to wake her up.

'Just then Val hears a car coming and realises she's only wearing her nin-on over none-on, so she dashes back into the scrub for cover. When she thinks about it she realises I'm not going to know she's missing till I stop at Goondiwindi in a couple of hours' time. She's got to get a lift.

'The next car she lets go by. And the next.

'She thinks, "I've got to get out there and wave. Next one. I've just got to."

'The next motor she hears is not for half an hour. Out she goes, waving madly. It's a bloke on a motorbike. Grey hair flying out from under his helmet. It's too late to change her mind, and she doesn't care now anyway.

'The bloke on the bike is a bit surprised to see this sheila out in the middle of nowhere in her nightie, but he stops and listens to her story.

'"OK," says Sir Galahad, "Climb on and we'll catch him." And off they go.

'In the meantime I'm sailing along, nice and easy so as not to wake Val, listening to some local radio fella spruiking on and playing country and western. Then I hear this horn.

'I look in the rear-vision and see this old codger on a Harley waving at me to pull over and stop.

'"Not on your Nellie," I says to meself. "Go on past, ya bugger!"

'He keeps blastin' his horn, and by now he's getting on me goat. I put me hand out and wave him on by. He doesn't go. I'm getting a bit mad. He's probably woken Val up by now.

'At last he pulls out, and I think, "Good, he's going!" But he doesn't. He draws alongside and starts pullin' faces at me and wavin' madly.

'That's when I see her. Blow me down! Val, hanging on for grim death behind the bikie! White face. Hair flying in the breeze. Wearing nothing but her nin-on over none-on.

'I dunno what happened after that. I think I tried to brake, but somehow I wasn't steering straight, and next thing I know me, the ute and the camper are flying through the air and there's a ditch coming up to meet us. There's the sound of screeching and crashing, and stuff is splintering everywhere.

'Val and the bikie, meanwhile, have sailed on past without so much as a scratch.

'I look out where the windscreen used to be and realise that at least I'm upright. The ute is on all four wheels. Up ahead, the bike's come to a stop and Val is running back towards me. All around it's a mess. One of Val's dresses is hangin' off a fence, and the bed from the camper is sitting in a ditch.

'An' the bloke on the radio is saying, "And here's Slim Dusty from 1978 with 'Some Things a Man Can't Fight' …"'

The Big Chance

Tamson Bryant
Scoresby, VIC

I was nineteen at the time and had been working full-time on our property for Dad since I left school. It had been a thrilling two years of picking dags off sheep bums. About the only excitement I had was provided by an old '82 Brumby ute which Dad gave me instead of wages when the cash was in short supply. No matter how hard I tried I simply couldn't kill that Brumby ute. Every time I went for a thrash (which was three times a day and all day Sundays) it just lapped it up and sat begging for more.

Anyway, there I was, dying of boredom and smelling like sheep dip, when I heard on the wireless that the local Stock & Station agent was looking for a 'bright young lad' to train in 'sales'; that is to say, ripping off local farmers.

Hmmm, I thought, I could be just the man for a career like that. In fact, it sounded like my big chance.

I sort of suggested to Dad that I might go for an interview, and after he gave me 912 reasons why it'd be a bummer of a job, he agreed to let me have a go. He obviously wanted to retain my dag-picking services for as long as possible. Anyway, after talking to the S & S bloke on the phone, I was asked to come in for an interview.

The night before the big interview we were having dinner when Mum said it'd be a good idea to really scrub up and look good for the interview. That was a cue for

Dad to offer to lend me his sports coat and daks. Dad was squirming like crazy. He hated lending me his clothes ever since I'd lost his one-and-only bow tie at my first B & S ball – in fact, he never got over it and mentioned it any time anyone talked about clothes, balls or good times.

Dad had just knocked down the last of the roast lamb and his second beer when he finally and grudgingly said, 'Well, you'd better borra me good coat an' daks, but don't bloody lose 'em like you bloody lost me bloody bow tie at that bloody B & S ball!'

He also kindly offered to let me borrow his Longreach ute for the drive into town. It wasn't so much because he trusted me or wanted me to look good. It was more because he knew my Brumby had a thick layer of accumulated crap all over the inside, and he didn't want his clothes to cop a coating.

While thanking Dad for his most generous offers, I toyed with the idea of asking if I could also borrow his new shoes – the ones he'd only just bought. They had little leather tassels hanging off the front of them and were really cool looking – much too impressive for an old fart like Dad. However, I wasn't game to push my luck. After all, I'd already got his coat, daks and ute.

Next morning, after Dad and the boys had left for a day of dag picking, I scrubbed up and got decked out in Dad's gear. I had to admit to myself that I looked pretty good as I paraded in front of my parents' bedroom mirror. The only shortcoming, as far as I could see, were my shoes: they were pathetic. Not only were they my old school shoes (which made them about three years old and too small), but they hadn't seen a whiff of boot polish since the Boer War.

There, by comparison, peeping out from under Dad's bed, were his brand new, shiny, tasselled shoes with the 'brothel creeper' soles.

The devil made me do it: I grabbed Dad's shoes, stuck them on and headed for town.

The interview went OK, but as I left the S & S office I was nervous as hell about Dad's shoes. What if I kicked the gutter, or lost a tassel? I decided I should take the shoes off immediately and not tempt fate any further.

Just as I was pulling my comfy work boots back on, Rough Rod the Roo Charmer (so called because he could get roos to walk towards him even without a spottie) screeched to a halt and yelled, 'Comin' down to the pub fer a quickie?'

Since all my saliva had run into my armpits at the S & S interview, my mouth was dry enough to soak up more than a few coldies. However, I remembered what Dad always said about parking a ute ('specially his ute) outside a pub – 'Yer just askin' for some frisky young cocky to take it for a joy ride.' So I piled into Rough's ute and headed down to the pub, satisfied that that frisky young cocky of Dad's apprehension would take Rough's ute for a burn, not mine.

It wasn't until later that night when Dad grabbed his sports coat and daks back off me that I suddenly realised that the shoes were missing. My mind raced and I remembered – I'd thrown them in the back of Rough's ute as we speared off to the pub. I waited till Dad and Mum had hit the sack, then I snuck out to the kitchen and rang Rough's place. 'No, not in my ute,' said Rough.

Should I tell Dad? No, if there was one thing I had to do it was to solve this one so he never knew. I didn't need a sequel to the bow tie story – it'd be handed down to the next three generations and I would never live it down.

The next Saturday I jumped into the old Brumby at dawn and thrashed the guts out of it, arriving in town before Brown's Shoes Emporium opened for business. I didn't even slow down to do re-runs over the odd bit of road kill; I was a man with a mission.

Through Brown's window I could see a pair of tasselled shoes just the same as Dad's. My troubles were over. Old man Brown finally arrived and unlatched the door. I grabbed the shoes. They felt a bit funny – but then, new shoes always did, I reasoned. Outside I scuffed them up a bit to make them exactly like Dad's. Aha, I thought. I've committed the perfect crime, and it only cost me two and a half days' dag picking!

So home I wheeled and stashed the shoes under Dad's bed. He'd never know.

That would have been the end of it except that about a month later Jack Appleton died. Being a good mate of Jack's, Dad decided he'd front up at the funeral. I'll never forget Dad's silhouette as he limped out the back door and climbed into the Falcon ute.

'Darn feet!' he said. 'Must be bloated – can hardly get me feet into me new shoes!'

Custard an' Shells

Lyn Chatham
East Geelong, VIC

Everything in the cupboard past its use-by date was goin' out. Flours an' rices an' Vestas. An' all those tins. It'd save Mum rantin' down the phone about food poisoning. She was always rabbitin' on and on about me doin' meself in before me time.

Anyway, the ute was the go. Load it all up and drive out to Pete's block for a humongous bonfire.

Pete's dark green EJ'd done heaps of stuff for the gang in the past – taken me sister's piano right across Melbourne, with Smitty playing 'Lady Madonna' all the way down High Street Road (funny name for a road, that); taken Cooky shootin' in New South whenever he felt like it. Now it was gonna help me (the name's Watty, by the way) clean up me flat.

The ute was special in its own right, too, 'cos it had original rego. I just wished Pete'd empty the ashtray occasionally. Once a year at least.

Anyway, we turfed the stuff out and onto the ute. I swear some of the tins were so old you'd need an archaeologist to open 'em.

Pete's block was on the far side of Buninyong – you know, t'wards Scotchman's Hill. It was scrubby and clayey gold country round there. You could almost see some poor bastard bent over the tailings wondering whether that shithouse-awful trip across the world was worth it.

Back to the story, though.

We parked the ute up the slope from the shack. Not that I thought it'd really matter if a spark got carried away. It was just a one-room shack, only good for boozin' in. And there was nothin' inside that you'd wanna keep. Yer 'specially wouldn't wanna keep the couch. Red floral, it was, and very stuffed, if you know what I mean. Anyway, Pete, Cooky and I supervised and Smitty unloaded everythin'. The mound of stuff was about three foot high in the end.

Cooky was allowed t' light the match. He dropped it in and then sat nexta Smitty on the tailgate to watch. I leant back on the side of the ute, watchin' those boxes and tins of crap slowly disappear in a fountain of red and orange. Bloody great, it was.

I closed me eyes and felt the October sun. The bonny talked and spluttered away. Someone told me once that we humans like fire so much 'cos it takes us back to the cave days. The ocean's the same, the way you can just sit an' stare at it for ages.

It's a funny thing. I've seen so many movies with ambushes in 'em that I'm amazed I still nearly shat meself when it 'appened.

It felt like there was ten of 'em firing at us. I hit the ground so quick I ended up with dirt up me nose. More than usual, that is. Cooky must've just threw himself right up into the ute's tray. I don' know what Pete did.

I wondered if we were bein' done over 'cos of something Smitty'd done to a jealous boyfriend. He always had girls hangin' round him, see. The bullets kept comin' and comin'. Hell, there was only four of us, why'd they need so many rounds?

And when it stopped there was nothin'. No screams of pain. No victory yells. Just the poppin' and crackin' of the fire. An' me heart, pumpin' like a freight train.

Then Pete must've had one of those flashes, as you sometimes have, 'cos I heard his voice coming from the scrub. 'Smitty.'

Smitty's head came up over the side of the ute. 'Yeah, mate?'

'Y'know when we took the stuff outta the ute?'

'Yeah?'

'Well, you weren't supposed to take it all off, you know. You weren't supposed to take the box in the corner. 'Cos, mate ...'

'Yeah, mate?'

'That was me shells for next week in Hay.'

Geez, what a shocker! Pete came up and fell on him. Laughin', mind you.

Well, after a while Pete let him go and leant 'gainst the ute facin' what was left of the bonfire. He lit a smoke.

It was then he got hit.

A two-litre lump of boilin' hot custard is pretty bad news when you get it in the groin.

Country Kids and their Paddock-Bashers

Sandra Wooderson
Blakehurst, NSW

The humble Aussie 'You-beaut-ute'!

Well, didn't every farmer have one, and didn't every country kid have a go at driving it? All the teenagers that lived on farms around me sure did. They were great for fanging around the paddocks, hence the descriptive name 'paddock-basher' that was part of our everyday vocabulary.

Of course, our dads believed that these utes were their fencing vehicles, complete with rolls of barbed wire, post-hole diggers and an assortment of tools. So, to keep them happy, we let them keep their tools in the back of our utes. The tools made grinding, screeching noises as they slid around the back gouging out metal as we did burnouts and skidded around corners.

Our ute had dodgy brakes, bald tyres and she leaked like a sieve when it rained. Her body had more dents and scratches than Elizabeth Taylor had husbands. The paintwork was a dull, faded grey, but I loved her. She just kept on going.

On weekends all the local farm kids would race each other up and down the quarry road that led down to the beach. It was a real back road, used only by local surfies and farm kids. The police knew we played up out there, and from time to time would threaten us with fines, but mostly they left us alone.

In our paddock-bashers it was a toss-up as to whose ute had the most 'character' – that 'been there done that' look. A boy named Bucktoothed Badger ultimately claimed that honour, as his ute had been rolled at least twice. Proof consisted of a series of serious score marks and dents on the roof.

One weekend I had a slumber party. It was my fifteenth birthday and a dozen girls, some of them Townies, were staying over. Like most teenage girls, our lives were filled with rock music, friendships, beaches and boys.

We all crammed into our faithful old ute, dogs and all. After a few pushes to get her started (the battery was well in need of replacing), we headed off for the beach along the quarry road. The boys from the next farm had tagged along with their ute.

The Townies wanted to learn to drive. We changed seats like a game of musical chairs. One girl, who wore glasses as thick as the bottom of a Coke bottle and snorted when she laughed, wanted to drive next, so we let her have a go. She had not the foggiest idea how to drive. We kangaroo-hopped for some distance before she floored the pedal to the metal.

We were off like a bag of prawns in the hot sun! The ute zigzagged at top speed along the tarred road until we reached the track that led to the sandhills. On the gravel the ute fishtailed wildly on its balding tyres and hit a large rock, rendering the steering useless.

Hysterical screams of 'Stop!' flooded the air and drowned out the song blaring on the radio.

'How do I stop it?' was all we got back.

'Put your foot on the brake!' I shouted.

'What's the brake?' came the reply.

'All the teenagers that lived on farms around would fang them around the paddocks, hence the name "paddock-basher".'

Shit! How could she not know where the brake was?

I scrambled over the top of the kids, packed like sardines along the bench seat, and yanked her foot off the accelerator pedal before shoving my hand down on the brake pedal – not an easy task with my head squashed between a set of thighs and my bum stuck in someone's face!

The ute left the road and sailed through the air, stopping abruptly when it hit the dry sand. I opened my eyes to see we had stopped inches from the precipice of a sandhill of some height. The ute teetered on the edge, its front wheels dangling over the drop.

'No one move!' I yelled. I looked over my shoulder to see if the others in the back were all right. The tray was empty except for the dogs still wagging their tails, their sloppy tongues happily hanging out of their delighted faces as if to say, 'Wow, that was fun!'

The road was strewn with kids doubled over, some laughing, some still winded from belly-flopping into the sand. They had all decided to cut their losses and opt for what they hoped would be a soft landing in the sandhills. The boys were having a great laugh, saying 'female drivers' and shaking their heads.

Everyone finally stopped laughing long enough to weigh down the back of the ute so that we on the bench seat could climb out. The poor ute still hung over the edge. We towed her back to solid ground with the other vehicle. The left wheel was badly bent and she was never quite the same after that day.

It wasn't long before I got a real driver's licence and drove a ute with all the mod cons – like brakes. And as for the Townie who drove like a demon possessed? Well, I only hope she didn't become a truck driver!

Back Fire

Ross 'Rossco' Moore
Raglan, NSW

Remember back in the old days when you could still buy real crackers for fireworks night? Real crackers. Penny bungers that'd demolish a letterbox or round out a galvanised-steel garbage can and punt it several feet into the air. Bungers with grunt that would drive dogs mad and worry your parents.

One cracker night me and three mates went cruising in my FJ ute. There were two of us in the cabin and two others sitting in the back. My mate in the passenger seat was having a bit of fun with the fellas in the back. He'd light a bunger and lob it out into the tray of the ute.

We'd all have a laugh, but after four or five goes at this my mate and I got bored and cruised along looking for other capers to cut.

It wasn't until a few weeks later, when it started raining one afternoon, that I decided to put my tonneau cover on the back of the ute. As I unrolled the tonneau I saw it was full of burn holes. My mates must have used it to shield themselves from the bungers we'd thrown in the back of the ute.

I'd wondered why they'd cacked themselves so much on cracker night; it wasn't that funny!

A Fella with a Ute

Margaret Large
Cootamundra, NSW

My husband John died fourteen years ago at the age of forty-seven. There were many issues that I had to confront in adjusting to life without him. One of my greatest practical frustrations was having to get my gardening rubbish to the tip in the back of my sedan. I decided that what I really needed was a fella with a ute.

Four years later, during a coach trip around Australia, the bus driver passed the microphone around and asked the passengers to introduce themselves and give a little of their history. When it came to my turn I proceeded to explain where I was from and outlined my various interests. I knew no one was listening until I announced that I was looking for 'a fella with a ute'. Within seconds every head turned in my direction, and from then on everyone had my measure. Somehow I even became a threat to the other women! For the rest of the trip the coach driver kept teasing me over the intercom whenever we passed a ute, suggesting that he pull over and let me 'check out the fella in the ute'.

I didn't find my ute-driving man during that trip, but some time afterwards I was at home gardening when, after copious pruning of shrubs, I again had the problem of getting the excess clippings to the tip. The wheelie bin was well and truly overloaded, to the point where I couldn't close the lid, so I wrote on a large piece of cardboard: *Sorry, Garbo, can't find a fellow with a ute.*

This sign almost caused several collisions. I live on an intersection, and everyone who passed slowed up to read the sign.

When I returned home that evening I found a 'P' plate stuck on my garbage bin. On it was scrawled the message: *Be back at nine pm with ute and mattress.*

I nearly had a heart attack! This was not the answer I had been anticipating! I promptly went inside and battened down the hatches. I was not even game to turn on the lights.

To this day I do not know who left the message. And I still haven't met my fella with a ute.

'I announced that I was looking for "a fella with a ute". Within seconds every head turned in my direction.'

Hiatus Years

Michelle Kitchin
Millgrove, VIC

There I was, minding my own business, when I heard voices approaching. Then I spied them: two of the roughest-looking blokes I had ever seen. They appeared to be coming straight towards me.

I could hear them talking. 'Man, what a beauty!' said one of them. Next thing I knew they were touching me all over, gibbering on like crazy men. Then they started whooping and yahooing. Finally one said to the other, 'This little pissa is gunna kick arse, whaddya reckon, Bub!' The other bloke gave me a kick and said, 'Yep, this'll make 'em sit back and take notice, Pete.' Then they took their leave.

The next day they were back. They didn't say much, just whipped around and pushed me off my blocks. The next thing I knew I was being winched up onto the back of a trailer and carried off. This was really distressing, as I had understood that I was to spend my hiatus years at this tip until I blended back into the earth.

After bumping along for some time the trailer finally rolled to a standstill. I sighed to myself, wondering what was going to happen next. I didn't have long to wait. Suddenly the street erupted with people. Beer cans were handed around, and lots of loud laughter and crude words filled the air. I hoped they would take me back to my tip to rust away in peace.

I was not to be so lucky, for the very next evening a whole heap of guys came around and started to delve into all my crevices. They pushed and pulled bits and pieces in and out of me until I felt quite red with embarrassment. They seemed to be enjoying themselves, though.

What followed next was a period of noise and activity. I honestly don't remember much about this time, but at the end of it I came out feeling like it had been worth the pain and distress. They had cut off my roof and welded a roll cage inside my cabin. They'd also put a racy new engine under my bonnet. My old wheels were gone and replacing them were a brand new set of fat tyres. All my life I had secretly harboured a desire for fatties, and now my yearning had been satisfied. I was starting to get to know and like these blokes by now. After all, they had been quite intimate with me.

One night Bub and Pete took me for a ride in the trailer to a big garage. Dozens of blokes with spray-cans in their hands started to jazz up my body. I felt like a princess with all this attention! They were still persisting in calling me a little pissa, though. I wasn't too sure what this meant.

There was a bit of a party after they'd finished that night. All the beer cans ended up in my back. Someone had jokingly said it was ballast, but I couldn't figure out what for.

The next day I went for a really long ride in the trailer. People were looking at me; I felt so proud! We got to a place where there were lots of other cars. They all had roll bars, just like me. I was feeling pretty special to be part of this until I heard some smarty come up and say to one of my blokes, 'This thing's feral! Where'd ya get it from, the tip?'

Well, Bub jumped into my driver's seat and Pete into my passenger seat. We went out on this dirt road and lined up with all the other vehicles. Suddenly there was this bloke on the side of the road furiously waving a green flag. Before I could grab a breath, Bub put my pedal to the metal and we were off.

Oh, to describe the thrill of the wind flying through my radiator! We went fast – I had never been so fast before! We slid around corners and into bends. We passed all the cars in front of us. My blokes were yipping and yahooing in the cabin, and I was feeling that this was what I had been made to do in life. The untamed beast in me had been set free at last; I was no longer just a humble HR ute.

My little heart was pumping those horses out like they'd never been pumped before. I could have gone on zooming around all night it was so exhilarating, but there was a silly little man out there waving a chequered flag at us, and Bub decided to take the pressure off the throttle. We ambled back into the parking lot and the blokes got out all excited. Pete was laughing and crying at the same time, and Bub was saying over and over again, 'Ya little pissa!'

This was the beginning of a whole new career for me. I was to become one of the toughest little goers on the racing circuit. Even Volvos looked at me with envy, and everyone referred to me as 'the quickest HR pissa in the west'.

Free Beer!

Nigel Nippard
Cheltenham, NSW

Aunty Doris said that Uncle Les only ever loved two things in his life – his pet ferrets and fishing. She said this loud and often, especially in front of company, hoping that Uncle Les would contradict her and confess that he loved her too. Trouble was that Uncle Les was a typical Aussie bloke: he never said anything about his feelings. However, deep down in his heart he knew that he really did love something else – his EH ute.

Riding in Uncle Les's ute was a scary experience, because Uncle Les didn't have a left hand. Where it should have been he just had a stump, ending at the wrist. When he drove his ute he'd hang his right arm, complete with hand and five valuable fingers, out of the window. Sure, it was illegal, but he'd been doing it for twenty-five years before it became illegal, so he figured he had a good excuse if ever he was pulled over. Besides, you can't teach an old dog new tricks, and what copper would be nasty enough to pick on a disabled driver?

Uncle Les conducted almost all of his driving functions with his left stump. He held the roughened end of it against the steering wheel when going straight, and poked it through the spokes of the wheel and wound it frantically to turn corners. He somehow managed to push, pull and twist the column gearshift with his stump to shuffle through the three-speed manual gearbox. He also used his stump to wave at mates and make rude signs at other motorists, although it was very hard to distinguish between a friendly 'g'day' and an 'up yours', since stumps don't display a lot of personality.

The only time he ever considered using his good right hand to drive was when he had to change gears while going around a corner. Even Uncle Les hadn't figured out a way to do that with just a stump. He often joked that he was busier than a one-legged man in a bum-kicking competition when driving with a stump, and that there was no loss of manhood associated with having to use his good right hand now and again.

Unlike a lot of his mates, Uncle Les never went off to war. While they were off fighting, he was out fishing. One night he and a mate were sitting in his rowing boat, throwing gelignite into the river, when he hung onto a 'cracker', as he called them, a bit too long. Off went his shirt, left hand and all his hair. His mate fainted and Uncle Les had to row the boat back to shore and drive himself to the hospital, all with a piece of fishing line wrapped around his raw stump to stop the bleeding. 'Bloody hurt, mate, I can tell ya,' he always added at the end of the story, waving his stump through the air for extra effect. Aunty Doris still felt queasy whenever she heard the tale, even after a thousand or so tellings.

The worst time you could have in the EH ute was being with Uncle Les when he thundered along corrugated dirt roads with the steering wheel vibrating and jumping around under his slippery stump. He always looked his passenger in the eye when he talked, so his attention to steering the vehicle seemed non-existent. Many a first-timer screamed 'Look out!' as Uncle Les slid around corners with his eyes and stump pointed in totally opposite directions.

Uncle Les loved telling yarns, as long as they involved fishing, ferrets or Frehd. He called his ute Frehd, because somehow he thought it was a hilarious twist of the English language to incorporate the 'EH' into his ute's name. Very few of Uncle Les's friends thought it was either funny or clever, because most of them left school at twelve and could hardly read and write. But that didn't stop Uncle Les, who annoyed even Aunty Doris by always referring to the ute as Frehhhhhhhd. He sort of elongated the 'h' sound into a drawn-out wheeze that lasted as long as his breath would allow, and usually ended in a severe bout of coughing. Like, 'I'm takin' Frehhhhhhhhhhhd [cough, bark, hack, snort] down to get a drink. Back before dark!'

One of Uncle Les's funniest yarns was about the time he took Frehd down to Sydney one Anzac Day, with Aunty Doris aboard. Uncle Les loved Anzac Day in Sydney because, although he never went to the war, everyone bought him free drinks when they saw his stump, figuring he'd had it blown off in the trenches. Here's how Uncle Les tells it.

'We was cruising southbound across th'Harbour Bridge, an' Frehhhhhhhhd [hack, splutter, cough, laugh] was purrin' along, hadn't missed a beat! Unknown to me, this joker was riding in the next lane on one of them Vespa motor scooters. Apparently it was a bit old an' the front brake didn't work. As the Vespa started to approach the toll booths the joker puts 'is foot on the rear brake pedal to slow up to pay the toll, but the brake cable snaps.

'There 'e is, rollin' towards the toll gates, gatherin' speed. Well, he pulls in the clutch an' tries to shift into a lower gear in order to slow 'er up, but he gets stuck in neutral – so 'e's got no flippin' brakes at all an' 'e's still gatherin' speed!

'Then he sees Frehhhhhhhd [wheeze, bark, snort, laugh], an' he spies the chrome grab rail 'round the side of the ute. So 'e steers over right next to th'ute, and grabs onto the rail, figurin' that he'll just hang on an' slow up as th'EH stops to pay the toll.

'All's well for a few seconds, but as me ute starts to slow up, the drag from the joker on 'is Vespa is just too much. Suddenly the rail breaks off, and there this joker is, riding along with about five foot of grab rail in his hand! I didn't see it at the time, but Doris was screamin' at the top of 'er lungs that we was bein' attacked by a city hoodlum.

'Anyway, the joker on the Vespa must've figured that he was in real trouble, 'cos next thing we know 'e's chucked the grab rail into the back of th'ute, an' off he sails, away from the ute. He shoots past us at a rate of knots, an' the last we see of 'im is that 'e's fangin' through the toll gates at about 50 miles an hour, whistlin' straight up York Street. We never saw 'im again.

'Trouble is, with Doris screamin' an' me bein' shocked by the crash of the grab rail hittin' me tray, I sort of freaked out. Me stump slipped off the wheel an' we collided with the wall of the toll booth. We weren't goin' fast, but we was a bit stirred up.

'The bloody toll collector was a bit stirred up too, so 'e calls the supervisor, who calls the cops. The copper finally turns up an' has a look, an' really admires Frehhhhhhd [cough, etc]. Reckons it was a shame that the grab rail was pulled out – said 'e felt like arresting the mongrel who did it. Then he says it seems like the damage to the toll booth ain't all that bad, so he asks me what I did in the war. I told 'im the truth: that I was on night manoeuvres when we took a direct hit, an' only me an' one mate survived. He said his old man was in the Navy, so 'e insisted on giving me a few shillings for a beer. An' off he went.

'Couldn't believe me luck. Just goes to show how an old codger in an EH can get a free beer no matter where 'e goes! 'Ere's to Frehhhhhhd [hack, wheeze, laugh].'

Brindle

Barbara Phillips
Donvale, VIC

Old Brindle, as the name would suggest, was a ute of many colours. She was waterproof in winter and had her own summer air conditioner – of a fashion. The windscreen had a strip of metal in the middle separating two sections of glass. The glass panels were hinged at the top and could be pushed open on a sliding arm. On hot days we would let in some fresh air, along with anything else that chose to fly in – dust, flies, grasshoppers.

One of the more exciting adventures we shared with old Brindle was to go spotlighting hares along the old abandoned airstrip on clear, still nights. There were four of us – Lewis, Jack, Tim and me. We didn't shoot the hares, we just had a bit of fun chasing them in the old ute. We would get close to them, momentarily confusing them with the lights. They were pure grace in motion as they bounded along, at first slowly with their long slender ears pricked, but faster and with their ears flattened back against their bodies as we gained on them.

As spring approached, so too did the lambing season, and every year foxes took many lambs. Dad suggested to Lewis that he should take the gun next time we went spotlighting, to shoot any foxes we came across. 'The Shire pays a bounty of five shillings for each scalp collected,' he reminded us. After a lecture on gun safety and common sense, we set sail for our night of spotlighting.

We had made several passes along the strip chasing hares but had failed to spot any foxes. Foxes are particularly cautious animals, cunning and fleet of foot. We knew that any chance to get a shot at them would be a fleeting one. As a last resort Tim produced a fox whistle from his pocket. He put it to the test.

Jack stood in the back of the ute, periodically sweeping the surrounding paddock with the spotlight, while Lewis sat poised behind the wheel, ready to fire Brindle into action. Tim complained his lips were getting numb, but neither Jack nor Lewis would let him stop.

'Over there!' whispered Jack as the sweep of the light picked up a set of eyes approaching the ute. Our eyes followed the light beam and in the distance we saw a pair of red eyes. Slowly the fox approached the ute. He seemed to sit and watch for a long time. Tim kept at his whistle. The red eyes disappeared, then appeared again, closer.

The fox was about thirty metres away. Lewis put his foot on the pedal and with a roar the old ute sprang to life. For a moment the fox stood mesmerised in the glare of the headlights, then he turned and fled down the strip.

We were gaining on him when he suddenly veered off the strip and across into the paddock. Lewis was like a man possessed. Spurring the old ute on to speeds she had never known before, he followed that fox across the paddock. We were gaining on him when suddenly the fox leapt through the air, clearing a new drain in his stride. For old Brindle it was not so easy.

We hit the drain at full speed. The old ute reared in the air, and as she became airborne one of the windscreen panels broke free and flew open. As we sailed across the drain there was an explosion from the back of the ute.

We landed hard and bounced a few times, then there was darkness. For a second or two we sat in stunned silence. Finally Lewis uttered a long string of oaths. 'Is everyone OK?' he asked. Tim and I were fine, but Jack did not answer.

We leapt out of the cabin and listened. A groan came from somewhere down in the drain. Lewis sprang down the bank, picked up the gun and sniffed it: it had been fired. 'Shit, Jack has shot himself!' he cried. Tim and I scrambled down the bank to join Lewis, who was now kneeling beside Jack, running his hands over his body. He felt something wet and pulled his hand away quickly, expecting to see blood. But no, it was water. Slowly Jack sat up and we all breathed a sigh of relief.

'What happened?' asked Lewis.

'Well,' said Jack, nursing his head, 'I had the fox lined up and was about to take a shot at him when you, you clown, tried to jump the drain. As I fired, the windscreen panel flew up in the air and I shot it instead. Next thing I knew I was flying through the air too! Then I landed in the drain and everything went black.'

Lewis and Tim helped Jack to his feet.

'Gawd!' said Jack. 'Have I got a thumping headache.'

Our trusty old Brindle, unharmed except for the one missing windscreen panel, was waiting to take us home. Tim, Lewis and I started smiling; the picture of Jack taking a shot at the flying windscreen was irresistible. Next thing we were on the ground laughing.

Only Jack didn't share in the joke. He was lost in his own misery.

The Driver's Friend

Kit Moodie
Bayview, NSW

He stood there, a lone figure on the dusty roadside.

I stopped the ute to pick him up. He nodded casually and climbed in beside me. I wondered what he was doing out in the middle of nowhere.

'Where you headed?' I asked.

'As far as you go,' he answered, settling back and folding his arms.

'I'm going to Sydney.'

'Fine.'

Now I don't mind a bit of company. It gets pretty boring by yourself just looking at the road hour after hour. But this fellow sure had buttoned-up lips.

'I'm Joe,' I said.

No answer.

I tried to start the ball rolling. 'You been on a holiday?'

'No, I work continually.'

I wondered what kind of work left a bloke stranded out on a country road.

'What do you do for a crust?'

'You might say I am the driver's friend. This year I'm helping ute drivers.'

So, he was an insurance agent! Any minute now I'd get the spiel. I waited, but it didn't come. All he said was, 'You are exceeding the speed limit by five kilometres.'

He said it gently, but my temper rose. Maybe he wasn't an insurance agent after all. Maybe he was one of those sneaky road cops trying out a new method of catching drivers going over the limit. I opened my mouth to say something to him, but the words dried up in my throat and my lips refused to move. This man's serene, grey eyes smiled as he directed me to keep my eyes on the road.

After a while my annoyance subsided and I started talking again. 'What do they call you?' I asked.

'Saint Christopher,' he answered calmly.

My hands tightened on the wheel. A cold chill started somewhere in my innards and spread to my limbs. A tough bloke I could handle, but a fruitcake ... I stepped on the gas, only to feel a soft tap on my arm.

'You are travelling over the limit again, Joe.'

I slowed down. Better humour him. For all I knew he might be carrying a knife or a gun.

'I suppose you live up there,' I said, jerking a thumb upwards.

'If you say so.'

'You work all year round,' I said, determined to be pleasant. 'This year on utes, next year ...?'

'Motorcycles. Steady, you took that bend too fast.' His voice was stern.

A god-damned back-seat driver!

Pointing to every road sign he kept me crawling while other vehicles flew past. He lectured me on the necessity of obeying the road rules. I let him natter on while I bided my time, thinking up a revenge. Just you wait, Saint Chrisso, until I'm within cooee of the checkpoint. I'll give you bloody road rules!

In the meanwhile I kidded him along, slowing right down and keeping my eyes glued to the road. I wasn't game to touch the can of beer I had in the Esky, though my mouth was itching for it. Occasionally my eyes went to the Esky and I was sorely tempted. Maybe he'd like a drink himself?

His voice cut across my thoughts: 'Drink and driving are natural enemies.'

Full of hatred I drove on. Then an idea hit me; such a simple idea that I wondered why it hadn't occurred to me hours ago. Why wait for the checkpoint? Why not just stop the ute and toss him out now?

I tried. I pulled up and faced him. His eyes looked through me, the pupils lit with a strange light. I tried to say two small words – *get out* – but I couldn't. My lips stayed stiff.

Defeated, I got going again. Time dragged. The ute moved as slowly as a hearse. The only sound was Saint Chrisso nagging away like a broken record. He was driving me up the wall; soon I'd be as nutty as he was.

Then I perked up. In a few minutes I'd be within sight of the checkpoint. I'd have to put my plan into action quick-smart before Chrisso's strange spell got to me.

Now! Do it now! I trod hard on the accelerator and let her rip, throwing back my head and yelling with unholy glee. 'Hang on, Saint Chrisso, you ain't seen nothin' yet!'

My passenger didn't bat an eyelid. He just sat there, arms folded. I took a bend, tyres screeching and sending up clouds of dust. The ute swerved madly across the centre lines, then righted itself. I laughed louder and louder. Exhilarated, I let the needle creep up. Then, above the roar of the engines, came a sudden, mighty explosion …

Surely it couldn't be night? Through the pitch darkness I heard shouts and screams. Someone said,

'He's gone,' and another voice said, 'He was the only person in the vehicle, so I guess he was the driver.' I tried to tell them about the loony in my ute, but nobody would listen to me …

I stood by the roadside waiting for the ute to pull up. Like all young smart alecs he braked too fast.

'How far you going?' he asked.

'As far as you are,' I answered, settling my back against the seat beside him.

'Been working?'

'All the time,' I said.

I touched his arm and advised him to keep his eyes on the road.

'What do you mean "all the time"?'

'I've worked day and night for twelve months. You are exceeding the speed limit,' I warned.

He was about to swear, but I stopped him with a stare.

He threw me a curious look. 'What's your name, mate?'

'My name is Saint Joe,' I answered, concentrating my attention upon his driving.

The Bum Sweat Brothers

Damien Winder
No Fixed Address, Oz

Damo and Keefy (Damien and Keith) had been on the tools ever since they left school a decade ago. They'd had a gutful of building project homes in Sydney. Like most other naive young builders, they were looking for a lucky break where they could make a pile of bucks for doing close to nothing.

To help realise their somewhat unrealistic dream, they called in at the local pub every afternoon to sniff out 'clues'. Their wives mistakenly thought they were wasting time and money just sitting there sinking schooners, when in fact what they were really doing was catching up on what was happening in the trade. News of scams and rumours flew at the speed of light and provided countless hours of speculation on the job. It helped occupy Damo and Keefy's minds while firing rusty nails into second-grade lumber. For them, the pub was sort of like the blue-singlet man's equivalent of the office typing pool: an absolute necessity if one was to be adequately informed.

One afternoon Damo was leaning on the bar listening to Skid, his de facto financial adviser, when Skid finally said something that seemed to make sense. 'If ya wanna make big money, ya gotta go to the bush, mate. Them poor bastards out there can't get doctors or builders, and they'll pay a fortune for either.' On top of that, Skid said he had a rellie out on a property at Thylungra who needed an extension done to his house. And he was prepared to pay top dollars to a pair of qualified carpenters who'd go and do the job quick-smart.

After lots of phone calls, and extensive assurances from Skid as to the creditworthiness and generosity of his rellie, Damo set out with Keefy from Sydney in Damo's old XF Falcon ute. It was loaded to the hilt with all their tools of trade: air compressor, welder, drop saw, mixer, saw horses, and a million and one hand tools. 'The only two-tonner XF in the west,' Damo bragged to his mates as they stared in disbelief at the rear end sitting on the turf and the headlights pointing to heaven.

Full of confidence, the Bum Sweat Brothers (so nicknamed because of the tendency of their Stubbies to exhibit long, thin sweat lines down an area adjacent to their bum cracks) pointed the tortured XF north-west, towards Thylungra, via Bourke.

They made it to Bourke OK, but by then the XF was doing it hard. It seemed it needed a few minor repairs, so they left it at the NRMA depot overnight and headed for the pub to check out the local rumours. Unfortunately for the Bum Sweat Brothers they walked into the wrong end of the wrong pub and immediately found themselves in the middle of an ugly situation.

To cut a painful story short, Damo and Keefy found themselves on the multiple ends of many knuckle sandwiches. So many, in fact, that they later gave thanks to the Lord for those nuggetty little legs of theirs that carried them swiftly to safety, after having been decked several times and relieved of the cash in their pockets.

The next morning the Bum Sweat Brothers were sore and swollen, and to make matters worse the local cop couldn't have cared less about their experience. 'What do yers expect if yer go in there?' he said.

To help lift his spirits and get his mind off his immediate problems, Keefy bought himself an Akubra hat from the local servo. It was a spiffy-looking model made from rabbit fur, with a feather hanging out the top.

'Ya look a bit daggy,' said Damo to Keefy, "specially with two black eyes and a swollen lip.' He pulled out the feather and flicked it behind the seat of his ute. It didn't have any effect, though: Keefy was already in love with that Akubra.

The sun was fighting its way out of the east as the boys set out for Cunnamulla, happy that Bourke was behind them. Somewhere between Cunnamulla and Charleville they passed a bright yellow XF ute parked about fifty metres off the side of the road in the scrub.

'An abandoned XF!' Keefy spluttered between battered lips. Damo stood up with both feet on the brake pedal, then executed a swift doughnut which brought them broadside next to the derelict ute.

When the bull dust drifted away, it was obvious she was a mess. There was no bonnet, both the headlights and rear window had been smashed, and the cabin roof looked like it had been used as a trampoline. The rear tray was rusted away, leaving a gaping rust hole through which you could see the busted exhaust pipe and what was left of the muffler dragging on the ground. Although the wheels were still intact, the tyres were bare canvas with maybe ten pounds of air between the lot of them.

The open-air engine was coated in so much grease and gunk that it was hard to see whether it was complete or not. Both door handles were broken and the doors were locked, so Keefy had to climb in through the driver's window to check out the inside. Surprisingly, there were keys in the ignition; they were probably the most valuable part of this once-proud ute.

'Lookf like she'f had the sword, mate,' Keefy spat between his cracked upper molars. 'There'f juft nuffin' left worf grabbin'.' It was just as well, as Damo's two-tonner XF was incapable of carrying anything more. Even an extra toothpick would have caused the rear springs to collapse.

The Bum Sweat Brothers soon forgot the old yellow XF as Willie Nelson got them on the road again, at dangerous decibellic levels. Half an hour passed before either of them spoke, and then it was Keefy who suddenly bellowed, 'Where'f me bloody Akubra?' They both shot a glance at the space between them on the bench seat where the Akubra usually lived. Apart from half a packet of Drum and three empties, it was bare. Nude. Vacant. Unoccupied.

'Oh no, you left your Akubra in that yellow ute,' moaned Damo, saving Keefy from having to lash his lips and suffer yet more pain. No further word was spoken as Damo wheeled the two-tonner around and headed back towards Cunnamulla.

About half an hour later they reckoned they were getting close to where they'd seen the derelict ute. Their four puffy eyes were peeled, searching the bush to make sure they spotted the wreck.

The excitement of reuniting with Keefy's Akubra was building and they were really hammering it as they came up over a small hill. As they topped the rise, there, to their utter amazement, was the yellow XF ute on the road, heading towards them going hell for leather. As the thing flashed past them in a blur of yellow paint and blue smoke, Keefy caught a fleeting glimpse of a black driver, grinning through the only piece of glass left in the vehicle and wearing an Akubra hat. His Akubra hat!

'That barftard'f ftolen me bloody Akubra!' shrieked Keefy.

The brakes groaned, the suspension snarled and the wheels nearly vibrated right off as Damo stood yet again with both feet on the brake pedal, this time with his head and one shoulder pressed hard against the cabin roof for extra pressure.

With the aid of the handbrake, and throwing the two-tonner down into second, it took Damo nearly half a k before he could slow her down enough to do a U-ie. As it was he turned her so fast that Keefy's cement-mixer shot out of the back and off into the scrub. 'Ferget the mixer, we'll get it later. Juz catch that bloody ute an' get me Akubra back!'

By the time they'd turned around and got back onto the bitumen, Damo reckoned they were about three ks behind the XF. He had the accelerator pressed so hard against the metal that he later developed arthritis and walked with a limp forever more.

That two-tonner was screaming; it sounded like it was blowing nuts and bolts out the exhaust pipe. After five minutes of frantic driving Keefy started looking worried – by now the derelict XF was an occasional flicker of yellow way off in the distance.

'We're doing over 120 clicks and she's pulling away from us. That yellow bucket of crap must be chewing off 150 or we're standing still!'

Well, the boys never did catch the yellow XF. Fortunately, however, they did make it to Thylungra, where they spent four weeks in non-stop day-and-night forty-five degree heat on top of Skid's rellie's house, banging and sawing and cussing. They proved yet again the validity of their nickname 'the Bum Sweat Brothers' – it just poured out of them!

Unbelievably, the two-tonner made it home, minus Keefy's mixer, that 'some turd knocked off while we was chasing th'Akubra'.

Skid's rellies did have money, and the profit on the job, after VB and expenses, almost made up for the load of cash that was stolen by their assailants at the Bourke pub.

And back in Sydney, in Damo's shed, stuck onto the Jim Beam mirror with a bit of masking tape, is a feather – a long, red and black feather – the only evidence that Keefy's Akubra ever existed at all.

Pushing the Wrong Button

Cathy O'Keeffe
Bowraville, NSW

The ute had more lives than a sackful of cats – she was in her sixth reincarnation when I got her. The old girl had been in the family since Pop bought her new after a rare three years of good luck, back in the fifties.

She'd been green then, polished to within an inch of her life. The ute had been purchased as a town car after her paddock-bashing predecessor had become a bit too dodgy to leave the farm gates. It was another ten years before the paddock-basher died disgracefully by rolling into the dam, and then the town ute became the only ute.

She had been resprayed at fifteen and again at eighteen. When the ute was handed on to Dad he painted her black, then added red and orange hot-rod flames up the sides. He was driving her when he met my mother.

Before the wedding they had a bugger of a time trying to paint her white without the black showing through. There are photos of Mum sitting on the bonnet showing a bit of leg, with Nan and Pop standing behind the guard and Dad with one foot propped on the bumper, looking smug. The glint in his eye wasn't me. It was my sister, Mary, who left home last year to work in Ontario.

Two months ago I turned eighteen and Dad handed over the keys to the ute. The next week I packed my stuff into the back, tied the tarp over my gear and headed off to uni.

It was there I met Lou. The first day, there I was, standing in line, when I heard her voice. It was the voice that made me look. And what I saw kept me looking. Constant glimpses of her around campus and a week's fantasising made up my mind for me: I asked her out.

Every day for the last six weeks I've spent at least some time with her. And it's still not enough.

But last night I blew it without even realising I was doing it.

Lou lives off campus with her parents, so every night she goes home for dinner. I always hate to see her go, but at least it gives me a chance to get my work done.

I live in the university flats, which is sort of a cross between a toilet block, a permanent party venue, a brothel and hell, depending on what the time is and who's around. Each resident has their own cell-sized room, with monastic comforts such as a bed, closet and desk. No carpet, fan or heater.

My room is at the end of the hall, so when the phone rings I usually let someone else get it. Last night it rang.

'Hendrix!' Isaac shouted. 'You home?'

'Yeah,' I said, coming out of my room.

'It's yer Dad.'

I took the receiver.

'Yo, Dad. How's it hanging?'

'Good. Good. How's the study?'

'OK. We haven't got much work yet. Just reading, and talks on how to use the library. Stuff like that. How's Mum?'

'She's good. Missing you. She keeps cooking too much food – forgets that it's just the two of us now. I'm getting fat just trying to keep up. How's the ute going?'

There was a beep on the line. Call waiting. 'Look, could you hold on a sec, Dad? There's a call on the other line.' I switched over.

'Hello, uni flats, Hendo speaking.'

'Hi.' A familiar, sexy voice was on the line.

'Hi yourself! I hoped you'd call. I missed you at lunch. How was the lecture?'

'Boring, but purposeful.'

'Lou, I hate to do this to you, but I've got Dad on the other line. Could I ring you back in five minutes?'

'Sure. But look, I'm not going anywhere. I was actually going to fold my washing while I was talking to you. So just switch back over when you've finished.'

'You sure?'

'Of course.'

'Back in a minute.'

I hit redial and the number for the other line.

'Back again, Dad. Sorry about that, but I've got someone on the other line. So you were asking about the old girl. Well, she's OK – not great. Expensive, you know. Takes a bit more to fill her up than most; I think I'll have to plug up that hole in her head. Anyway, now that I've got my hands on her I'll have to treat her nice. Don't want her to get cranky on me, do I? She can be really temperamental, you know. And she's still got a lot of rough edges, especially across her tail end. But I'll deal with them once I get used to having her every day.'

The line went dead. I pressed redial and the number for the second line. It was dead too. I tried both lines again but they were engaged, so I decided to leave it. Dad would call me back some time, and I'd see Lou the next day anyway.

It was strange that Lou didn't show up at our usual meeting place outside the cafeteria before class. Oh well, she was probably running late. I'd see her at lunch.

I was a few minutes late for lunch when I saw Lou heading outside with her tray. She saw me and with an angry shake of her head began to walk in the opposite direction. I went after her.

'Lou! What's up?'

'Bugger off!' she spat.

'Why? What have I done?'

'You should be able to figure it out.'

'I've no idea!'

She turned and started to walk away again. I grabbed her arm.

'Leave me alone,' she snapped.

'Why? What the hell's the matter?'

'You're the matter! You treat me like dirt and you can still ask?'

'Yes, because I have no idea what you're on about.'

'Oh, no? You thought you were talking to your father last night, but you switched back to me. You started talking before I could tell you. Once I heard what you had to say I kept listening. Let me refresh your memory ... You said I'm OK, but not great. I cost you too much. I'm temperamental. And you'll deal with my rough edges once you get used to having me every day. You are a pig! I never want to speak to you again.'

Bewilderment gave way to relief, but for the moment I was laughing too much to explain ...

Boys will be Boys

Kevin Duddy
Broken Hill, NSW

This is a true story of three teenagers with a taste for adventure and a lime-green 1979 HZ Holden ute. This story is typical of the exploits of many young lads brought up on a farm – lads who have lived most of their lives in blue jeans, flannel shirts, riding boots and with the old farm ute close at hand.

It all began when three teenagers growing up in a small rural community in New South Wales took it upon themselves to make one particular couple of days a weekend to remember. What better way to do this than to borrow Dad's ute and set out on a camping expedition? With the usual obligatory assurances of 'yes, we will be careful' and 'no, we won't be silly', and posing as three extremely trustworthy young males, they were given the go-ahead for complete freedom for a Saturday night.

The supplies for the trip were packed. The basic essentials were there: a two-man tent, a deck of cards, a torch, blankets, enough steak, sausages, eggs, onions and cans of baked beans to feed an army, and as many *Playboy*s as they could hide from Mum. After loading up the ute and looking under the bonnet to make sure that the motor looked the same as it did ten minutes earlier, they were all set to go. Only one more obstacle stood in their way: was it to be Jimmy

Barnes's 'Working Class Man' or Jon Bon Jovi's 'Ride Cowboy Ride' that would see them on their way?

With a smell of anticipation in the air, the ute disappeared down the road, leaving behind the homestead and Mum running down the steps waving a cake of soap and three bath towels.

All was going as planned. The thirty-minute drive across the property had gone without mishap, not permitting the quickening of the lads' heart rates on one occasion when the ute was propelled towards a menacing gum tree as a result of uncontrolled circle work. The prospective campsite was across the river, so the boys carried their equipment above their heads through waist-deep water.

The tent was pitched, a bonfire was lit and a meal was cooked and consumed. All that remained to be done then was to participate in the normal teenage antics that youthful vigour and a bit of Bundy and Coke fuelled. Stories were told and the truth was stretched almost to breaking point. Like their forebears, these young blokes never liked to let the truth get in the way of a good yarn.

Just as a cosy feeling of sleepiness was descending upon the weary revellers, things started to go wrong.

It was nearly midnight when the storm struck, its gale-force winds bringing torrential rain. Because foresight was not a concept taught in high school, and stubborn determination was an inherent quality in most country boys, the situation reached crisis point before any action was taken. The tent was torn from its moorings. Everything was immediately drenched, including the boys. But it was not until a limb from an old gum tree came crashing down beside the campsite, creating a shocked silence after so much noise and bravado, that the suggestion was posed that the trip be abandoned in exchange for the comforts of an open fire, a cup of hot Milo and a packet of Tim Tams back at the homestead.

Without wasting another second the boys shoved their camping gear into packs, hoisted them above their heads and, with a couple of falls in the rapidly rising river, successfully crossed over and clambered into the ute.

What to do now? The pouring rain, the fogged-up windscreen and the long grass, which grew up past the bonnet of the ute, made the chance of navigating through the scrub without hitting any of the hundreds of rocks and stumps that lay scattered throughout the paddocks almost impossible. They had two choices: to spend the night in the ute, or send someone running ahead of the vehicle to guide the way. With a little persuasion, a member of the party courageously volunteered for this position and began leading the way.

Unfortunately for the boys, the noise and spectacle of the labouring ute drew the attention of a nervous herd of Hereford cows and a couple of Black Angus bulls. In the darkness and confusion of the storm, the cattle stampeded. The guiding knight in shining armour fled for his life, and somehow, in the confusion of everything, the ute positioned itself on top of a granite boulder.

It was immovable. No matter how much encouragement was provided by the combined strength of three normally unstoppable males (the guide had been rounded up by now), the ute would not budge. The boys had no other choice than to trek back to the machinery shed and sneak the tractor out to retrieve the vehicle. No young male growing up on a farm feared anything more than the wrath of the old man, so several weary hours passed in lifting the ute off the rock and negotiating the way back through the paddocks to the farm.

They arrived just as dawn broke. With the tractor returned to its exact position in the shed and the ute safely stowed in its usual place, the boys entered the house to be greeted by Mum and Dad asking, with a twinkle in their eyes, 'So how was your weekend, boys?'

Creation, Evolution or Utin'?

J. W. Straney
Hervey Bay, QLD

I knew these two brothers who owned adjoining properties, which they operated by helping one another. They were sheep graziers.

The elder brother, Clarrie, had moved to town to live, while the other, Jeff, still lived on the farm. Clarrie was in the habit of going out to his farm on Sunday afternoon and staying until Friday, when he'd drive back into town for the weekend.

This particular weekend Clarrie went out to his property on Sunday as usual, and on the Monday morning went over to Jeff's to give him a hand. It was about ten o'clock. While he was waiting for Jeff to finish what he was doing, two Jehovah's Witnesses turned up and started talking to him.

Now Clarrie and Jeff were real bushies who rated their sheep first, their dogs second, then perhaps their wives third. They weren't particularly concerned with things in the celestial kingdom.

The Jehovahs were still talking to Clarrie as Jeff wandered across towards them. Just as he was approaching, one of the Jehovahs asked Clarrie how he had got here – by Creation or evolution. Clarrie replied, 'Buggered if I know.'

But Jeff, not hearing the question properly, answered, 'No, he came out in the ute yesterday.'

The Brute in the Ute

A.D. Carroll
Engadine, NSW

Brad was an enigma. Although he was only young, he had an old-fashioned, easy way about him. He didn't drink or smoke and he never told risqué jokes. Despite all that, he was well liked by his peers.

Brad was a snappy dresser. That and his easy-going personality stood him in good stead for his job as a representative for La Femme, a women's shoe company specialising in top-of-the-range fashionable female foot attire. Brad's job as representative involved displaying the new ranges of La Femme shoes to prospective retailers.

On the morning that he was due to begin a fresh sales campaign he woke later than normal. He dressed hurriedly and left the house.

In his anxiety to make up lost time, Brad took risks with his driving. At one crucial point he changed lanes without warning, causing the vehicle behind him to brake sharply. That vehicle was a thirty-year-old uncared-for utility. Its driver looked to be of comparable age and condition. Glancing in his rear-vision mirror, Brad didn't have to guess that the ute had had serious skirmishes with rust, mechanical failings and bald tyres. One door, of a different colour to the rest, had obviously once belonged to another vehicle, and the paintwork overall could politely be called shabby.

The sudden application of brakes had caused the faulty tyres of the ute to skid sideways. The driver leant out of his open window and shouted a mouthful of inventive obscenities. Although the personalised numberplate read 'BRUCE', Brad immediately dubbed his opponent 'BRUTE'.

The Brute, not about to let Brad forget his driving error, continued his stream of insults. What followed was a relentless cat-and-mouse chase. The Brute drove as close as possible to the rear of Brad's car. If Brad accelerated, so did the ute; if he slowed, so did the ute. Even though Brad waved a white hanky of surrender, the persecution continued.

Desperate, Brad turned sharply to the right without indicating. The Brute was obliged to continue straight ahead. Shaken but relieved, Brad waited ten minutes before rejoining the traffic. He was certain that The Brute in the ute had gone.

Brad looked at his watch. He was going to make his first appointment after all. Relaxing the tense muscles of his shoulders, he sat back in the driver's seat and focused his thoughts on the job ahead. Selling the most recent range of La Femme shoes was going to be challenging. The Stavron Slingback was the problem. Whereas most of La Femme's shoes were highly priced, the Stavron Slingback was tagged well under the usual mark. It still carried the company's stamp of beauty and style; trouble was, at that price it was going to be hard for Brad to convince buyers that the rest of the range was worth purchasing. It was going to take all his powers of charm and persuasion to move this lot.

Thinking such thoughts, Brad glanced in his rear-vision mirror. With horror he saw that the ute was back! He formulated a hurried plan. If he employed the same tactics as before but this time lay low for longer, hopefully The Brute would lose patience and go on his way. His first three retail appointments could be delayed; a couple of phone calls would sort that out. Staying alive was now a higher priority than making his appointments on time.

He put his plan into action, pulling out of the traffic without warning and concealing his vehicle in a quiet back street. The whole incident had certainly rattled Brad. His normally easy-going demeanour was shaken.

At noon Brad decided to drive a short distance to the estuary and eat his lunch by the water. The atmosphere was peaceful. Seagulls made graceful arcs in the air, and the broad expanse of water shivered gently in the breeze. The unpleasantness of the morning was starting to feel far away.

Just as Brad was swallowing his last mouthful of sandwich there was a tap on his half-opened passenger-side window. He looked across and with a sudden grip of the heart recognised The Brute. The man was two metres tall and must have weighed 120 kilos. He had long, unkempt hair and sported tattoos on his arms. Two of his front teeth were missing.

Brad started to consider the alternatives; survival was uppermost in his mind. He could drive off at full speed, leaving behind tyre marks and crushed toes. Or he could abandon ship and sprint away on foot. Then there was the option of feigning a heart attack. As a last resort he could try talking his way out of it, though The Brute didn't look particularly amenable to conversation. One thing was for sure: there was no point in slugging it out. He wouldn't last two seconds with this giant.

These thoughts were all hypothetical, because it was too late now. The Brute's massive right arm was thrust through Brad's half-open car window, his hand rolled up into a fist the size of a leg of lamb. Brad sat back and waited for the inevitable. He was dead meat. Suddenly the circling seagulls seemed like vultures waiting for the corpse to hit the deck.

When the fist was about ten centimetres from Brad's face, it suddenly opened and the voice behind it spoke.

'How lucky that I pulled up next to you just now! This gives me a chance to apologise for this morning. See, I had a terrible fight with my wife last night and she kicked me out. I had to sleep in the back of the ute. Wouldn't you know it, it started raining and not long after that you came along. I shouldn't have behaved as I did.'

Without the vulgarities and anger, The Brute seemed a different person. Brad reached out to accept the hand of friendship offered to him, wondering for an instant whether this was a mistake. This man's grip could crush a brick. Relieved to find himself at the end of a peaceable handshake, Brad didn't notice the direction of The Brute's gaze.

'I'd love a pair of them,' he said. 'For Wendy.'

Brad looked and saw the Stavron Slingbacks on the back seat.

'It'd get me out of hot water if I could buy 'em off you.'

The salesman in Brad resurfaced. He was once again in charge. Brad finalised the sale when he offered him a 'special price'.

The Brute departed. That afternoon was one of Brad's most successful ever.

The Wet

John Fowler
Mandurah, WA

'We'll all be ruined,' said Hanrahan, 'if this durn rain don't stop.'

Someone said that that poem was written by Banjo Paterson, or Henry Lawson, or someone like that. I don't know much about arty things, but I do remember getting caught in the rain.

I took this Pommy bloke out to the bush one time to see some roos. The station we went to had been in drought for the past three years. We drove in wearing a billowing cloak of red dust and stopped in the shade of a gum tree. Two blue heelers, roused from their torpor, yapped over to investigate. They checked the telegraph service on all four wheels, left return messages, then jumped onto the steel tray at the back of the Land Rover ute.

'Come out of it, dogs!' roared the owner as he came down the steps of the verandah. The dogs retired to the shade. 'Hello, boys, what are you doing out this way?'

I introduced my passenger, explained that back in England he'd heard that roos had all been exterminated in Australia, and asked if we could drive out and find a few healthy examples of these supposedly extinct creatures.

The owner gazed imploringly at a bank of clouds low on the horizon. 'Go past the sheds and turn north; you cross three creeks on the way out. Turn right where we bogged the truck three years ago, go a couple more kilometres and turn left, then head for the hump you can see on the ridge about fifteen kilometres further on. The rock pool is just below the hump. That'd be the best place to see roos at the moment.'

So off we went. We drove past some sheds and on towards a distant line of trees that indicated the first creek. The ute crossed the stone causeway without a problem. A further three kilometres brought us to the next crossing, then the third creek a kilometre beyond. We turned right and continued along a rougher track.

I had been concentrating on driving and hadn't noticed the clouds roll out like a carpet across the sky. Then the first raindrops hit the windscreen and turned the dust into mud. I glanced at my passenger.

'Sorry, we can't finish the trip,' I told him. 'We're turning back now this rain has started.'

'But this is only a Scotch mist,' he protested.

'Mate, out this way a Scotch mist turns into the Loch Ness monster. We're heading back while we still have a chance.'

We skirted carefully around a wallow and picked up speed for the run to the first creek crossing. The first line of trees came into sight through the steadily increasing rain. I changed into four-wheel drive, eased the ute down the bank, crossed through the swirling mud that was already halfway up the wheels and climbed the other bank. I stopped, jumped out, rummaged in the toolbox until I found a roll of insulation tape, then sprinted around to the passenger-side door as my passenger started to disembark.

'Don't open your door. I'm just going to tape them to keep the water out when we hit the next creeks.' I could see he thought I was being overly cautious.

We made it to the next line of trees.

'Where did all this water come from?' he asked.

'Out of Loch Ness,' I muttered, and concentrated on driving a straight line on the now invisible rock causeway. Eventually the ute's nose tilted up and we emerged on the other side. Only one more to go.

We slowly churned through three kilometres of cloudburst, with the windscreen-wipers only pretending to do their job. Then I saw the vague silhouette of the next line of trees.

'Don't open your window, mate. We need the bubble of air inside in case we go too deep on this crossing.' I could see he thought I was really going too far now.

The vehicle suddenly lurched and tilted to an alarming angle. We jolted and jounced, bucked and bounced, swayed, slewed and submerged as we crabbed towards the line of trees. Fortunately a diesel motor will keep running half-submerged in water. After an eternity we reached the banks, crawled through the trees and headed for the homestead.

The owner was cavorting uproariously in the front yard as we approached. He snatched his hat from the mud, tossed it in the air and watched as it was grabbed by one of the dogs. The other dog promptly took a mouthful of the hat for a tug-of-war before the owner snatched it back and tossed it in the air again. His saturated hair was plastered across his face, his shirt clung to his chest, his trousers were spattered with mud up to the knees, his boots sloshed water each time he jumped, and by this time his hat was beyond description.

He stopped carousing long enough to say, 'I'm glad to see you boys, but I'm more pleased to see this rain!' before continuing his corroboree. The rain gods were probably laughing their silly heads off; another couple of days and he would be wailing like Hanrahan!

We went in raising dust and came out slithering through the mud. The ute was pleased to see the sealed road again. That Pommy bloke still believes kangaroos have been exterminated from Australia.

Dangerous Drivin'

Peter Rosenhain
Tennant Creek, NT

'Wanna go for a ride in th'ute?' I asked Cuthbert. It was a stupid question, sort of like asking, 'Could you use a little extra money?'

I had to quote on a building job up north. The quote would take all of thirty minutes, but the 200-kilometre round trip from Sydney was just right for a Saturday-arvo run. Cuthbert was weak-willed when it came to anything to do with uting, and I knew that even if he was in the middle of his weekly bath he'd pull the plug and turn up carrying the soap.

As we headed north we chatted away about all the utes we'd ever owned, and the ones we'd like to. Cuthbert lamented the fact that the new XR8 ute that had gone on sale recently had sold out at all the dealers he'd visited. He suspected a conspiratorial marketing ploy aimed at driving innocent ute owners into a buying frenzy, leaving them unable to exercise free will when huge numbers of new XR8s were suddenly released in the middle of Ute Shortage Month. The intricacies of Cuthbert's theory lasted about twenty kilometres. Flecks of froth peppered the windscreen in front of him. I accelerated to try and make this trip as short as possible.

Realising that Cuthbert was getting pretty worked up about not being able to view this latest piece of Ford whizz-bangery, it suddenly occurred to me that we'd be passing pretty close to Causby's Motors, who just might happen to have an XR8 in their yard. Should I mention it to Cuthbert, or would disappointment lead to another fifty kilometres of incoherent moto-twaddle?

Well, he was my mate, I reasoned, and mates, even like Cuthbert, were hard to get.

'OK, Cuthbert, if you promise to stop blabbering we'll stop off at Causby's and see if they can show you an XR8.' Silence. Cuthbert's mouth shut down as his overactive brain processed the probabilities. I just prayed that even if Causby's didn't have a live XR8 on the showroom floor, at least they might divert his attention with a glossy brochure for bedtime reading. He'd be unbearable on the way home if he didn't get his fix!

After getting assistance from a local man who pointed out the directions with the ghost of a missing forefinger, we tracked the last 200 metres by the smell of sausages. Yes, Causby's free Saturday barbecue was in full smoke. I climbed out of my ute and was in the midst of grabbing bun, sausage, steak and onions when a booming voice almost exploded the gas bottle.

'They've got one!'

With sauce dripping through my fingers and onions trailing in my wake, I rushed into the showroom to find Cuthbert sitting inside a bright red XR8. His grin ran all the way from one side of his mouth, down through his armpits, under his crotch and up the other side again, meeting in a vortex on the very top of his bald patch.

'Sonovagun, mate, whaddyareckon?!'

After waiting a discreet interval I dragged him out of the cockpit and suggested we look at the fifty or so other Fords on display. No hope. Cuthbert's mind had been hijacked by aliens and injected with XR8 serum. His eyes were glazed and he started talking like a man possessed.

'No – I'll never sell my old XD – far too enjoyable a ute to ever relinquish. Swaggin' it an' the XD go together like love an' marriage and eggs an' bacon. But I need that XR8! It's a have-to-have-before-I-die ute. It has my name on it.

'Did you see those almost-concealed headlights, like a Ferrari? They winked at me – fair dinkum, mate, winked! Look under that bonnet at those cylinders – eight of 'em. Count 'em if you don't believe me. And fat tyres. Those are the mother of all fat tyres. Yessir, the absolute Queen of Fat. An' I s'pose you missed the leather steering wheel an' the cruise control an' the air conditioning an' the power mirrors? Power mirrors: that's technical innovation. Even the space shuttle doesn't have power windows! Do you realise what I could do with a ute like that?

'OK, realistically, sensibly, in the cold hard light of day, I don't need that ute.

'But I have to have it.

'How can we do it? Can you lend me forty grand? You've got credit cards ... What about your company chequebook? What sort of overdraft do you run? You must have stuff you could sell! Your old man owns his own home; does he have a mortgage? Interest rates are low, wouldn't cost him hardly anything. Don't tell me there's not money somewhere!

'Look, we're mates – don't hold out on me. Man, that sucker could be getting sold while we're standing here trifling over something as insignificant as money!

'So com'on now, be reasonable. Remember it is more blessed to give ... God wants me to have that ute. He does. Please!'

Well, things were getting embarrassing. Cuthbert had slid down onto his knees and had his arms wrapped around my ankles. His tears and slobber were messing up my Nikes. What's more, a crowd was starting to gather. Cuthbert's thunderous sobbing echoed through that place, drowning out even the occasional revhead as he fanged out of the car park next door.

All dignity was gone. Raw carnal lust was rolling around the showroom floor as he kicked and flayed.

'Come on, Cuthbert ol' mate, be a big boy – don't goober on my Nikes. Dry your eyes, be a tough soldier. Ute drivers don't cry just because everything doesn't work out right! On your feet, we don't want to visit Mr Smack just now in front of all these nice people, do we? Now let's go see the salesman.'

I don't know whether it was my tender admonitions or those last few words, 'let's go see the salesman', but Cuthbert went from 100 per cent horizontal blubber to 110 per cent vertical excitement, his famous smile crashing so hard at the top of his cranium that the shock wave must have caused his teeth to ache.

The salesman couldn't have been more helpful. He cancelled the call he'd already put in to the police, realising that there was no need to forcibly eject this snivelling tyre-kicker. No, the pavement could remain vacant, free from the riffraff that so often fantasised about XR8 buying but lacked the wherewithal. He sucked in his gut, tucked the bottom of his sauce-stained shirt into his duds, moistened his lips and prepared his jaws for the premier negotiation of the day.

He had almost got his mouth open when Cuthbert threw him right off balance with his cunning opening negotiating stance: 'We'll take it.'

The rest is history. New keys on the ring, staying up late reading the handbook, lying underneath th' XR8 checking every marvellous nut and bolt, re-counting the cylinders and exhaust outlets to make sure they're all there, showing her off to mates, applying for the special licence plate THXR8 ...

That's almost the end of the saga, except I haven't told you where Cuthbert got the money for that ute.

Well, there's no doubt that the most impressive attribute of a desperate ute fanatic is cunning, and Cuthbert's no exception. In my safe at home is a contract he forced me to sign, witnessing the fact that the new XR8 is owned jointly – in two names, mine and Cuthbert's. Yep, we both put up half the money and bought her together.

As Cuthbert reasoned, a man can't drive two utes at once. Every man needs at least one well-used old ute that can be safely parked on a building site, but that doesn't stop him owning half a brand-spanking-new XR8 too!

It's dangerous going ute-driving with a mate like Cuthbert.

Miss Ute Girl '99

Robyn Turner
Jerseyville, NSW

From the moment I opened my bloodshot eyes I knew that the day was going to end in disaster. This wasn't a startling premonition; I felt like this most days, because I was married to Snowy, and had been for ten years. The depletion of our home-brew stocks the previous night was testimony to the fact that we still had one thing in common, even if it was only a mutual love of booze.

Gingerly I swung my legs out of bed. Where in hell was Snow? I knew without even turning to look at the other side of the bed that he wasn't there. The air in the bedroom was fresh and unpolluted – meaning that he had already vacated the boudoir some time ago.

Two cups of strong black coffee and six pain-killers later, I felt a tad chirpier. Then I remembered what the day held in store. Snowy was entering his ute in the Great Ute Race and I was supposed to stitch up the Miss Ute Girl 1999 title. I had just four very short hours to turn myself into a raving beauty. The 'raving' part was already a long-established trait of my character. It came naturally, being married to Snow.

I thought that a good soak in a tub of warm water and bicarb might smooth out the old body wrinkles and freshen my skin a bit. Snow found me half an hour later, still in the tub and sound asleep. I pulled the plug and set to work to complete my camouflage operation while

Snow dashed back outside to give his beloved ute just one more polish (which directly followed the three he'd just given her). As far as he was concerned his beaut ute was already the winner.

Snow whispered sweet endearments all the way along the fifty-kilometre dirt track to where the shindig was to take place. I sat stony-faced as the ute lapped up the compliments, motor purring contentedly.

Well, they ran the race and Snowy and his ute blitzed 'em. I commented to Snow that he was going to have to give the ute another polish to get all his lip marks off the duco. He parked outside the beer tent and disappeared straight inside, but not before giving the ute another smooch and me a sound slap on the fender.

I figured that I needed a quick drink to settle my nerves before the pageant, so I strode in after him. After two or six beers (who's counting?) I felt a bit fuzzy so decided to have a quick lie-down in the back of the ute.

I awoke suddenly, thinking that I was still in the tub at home: I was drenched! Then I realised, in horror, that the heavens had opened and the ute was moving. As I hauled myself up in panic, the ute hit a stump and in the twinkling of an eye I was airborne. I came down face-first on the ground, so hard that I thought I could see the end of the universe. I opened my mouth to scream but found it was full of mud.

Needless to say I never made it to the beauty pageant. Christy with the henna head grabbed first prize – a plastic tiara coated with silver sparkles, and a bistro meal at the local pub. To Christy's chagrin she didn't, as expected, make it onto the front page of the local newspaper. I did.

There, in all her glory, sparkling, shimmering and (some would say) smiling, was the ute, and beside her

Snowy, her proud owner. Both were draped in bright red ribbons – the perfect couple. And if you looked very carefully (as all the locals did), there in the background, standing slightly to the left, face smudged with mud, auburn hair sticking out at all angles, one foot poised directly behind the ute's rear end, was me.

The Finger

G.R. Madsen
Frankston, VIC

A few years ago Lazy Ted got lucky at this little bar in Mayfield. She was a good-looking girl and she'd said to him, 'I can never resist a man with a ute.'

He drove her around to the local park for a little bit of privacy. They were getting along just fine when a bunch of louts happened by.

Lazy Ted locked the doors, so the louts had to content themselves with rocking the ute back and forth and banging on the roof.

Lazy Ted decided he wasn't going to hang around for any more nonsense. He stuck the ute into reverse and lurched out of the park, scattering bodies in his wake.

Now Lazy Ted didn't like to waste any mental energy remembering bad experiences and would have been happy to forget all about the incident in the park, but the very next day he was watching his wife Betty wash his ute when he noticed something sticking out of the front grille. A human finger!

He shook his head and was about to tell Betty to toss it in the rubbish when she stopped him short.

'That finger,' she said, 'must belong to someone. We'd better take it down to the lost and found.'

So down to the local cop station they went. The police were very helpful. Luckily for Lazy Ted they were more interested in the particulars of his ute (what make it was, how old, how many miles per gallon . . .) than in how a finger happened to find its way into his grille.

Lazy Ted had forgotten all about the finger episode when one day a cop came to the door and presented him with a small frozen case. The finger!

'According to Section 4 of Article 8 of the Mislaid Articles Act of 1983,' the cop spouted, 'found lost goods, if unclaimed by the owner and the loser of the aforementioned found lost goods, after a period of three months should be returned to the finder who will thereafter be considered the owner, and therefore the loser, in the event that the aforementioned found goods be re-lost.'

Lazy Ted scratched his head. He took the finger, thanked the cop for his trouble and told Betty to put it in the freezer.

Soon after this the phone calls started.

First a man with a deep, mean voice would ring and say, 'You got my finger. Give it back or you get rubbed!' Night after night, the same man rang with the same message.

Then, during the day, the Health Department started ringing, saying, 'Keeping a finger in your freezer contravenes Section 17 Article 12 of the Body Parts in the Kitchen Act. If you persist in infringing this regulation, we will be forced to proceed with legal action.'

Then a bloke called and asked, 'You the bloke with the finger?'

'You can't have it,' Lazy Ted told him.

'Oh, I don't want the finger,' the bloke told him. 'I was just wondering if you wanted to sell the ute.'

The final straw came when a surgeon started calling on a regular basis. 'Listen, we get kids in here every day with their fingers missing. Car accidents, gun accidents, you name it. Some will never use their hands again. With that one finger, you could help a child.'

All these phone calls got too much for Betty.

'Listen, Ted, do something. Raffle it, auction it, give it to the hospital, sell it to the sausage factory – just get rid of it. It's no use to you.'

It was all to no avail; Lazy Ted wouldn't hear of it.

But you know Lazy Ted – he'd never lift a finger to help himself or anyone else. He just snatched up the keys and went for a drive in the ute.

To Paradise in a Ute

Lorna Brennan
Frenchs Forest, NSW

Nineteen fifty-six. Newly married. Bernie and I rattled northwards in a dilapidated Holden utility (otherwise known as the Flying Bedstead). Our honeymoon destination was Surfers Paradise, with an overnight stop to visit Bernie's cousin in Grafton. I was navigator; in retrospect, that was not a good idea.

After some hours of travelling we noticed an absence of traffic. The road had become a rutted nightmare. We stopped to check maps and stretch our legs.

'Oh no!' wailed Bernie, examining a spreading pool of oil beneath the ute. 'The bloody thing's busted!'

A gravel truck pulled up beside us. 'G'day,' bawled a throaty voice. 'What're you doing, mate?'

'We're on our way to Grafton,' replied Bernie, 'and the ute's broken down.'

A bellow of laughter. 'Grafton's north, mate! You're heading due west! Stay put and I'll tow you into Scone on my way back. Won't be long.'

The truck vanished in a cloud of diesel smoke, leaving us in the middle of nowhere, our only company 20 million flies.

Four hours passed; four long hours. No conversation flowed and the silence was profound. We were beginning to believe we'd surely perish when the truck reappeared. Its driver, an enormous man, made short work of hitching up the ute, and soon we were majestically entering Scone. Our Good Samaritan delivered us to a mechanic, who looked at the ute, clucked and shook his head sorrowfully.

'Can't do it today, mate,' he said glumly. 'Tomorrow arvo's the best I can do.'

Bernie and I looked at each other in dismay. This would mean spending precious cash on accommodation for the night.

The hotel was old. In fact, it appeared to be disintegrating. French doors opened from our room onto a long verandah. Tired and grubby, we went in search of bathrooms.

There was no shower in the female bathroom. As I sat in the bath I noticed a hole in the wall beside me. I applied my eye to it out of curiosity and gasped when a large eye looked back at me. Bolting back to our room, I was passed by Bernie travelling at an even higher speed.

'This is a weird place,' he puffed, as we burst into the room.

'Why? What's happened?' I asked, not about to tell him of my peephole experience.

'I was sitting in the bath, holding the tap because it kept turning off, and someone banged on the door. Next thing, the door lifts off its hinges and this bloke marches in holding it in his hands. Gawd! I nearly died! He set it down, said "G'day", then proceeded to have a shave, with me sitting there in the bath.'

We fell about laughing. Then, too tired to eat, we went to bed.

* * *

I woke suddenly and jabbed Bernie in the ribs.

'Wassup?' he snorted.

'There's somebody on the verandah,' I whispered.

We both shot upright, clutching the sheets to our chins. We could hear soft footsteps approaching. Signalling me to be quiet, Bernie crept from the bed, grabbing a shoe as he inched towards the door.

The door handle turned slowly.

My hero stood there, bathed in moonlight, the quivering weapon held aloft in his hand.

But the opportunity to defend me never arrived, for the door handle stopped turning and the footsteps retreated. Bernie remained where he was. He stood there for an hour, ready to deal out mayhem with a slipper.

Time meaning little to the mechanic, we endured a second sheet-clutching, slipper-gripping night of inexplicable happenings before the ute was ready.

'Keep your eye on the oil gauge,' warned the mechanic. 'It's only a temporary repair.'

As we neared Tamworth I noticed a sign that said *Grafton 104 miles*. A man riding by on a hapless-looking horse assured us, 'It's a good road, mate,' so we took the short cut.

A good road? It was horrendous! Our ute's wheels balanced precariously on the ridges left by timber jinkers and I nearly went blind watching the oil gauge.

'There's a place called "Ebor" around here,' I volunteered, as we inched through a swarm of grasshoppers.

'Where?' asked Bernie.

'I think we just passed it,' I replied helpfully, consulting the map.

There was silence until we came across a lake covering the road. 'You walk through to see the depth and I'll follow you with the ute,' said Bernie.

The idea didn't charm me. 'What if I disappear?'

'Then I'll know not to bring the ute through, won't I?'

Twelve hours later we arrived in Grafton. Bernie's cousin was amazed to learn that we had 'crossed the Dorrigo', as the road was officially closed.

'Well, nobody told us,' Bernie growled.

Grafton was wallowing in the aftermath of flood. There was black silt everywhere, and a terrible smell.

Sinking gratefully into a hot bath, I eyed the mass of insect life partying about on the ceiling. Suddenly, a huge frog launched itself through the window and into the tub. Grafton was treated to its first streaker as I fled, naked and screaming, from the bathroom. Bernie's cousin must have marvelled at his relative's choice of a bride.

The gallant Bedstead took us to Surfers Paradise and, after ten glorious days, all the way home again, its oil filter clinging together precariously.

Now, forty years later, we recently farewelled our newlywed daughter and her husband as they boarded a jet to Hawaii. As we strolled, arm in arm, out of the airport, Bernie gave a hoot of laughter.

'I wonder if they'll have as much fun as we did,' he said.

'Not without a ute,' I replied.

The Flaming Green Ute

Kylie Baker
Sorrento, VIC

I was doing 120 kilometres an hour, singing along with Gina Jeffreys on the radio, when the green ute started to lose power. 'C'mon, you old ute, you can still manage over a hundred!' But the green ute was down to 60 kilometres an hour and things weren't looking good.

Shit! Where was the button for the hazard lights? As I searched the dashboard the ute hit the gravel. By the time it came to a halt the hazard-light button had mysteriously appeared on the steering column. It was a wonder I hadn't seen it there before.

I looked up and, as luck would have it, there just ahead of me was a service station.

OK. Be cool. Switch off the hazard lights. Just drive in quietly and ask for a bit of professional advice.

No sooner had I switched off the engine than the panic started.

'Fire! Fire!'

Had I heard it right? I wound down the window.

Louder this time, I heard it again: 'Fire! Fire!'

I jumped out of the car like a female James Bond and scanned the servo. Where? Where was the fire? I could smell it; I could tell it was close by. I turned back to the green ute.

Agh! My wheel was on fire!

I ran inside to the woman at the counter. 'Ah, excuse me. My ute's on fire. Do you have a, um, fire extinguisher?'

She pointed vaguely outside. 'Over there.'

Great help!

I had a quick look around for the fire extinguisher. The smoke was really belching out from underneath my ute now. I spotted the extinguisher, but when I tried to grab it I discovered that it was locked onto the pole. I didn't see the release pin, but it didn't matter because I didn't know how to use an extinguisher anyway.

Then I noticed a guy at the next bowser with his head in the engine of his car. He looked like he knew what he was doing, so I asked him if he could use a fire extinguisher.

'Nup.'

By now it must have been apparent to every person within a one-mile radius of the service station that my ute was on fire, but the man just kept pretending to fix his car. Geez, I thought, if you know how to fix a car you'd surely know how to use a flamin' fire extinguisher!

The woman who'd raised the alarm was still screeching: 'Fire! Fire!'

'Yeah, lady, I know,' I said.

She settled down once I'd convinced her that I'd noticed the fire. Obviously she'd just needed some reassurance.

Next thing I knew the woman from behind the counter had grown legs and was using them to run straight towards me. With her were two burly young men who'd appeared out of nowhere.

'Oh my goodness! Oh quick! Quick, over here!'

At last: people who'd know just what to do! What? Why were they just standing there?

One of the men rubbed his chin a few times, then crouched down and had a closer look at the wheel. The other one even tried to touch it.

I thought about making a run for it, but figured that the service station would probably scatter itself over the whole block when it blew up, so I'd only be wasting the last of my precious time.

Just when I'd resigned myself to perishing beside my green ute, one of the blokes picked up a bucket of water, flung it over the wheel and lay the flames to rest.

Why hadn't I thought of that?

So, what of the mystery behind the wheel that caught fire? The mechanic said that the person who'd changed the brake pads had used transmission fluid instead of brake fluid. Can you believe that? What an idiot!

My boyfriend knew exactly who this person was, but he didn't say a thing because I was the one who'd handed him the container. It's just that they all looked the same to me ...

The Old Man

Chris Thomson
Windsor, QLD

Lots of fellas complain about their fathers. They seem to emphasise their dads' failings rather than praise them for their good points.

Well, my old man was a bloody good bloke. Was, I say, because he's gone now. A dicky ticker took him off in the middle of the night when he was all alone at the age of eighty. Mum had gone a few years earlier. Actually, he wasn't really all alone; he had a really strong faith in God and was looking forward to sharing eternity with Mum and the One who created him.

One of the reasons I loved the old fella was that he was a real trier. He wasn't a famous person, he never won any awards, but he busted his butt to do the right thing by his wife and kids. He often joked about how highly qualified he was, being the only bloke in the district with a PhD. Of course, his punchline was that PhD stood for 'Post-hole Digger'. Dad loved all of us with an unselfish devotion that set a high standard for us to live up to.

I'll never forget his words as he'd come in for dinner each evening. He used to always say that he'd been 'striking blows' – that is, that he'd been making progress in whatever task he'd set himself for the day. He'd never come in for dinner until he'd met his goals, which sometimes meant that he came in very late. Then he'd flop down in a chair and give thanks to the Lord for the simple but enjoyable food Mum always had on the table.

Perhaps one of the most memorable days in our shared experiences was the day when Dad copped what he always dreaded: three pieces of bad luck in one day. He had always maintained that good and bad luck came in threes. This simple, illogical and unproved principle was about the only non-biblical belief that seemed ingrained in his heart. Mum said it was the only thing she ever disagreed with Dad on, but Dad stuck to his guns whenever challenged.

On that Black Day I was about fifteen and still at school. When I got home, Dad wasn't there. I was disappointed because he'd promised to take me bunny shooting that afternoon. Mum said he'd gone into town to get a tyre on the ute mended. Apparently earlier in the day he'd had some trouble starting his chainsaw. He removed the air filter and found that the motor started immediately. While he washed and re-oiled the air filter he left the chainsaw idling on the shed floor – 'warming up'. Just then Mum poked her head round the door and shouted to Dad that his brother wanted him on the phone for a quick word.

Dad went inside to take the call. In his absence the idling chainsaw slowly vibrated its way across the floor until the spinning chain was chewing gently against the rear tyre of the then-new Valiant ute. Dad was still engaged in the 'quick word' when, about ten minutes later, he was forced to cut short his conversation due to the sound of a muffled explosion in the shed. He rushed out to find that the chainsaw had chewed right through the sidewall of the ute's tyre and inner tube. The loud noise had been the sound of the whole thing letting go. That was the first disaster for the day.

I'd only just finished hearing Mum's version of Disaster One when a ball of dust rolled up the driveway. Inside it was Dad in his ute, complete with new tyre. 'C'mon, boy, let's go get them bunnies!' he grinned, forgetting about the $110 he'd just forked out on the new tyre and tube.

The thing about this expedition was that I was allowed to drive. Most kids would probably rather have done the shooting, but for me driving was a far bigger treat. Dad stood in the back of the ute, his .22 resting on the cabin roof, his earmuffs sitting snugly on his head. He had taught me, through a series of bangs and thumps on the roof, to drive faster or slower, or to stop, go left or right. An almighty thump on the roof meant, 'I've bagged a bunny!'

We'd only been driving for a few minutes when Dad let out a yell, loud enough to scare any bunnies within miles. I slammed on the brakes and leapt from the ute.

Dad's earmuffs were in the scrub and he was hanging onto his head, howling like a wounded pig. Apparently we'd run into a bee, which had somehow got wedged between his earmuffs and his head. The bee had stung him just in front of his left ear.

Dad's head started to inflate like a balloon. It was incredible: within five minutes he looked like an alien with his lopsided face and puffed-up left eye. In addition, he'd developed a really crook headache. Disaster Two had struck!

We decided to leave the bunnies until another day and head home. We got there just as the sun was going down. Mum fussed around Dad, putting a bag of Blue on his sting site. Forcing him to sit down on the lounge, she switched on the TV and insisted that she would serve his dinner on his lap – a rare treat in our household.

Dad took this opportunity to bewail the fact that he'd now had two disasters. 'Wait an' see,' he prophesied, 'I betcha something else crook happens before I hit the sack.'

Mum responded by giving Dad a tongue-lashing and assuring him that if he just sat and ate quietly, and then got an early night, he couldn't possibly suffer any further mishaps on that day. She plonked a plate of food down on his lap and we left him there in front of the TV while we ate in the kitchen.

'Stubborn ol' bloke,' Mum said. 'I'll eat his earmuffs if he gets into any more trouble tonight!'

We were just about to wash-up when it happened. Dad let out a whooping noise from the lounge room that made my blood run cold. We rushed in to find him spread-eagled on the floor, a broken plate to one side. He was writhing around, hanging onto his bottom lip and sobbing.

'What's happened, love?' Mum cried out, but the only sense we could make out of his moaning was, 'Disaster Three! Disaster Three!'

When finally he quietened down, his pain subsiding, we learnt the cause of his misery. It seemed that when he collected the bee in the side of the head, unbeknown to him he had also caught one on the front of his jumper. The bee must have got stunned as it hit Dad's chest, and then lain there tangled in the wool. Dad had been eating his dinner when he glanced down and saw something on his chest. He wasn't wearing his specs, so he assumed it was a crumb of food he had dropped. He picked it up and popped it into his mouth. The bee rallied and stung Dad on the inside of his bottom lip! I wince now as I think of it; no wonder Dad went berserk!

After that 'Black Day', Dad and I had many many good days. Once Dad's head had shrunk back to its normal size we were able to look back and laugh about chainsaws, utes and beestings.

However, those three events did nothing to dispel Dad's superstitions; in fact, they only served to refine his theories about disasters. Anyone who would listen would hear him deliver a lecture on the Law of Misery. I reckon maybe the old fella had a point.

Of course, Mum still maintained that it was all a load of old codswallop. I never reminded her of her promise to eat Dad's earmuffs if a third piece of bad luck struck him that night ...

A Dog's Life

Kelly-Anne Brand
Nana Glen, NSW

Ever since I was a pup I've spent most of my life in the back of Russell's ute.

Deep down I'm a pretty good dog, although there have been some rough spots in my life that have brought out the worst in me. Most of it I can trace back to my puppy years. Russell used to grab my head and put it between his knees, then rough me up by tweaking my ears while pounding on my back and sides. I'd go mad with excitement, growling, barking and squirming until I'd finally break free. Then I'd savage Russell, ripping his trouser legs and biting him anywhere I could reach. It wasn't such a big deal way back then, but I can sure do a lot of damage to Russell now that I'm grown up!

When I was a pup Russell usually laughed a lot when I did this. It was only when I drew blood that he'd start to get a bit cranky. I'd always see his mood change coming and try my best to stay out of the range of his swinging boots when he started to have a kick at me. 'C'mon fella, that's enough fun now,' he'd say, hoping that I'd suddenly shut down adrenaline production and quit.

Nowadays I don't even wait for Russell to start the rumbles. I lie in wait for him, especially on dark nights as he struggles up the garden path with an armful of shopping out of the back of the ute. I go straight for his calf muscles as he curses and tries to kick his way inside the house.

The beginnings of my love–hate relationship with Russell didn't just come out of play times. Daily life provided opportunities for dissatisfaction, too. Like, he'd whistle me up into the back of his ute when he was going anywhere. I was a mug, thinking he just enjoyed my company, but it finally dawned on me that I was actually there to protect his tools and stuff. I'd always fall for it, though, and leap up, trying not to skid too far across that darned slippery tray top before coming to a halt.

In the early days he let me run around the back of the ute untethered while he was driving, but one unfortunate day I fell out. It happened just as Russell swerved to miss the local bushfire truck which was blasting down the main street to attend a false alarm. This violent evasive action made me skid right across the tray and shoot off into the newsagent's. Papers and customers flew everywhere. 'Stay in the ute, you stupid bloody dog!' he yelled at me as he grabbed me by the skin of my neck and chucked me roughly back onto the ute. I'm sure he did this just to make passers-by think that I was the problem, not him.

Oh yeah, by the way, Russell seems to believe that false story about the skin of a dog's neck being a convenient and non-painful way to carry a dog. Well, that's rot! It's darned painful, believe me. Try grabbing a bunch of your own skin and lifting yourself off the ground; it just ain't a nice feeling. I grabbed hold of some of Russell's spare skin once when I ripped into him during a 'game'. He lay moaning on the ground for ages before going to the doctor's. He got a certificate for a week off work. Seems Russell has very weak 'fourskins', whatever they are.

Nowadays, whenever we go out, Russell tries to tether me to the headboard of the ute. I try my best to bite the bugger. It's quite a contest, really. A crowd often gathers to watch in amazement as Russell tries to look cool and in control while his own dog does its best to savage him.

Another point I should mention is that a lot of people get the wrong impression about us dogs. We don't like riding in the back of utes at all, especially not in utes like Russell's. The thing I hate most is all that wind blowing at me. If I face forward into the wind, my eyes water and fill with grit, my lips dry out and I lose a hell of a lot of spit. It's much worse if I face backwards, since I've got one of those upward-pointing tails which leaves my bum area very exposed to the elements.

Then there's the problem of meeting other dogs. Hanging out of Russell's ute I don't get a chance to socialise properly, 'cos we just fly past those other dogs. Try as I might, I can never get a good whiff of them; the smell's disappeared long before I get a good go at it.

And whoever thinks about the problems caused by all those lampposts a dog sees from the back of a ute? Everyone knows that the sight of a lamppost triggers a dog's urine production. It's a known fact that dogs' bodies produce urine in direct proportion to the number of lampposts they see. So as I flash past millions and millions of lampposts while Russell is thoughtlessly gunning his ute, my urine pumping station is sending gallons and gallons down to my bladder. Trouble is that my bladder doesn't have actual access to the posts – no outlet, see – so it just stores the stuff on board. By the end of a long trip my body weight is ninety per cent urine and only ten per cent meat and gristle.

It's no wonder I go berserk when the ute finally stops. I'll squirt at hubcaps, boots, doorways, trees, posts, people and anything else within range.

My advice to all young pups is to think hard before you start to train your human. Instead of pretending that you love riding in the back of his or her ute, consider the restrictions of tethering, the social isolation, the piles that you'll contract through having a permanently cold bum, and your limited bladder capacity.

Maybe it would be wiser to consider a desk job.

Dented Pride

Peter Sinclair
Goulburn, NSW

It was just on three weeks since my Holden ute had been resprayed, and with all the other work I had done on her over the last six or seven months she was looking good.

Then along comes Darrell the Barrel, the nong in thongs. He wants us to take his Honda 250 trail bike into town to have some work done on it.

Darrell runs a piece of timber up into the back of the ute.

'I'll ride it up, mate. No worries.'

Contact. Front wheel up onto the timber, back wheel up, onto the tray. So far so good.

KERASH! Full flaming throttle into the back of the cabin.

The bike does a lovely little pirouette. The back wheel comes floating around like a wanton butterfly and drives the muffler straight through the back windscreen. Glass everywhere. The bike then realises that it shouldn't be hanging around any longer, so it ever so gently sneaks away over the side of the ute, leaving a gash the size of Bungonia Gorge just behind the door.

'Good onya, Dickhead!'

During all of this, Darling Darrell has gone over the handlebars, plonked his fat arse on the roof of the cabin and caved it in before sliding his dainty figure down the windscreen, ripping off one of the wipers and coming to rest in the middle of the bonnet, which I reckon is just about touching the carby.

'Geez, sorry mate. I thought ...'

'You mongrel-bred bastard! If your brain was made of ink you wouldn't have enough to make a full stop.'

Darrell picks himself up off the bonnet and I ask, 'What were we taking the bike to town for, Dickhead?'

'Ah, to fix the sticky throttle and the brakes.'

God give me guidance to bury the body where it won't be found!

The Bench Seat

C. Dunstone
Jan Juc, VIC

'We'll have to move this stuff out of the shed, Dad. We never use most of it.'

'I know it's untidy, son, but I hate to throw things away. Most of it is family history.'

'We haven't got enough room to be sentimental, Dad. Look, that old tractor hasn't been started in years.'

'Yeah, but that was my father's first tractor. You can't get rid of that.'

'And this old motorbike?'

'That's your Uncle Bill's bike; had it before he went to Vietnam. Couldn't possibly throw that out. I think of Bill every time I see it: flying down the road, dirt billowing out behind him, your Auntie Jean hanging onto the back. Imagine her on it now! Bill gave me that bike before he went. I think he knew he wouldn't be back ... I'll get it going one of these days.'

'OK, keep the bike. But that ute has to go.'

'Get rid of my old ute? No way! That ute has more history in it than any book you could read. If that ute could talk it could give you the life and times of this farm and district for the past forty years.'

'Look, Dad, when you went to live in town you told me I was in charge and that if ever you came and bothered me I was to tell you that I was the boss now. So that's it, we start with the ute.'

'Gee, mate, the day the fire broke out at Kenton's that ute flew down the road to phone for the brigade; no bloody mobiles then, eh! And when the big cyclone wrecked the pub, who ran to Boorcan for beer? That old ute, of course. You were too young to remember the day Bob Williams got caught in the power take-off. We laid him out in th'ute and saved his life by rushing him to the hospital. Never let us down.'

'Well I know all that, Dad, but I'm still making the decision.'

'Just before you make up your mind I'll let you in to a secret. When your mum and I first married we were pretty young and thought we'd have a family just like everyone else. Well, we were married for almost three years and still no sign or reason why not. I knew she was worried, and to be honest I was too.

'It was summer and I'd just finished harvest. Your mum had worked hard too. It had been as hot as hell – and of course, no air conditioners then. I'd taken my last load to the silos and when I got home I saw your mum sitting out on the verandah. I remember thinking how exhausted she looked. I told her we'd pack up some tea and go out to the lake for the night. That was the only place you could get a bit of a cool breeze. Well, she sparked up immediately, so we got our things together and off we went – in the old ute, of course.

'We swam and lazed till we were so cool and fresh. It was beautiful – just the two of us. We'd brought a mattress to sleep on in the back, but the mozzies gave us hell so we ended up in the front seat. The radio was on and we sat there talking. We were feeling very close, and so you don't need to use your imagination to know what we did then.'

'What, in the front seat of a ute, Dad?'

'Well, it's a bench seat as you well know.'

'Why are you telling me this, Dad?'

'It was nine months later to the day that you were born, son. I've got a lot of respect for the medical profession but I think there was a little bit of magic in this old ute. I always used to tease your mum and tell her we had to do it again in the ute to get it to work, but she always threatened to kill me if I told anyone. So make sure you never let on to her.'

'OK, Dad. I promise.'

'Now that reminds me, son. How long have you and Mary been married? Twelve months now and no sign of a grandchild! You'd better leave the old ute where she is – just in case there's an emergency, eh?'

The Miracle

Kathleen Shertock
Penneshaw, SA

Only the radio could be heard as Skeet pushed open the pub door. He knew better than to yell his normal crude greetings – the third in Melbourne was running. He squeezed in at the bar next to his two mates, Yogi and Swampy. A chorus of moans and groans signalled the end of the race, and torn tickets fluttered to the floor as the hum of conversation started up again.

'Hi, Skeet, what are you havin'?' Yogi asked as he made room.

'The usual. Hi, Swamp. Where's the automobile? I couldn't see it.'

'Parked 'round the back. Cost me an arm and a leg to get it fixed this time. They think a man's made outta money.'

'Why don't you trade it?' asked Yogi. 'The repairs are costing more than the truck's worth.'

'I've told you before, it's not a truck, it's a ute. I'll spell it for you: U-T-E. And I'd trade me missus before I'd part with the ute.'

Yogi nudged Skeet and winked as he said, 'It's a rust bucket, Swamp, and bloody dangerous. It'll fall to pieces when you're driving it one day and break your bloody neck.'

Swampy placed his glass slowly and deliberately on the bar and faced him. 'Is that right, mate? Is that bloody right? Well, I don't suppose you'll want to come with me and Skeet when we go fishin' in the morning. Good weather, tide's right, and an Esky of cold stubbies ...'

'I'll consider the offer,' grinned Yogi. 'What time are we leavin'?'

''Round five. All dob in for the beer now, 'cos I'm going home to pack the old rust bucket.'

The men carried a carton of beer to the ute. Swampy stood back examining his vehicle. Peeling paint and rusty doors took nothing away from its dignity. It knew it was loved, knew it was top of the totem pole in Swamp's life, coming before wife and kids, even before his mates. That ute knew it would never end up in the scrapyard while Swampy was alive.

Skeet kicked the tyres. 'Tyres are a bit bald, Swamp.'

'Will you blokes lay off?' said Swampy, patting the ute as though soothing its hurt feelings. 'I'll get some retreads when I can afford them. We might catch some biggies to sell at the pub; who knows? See you tomorra at sparrows.'

He climbed into the seat and sped off in a cloud of dust.

The fish were biting and the fellas soon had a decent catch, although nothing big had been sighted. Leaving their lines in the water they stopped for a beer.

'Wonder what the poor people are doing?' said Skeet, laying back looking at the clear morning sky and drinking slowly, the cool bottle against his face.

'We're fishin',' smartmouthed Swampy. His mind was still on his bald tyres.

'Maybe you'll get lucky and catch enough to get you those tyres,' said Yogi, chaffing at Swampy for his optimistic comment of the day before. 'Miracles do happen, you know.'

'Oh yeah, ever seen one?' Swampy didn't believe in divine intervention.

'I've heard of 'em.' Yogi was grinning.

'We're listening,' said Skeet.

Yogi rested back on his elbow, one hand lightly holding the fishing rod.

'Well, there was these three blokes, see? One was blind, one was deaf and the other was a cripple in a wheelchair. They were lost in the desert and dying of thirst when they came upon an oasis, see? The deaf bloke races to the water and dives in, splashing water all over him. When he stands up he looks around and starts yelling, "It's a miracle! I can hear, I can hear!"

'He runs back and leads the blind man into the water, ducking his head under and splashing him excitedly. When the blind man opens his eyes he starts screaming, "It's a miracle! I can see, I can see!"

'They both rush back, grab the crippled man and lift him, wheelchair and all, into the water. "Stand up," they say. But he can't. He tries again but his legs won't support him. As they're carrying him back to shore he suddenly points to the wheelchair. "It's a miracle, it's a miracle! Look!" His wheelchair has got four spanking-new tyres!'

Yogi had hardly finished telling his joke when suddenly the line screamed in his hand. Grabbing the rod before it was pulled overboard he started winding.

'Must be a bloody Great White!' yelled Skeet.

'How about a marlin?' beamed Yogi between gasps. His face was becoming red with the effort of pulling in the line.

'Get the gaff, will you, Swamp? I'll slash me wrists if I lose this one.'

The snapper weighed twelve pounds. Excitement mounted when Skeet's line suddenly took off. In a matter of five minutes the score was Yogi three, Skeet four, Swampy nil. Then silence. The fish had moved on.

'It's just not my bloody day!' said Swampy in disbelief. 'Not even a bite!'

'It's arse, not class, Swamp,' said Yogi, attempting to lighten the atmosphere. He knew how he'd feel if he hadn't got one.

'D'ya mind if we call it a day?' asked Swampy. 'I've suddenly lost interest in fishing.'

'Here's Yogi now,' said Skeet. He and Swampy were sitting at their favourite watering hole, discussing the fickle sport of fishing while waiting for Yogi to meet them. Skeet raised his eyebrows at Yogi and got a slight nod in response.

'What did you blokes end up doing with those fish?' asked Swampy. 'Did you smoke any of 'em?' He was feeling just a little hurt that the other two hadn't offered to share the catch with him. After all, the unspoken rules of fishing were that you divided the catch, no matter who did the catching.

Before they could answer, Mick the barman leant over and said, 'Hey, Swamp, someone's messin' with your ute!' Swampy slammed his glass down on the bar and raced outside. Skeet and Yogi followed at a more leisurely pace.

Swampy stopped abruptly. There stood the ute, its four new tyres incongruous against the chassis with its rust and peeling paint. It was magnificent.

'It's a miracle! It's a miracle!'

Skeet and Yogi were grinning from ear to ear.

The Carport

Coral Petkovich
Spearwood, WA

'You're crazy,' said my husband. 'Drive eight hundred kilometres just to pick up an old wardrobe? It doesn't make sense!'

'It's solid wood,' I said, 'practically an antique. I always loved it and I don't want it sold. My father left it to me.'

Peter scowled at me. 'I've got better things to do on the weekend.'

'We can stay overnight,' I cajoled. 'Go bushwalking, sightseeing. It could even turn out to be a pleasure, not a chore, to be alone with your wife for a change ...'

That took the scowl off his face. He became more appeasing. 'It's not that. You know I'd love to get away – with you. But wouldn't it be better to go away for a few days or a week, not just there and straight back?'

'OK, you don't have to go with me. I can go by myself.'

I left him sitting there, his mouth slightly open. I knew he'd be reluctant to let me drive his precious new ute all that way by myself. I knew that we'd both be going.

I spent a very pleasant hour or so working out exactly where I would put the wardrobe, and what I would put in it.

Saturday morning was grey and windy and Peter said it was going to rain. How did I think we were going to bring the wardrobe back in a rain storm?

'They said it's clearing tomorrow,' I said. 'And anyway, it won't be hard to cover it with a tarp.'

We set off in an uncompanionable silence. A fine drizzle was falling, obscuring any views.

At last we arrived at the small farmhouse where my father had spent the last years of his life. The place had been sold and was currently uninhabited. I spent a few anxious minutes wondering whether the wardrobe had been sold or stolen, but when we got the key from a neighbour and went inside to check, I was very relieved to see it.

Even Peter was impressed.

'I expected something heavy and ugly – this is really beautiful!' He ran his fingers along the softly shining surface. 'No wonder you remembered it so fondly.'

We slept that night at a nearby motel that differed from others of its kind only in that neither the heater nor the television worked, and there were no spare blankets. Peter refused to go out in the rain to the office and ask for more blankets. Neither of us mentioned bushwalking or sightseeing.

The next morning the sun was shining.

'Let's go for that walk, it's a beautiful day.' I looked at Peter hopefully.

'Why not?' he said, putting his arms around me. 'We can head home after lunch.'

The first part of the walk was all I had hoped for, and more: wonderful scenery, perfect weather, and Peter at his most charming. It was only a pity that we made a detour off the path. It was even more regrettable that I was the one who suggested it. The swarm of bees ignored me and went straight for Peter. Two of them stung him on his cheek and another one under his eye.

His mood changed dramatically with the onset of pain and swelling.

We returned to the motel much faster than we had left it, and spent the rest of the morning tracking down a doctor and buying some medicine. Peter never stopped complaining, but there were worse things still to come.

After lunch we laboured to get the wardrobe onto the ute. We packed it so that nothing could damage the polish, and tied it down securely. That accomplished, Peter realised what I had suspected for some time – that he was in no condition to drive.

'Peter, I'm perfectly capable of driving the ute, you know. I've driven it before.'

'It's too heavy for you, you can't drive all that way. Besides, you've only ever driven it around the block.'

The argument went round in circles. Finally I had to bring it to a close. 'You have two choices, Peter. We either stay here until you've recovered, or I drive. When you've made up your mind, come and tell me.' I stomped around to the back of the house, sat in the garden and waited.

Of course he finally decided to let me drive.

'And don't sit there criticising,' I warned him. 'You'll make me nervous.'

He was really very good, considering how worried he was about his ute, and how much pain he was suffering. Little by little, as we neared home, he started to relax. At last we were driving up our street.

'I guess there's no harm done,' he volunteered. 'I should be back to normal in a day or two. And you have your wardrobe, safe and sound.' I turned to catch his smile as we drove into our driveway, and was just in time to see a look of horror flash across his face. A split second later there was an almighty, splintering crash. I thought that I had destroyed the house, it was such an impossibly loud and unexpected noise.

But it wasn't the house. It was the wardrobe.

We got out to inspect a pile of splintered wood. I had forgotten about how high the wardrobe stood on the back of the ute and had driven straight under the carport …

On the Way to the Church

Marie Pond
Wangaratta, VIC

It began with a phone call on a hot January day.

'Yeah?' my brother said into the telephone.

'Mick Harrington here. Need your help. Your ute running OK?'

'Was the last time I drove her. Why?'

'My daughter's getting married in two hours' time and the effing bridal car won't start. Spent four hours polishing the bastard yesterday, too!'

'Surely a ute's not the thing for ...?'

'Yeah, it is, mate. When there's no other bloody car left. Mum's gone with the bridesmaid and everyone else is on their way. You're the last set of wheels around – don't think I haven't tried. I'm desperate, mate.'

'But how ...?'

'I'll sit up in the back, Dawn goes in front with you. Geez, mate, pull your finger out and get over here, will you!'

My brother flung an old mattress into the back of the ute and sped to the rescue. He was suddenly forced to brake at the sight of a figure slumped by the roadside, waving him to stop.

'It's me leg. Broke, I reckon.'

The leg's owner, Pop Cook, had spent a painful two hours crawling up from the valley floor. My brother decided that all he could do was take Pop to Harrington's place, then arrange for an ambulance to collect him.

After much heaving Pop was levered into the ute's front seat, where he promptly fell into unconsciousness.

Mick Harrington stood staring anxiously down the dusty track, his face scarlet from heat and anxiety.

'Good onya, mate. Won't forget this. What's bloody Pop Cook doin' in there? Drunk?'

My brother explained the situation as he tried to lift his passenger out. Pop let out a scream of such agony that my brother swore his own heart stopped beating for minutes. Obviously Pop was not to be moved.

Mick stated, 'My Dawn's going with you and that's that. We'll both travel on the back.'

The bride came out, her make-up melting in the heat. Suddenly she grabbed hold of the hem of her billowing wedding dress and made a run at the ute's tray. Just as she leapt, my brother stepped forward to assist and a horseshoe, wrapped in ribbon and tied to her wrist, hit him in the left eye. It was a real horseshoe, from Dawn's first horse. His eye began to sting, then ache, and finally to close.

The bride began winding her veil around her head to keep her hair in place. My brother felt the bounce of Mick's weighty bulk as he clambered up onto the tray. He took off, Pop Cook moaning beside him.

There was a banging on the rear cabin window. My brother glanced over his shoulder and found himself looking into the drooling face of a red heeler, her lips blown sideways by the wind. Where did she come from?

The banging continued. He looked again and saw Dawn gesticulating at him.

'We've left Dad behind,' she announced as soon as the ute had come to a stop. 'He was getting onto the tray when Red leapt on and knocked him off balance. Can't go back now, we're late as it is. Dad'll understand.'

My brother shrugged and drove on as instructed.

He hadn't got far when a young man suddenly ran out onto the road, arms akimbo, face contorted.

'Give us a lift please, mate! I've crashed me car and I'm late for a wedding I just have to be at!'

Before my brother could protest, the young man leapt up on the back in a single bound. A border collie sprang up behind him with the same alacrity. My brother knew nothing of this extra passenger as he drove off cursing brides, weddings, horseshoes and ... then he heard it. The muffled snarling and growling of dogs fighting.

When he looked through the cabin window his eye met the four upturned legs of a red heeler. When he looked again the legs were upright and four collie legs were upturned. He braked and ran to the back of his ute.

No bride. No young man. Only the two dogs panting in apparent truce on opposite sides of the mattress.

The story, it turned out, was this. Apparently that young man had been in love with Dawn for years. Dawn had only been marrying someone else because the young man had never proposed to her. In the back of the ute the two lovers had sorted out their differences. When my brother stopped at the town's only traffic lights they had alighted, gone to the nearby railway station and caught the next train out.

'Awful for the jilted groom,' I commented when I'd heard the story.

'Not really,' my brother explained. 'It turned out he'd only been marrying Dawn for Mick's dairy farm. Said he liked cows better than women any day.'

'To top it all off,' he continued, 'those bloody dogs tore the stuffing out of my mattress. I arrived at the church in a cloud of feathers. Teddy Bridges fined me for littering, and Pop Cook got hauled up for using obscene language.'

When old Mick had heard what had happened to his daughter, he'd sighed and said, 'Oh well, at least the ute performed all right. Some things you can rely on.'

My brother had agreed, and the two of them had settled down to a couple of quiet beers together.

How I Became a Man

Bob Wallace
Tennyson, NSW

I was a kid, just eight years old, when first I got the urge
To own a red-hot motor car, to stand out from the herd.
I craved the smell of engines, loved tinkering with pliers,
I loved the sound of smashing glass and screeching rubber
*   tyres.*

So as I grew I saved my bucks and read the motor mags,
I eyeballed all the muscle cars, and watched them at the
*   drags,*
And by the time I reached my teens, with pimples on my
*   face,*
I couldn't wait to get a car and join the human race.

Then finally the day arrived to take my driving test,
I passed it oh so easily – heaps better than the rest!
So out I went to buy a car, to climb behind the wheel,
To crash the gears and trash the brakes, to make the
*   ladies squeal.*

And as I searched all over Oz, one thing started to be
*   clear,*
I wasn't gonna find a car to make me shout and cheer.
Instead I saw that all the blokes who had the brains and
*   clues,*
Were getting into bloody utes ... Holden HQs!

So start to search the yards I did, looking for a beast,
HZ or maybe Falcon, big donk with guts at least,

But not a Jappo crapper, lest all me mates would laugh
And piddle on me piddling ute, and I would end up last.

Then finally my dream came true, as walking down the
    street
I spied this Holden HQ ute, an old bloke in the seat.
Up on the screen it had a sign, 'For Sale' it shouted loud,
And underneath it told the tale, it sounded mighty
    proud.

I grabbed the old bloke by the sleeve, and offered him my
    bucks,
My heart was nearly dying with love, it was the king of
    trucks!
He said 'yes' and there I wept, kneeling in the street,
The ute was mine, the deal was done, an HQ with bench
    seat.

So home I roared to show my Dad, who dribbled with
    desire,
'Cos years ago he'd had one too that'd set his heart on
    fire.
We looked into the glove box, we climbed into the back,
We crawled into the motor, we knew she was no hack.

In fact she was a V8 – a one-owner, too, at that,
The miles were low, she'd not been thrashed
    (I'd soon change all of that!)
And shedding tears of joy we found there wasn't any
    rust.
Who said that God above was dead, and in Him we
    couldn't trust?

We stuck her up on blocks right there, protected in the shed,
We ripped off all her panels, we shaved her lovely head,
We bolted on extractors, we changed her cam as well,
And just for luck resprayed her, with paint called 'Black
      as Hell'.

We fiddled with suspension, and lowered her right down,
Till her chrome-plated private parts nearly touched the
      ground.
And with her cavernous exhaust she gave a throaty note,
A warning to the Volvos, 'Move, or I'll slash ya throat!'

But now the greatest fun of all, installing special parts,
Nothing small or wimpy, not like the Jappo farts.
One humungous bullbar, five-poster, heaps of mesh,
Perfect for protection and bulldozing cattle flesh.

And then we added spotties, for turning nights to days,
For searching out those wallabies, and bagging big old
      grays.
And hanging off the front of her, maybe just for show,
The tallest CB aerials you'll see at any Show.

But on the back where all could see, sticking to the glass,
A collection of ute stickers, plus me annual B & S pass,
And underneath the tailgate, for those who eat my dust,
A Caterpillar mud flap, hiding all the rust.

Yes, my friends, I am a man, and it took me just a week,
To change myself from scrawny lad to man of great
      physique.
It's not the food, it's not the air, it isn't just a daydream,
I owe it to my HQ ute, the ultimate machine!

THE MAN FROM
DAKOTA

ALSO BY PETER BRANDVOLD

The Peter Brandvold Introductory Library

The Bells of El Diablo

Blood Mountin

Shotgun Rider

Spurr Morgan

The Weird West Double

.45 Caliber Series

Bloody Joe Mannion Series

The Saga of Colter Farrow

Lonnie Gentry Series

Lou Prophet Series

The Revenger Series

Rogue Lawman Series

Sheriff Ben Stillman Series

Yakima Henry Series

And many more…

THE MAN FROM DAKOTA

NORDIC & FINN
BOOK TWO

PETER BRANDVOLD

WOLFPACK
PUBLISHING
— EST 2013 —

Paperback ISBN 979-8-89567-216-7
Ebook ISBN 979-8-89567-215-0
LCCN 2025939585

THE MAN FROM
DAKOTA